God's **Entrepreneurs**

About the Author

Joe Humphreys is an author and senior staff journalist with *The Irish Times.* He has written extensively on African affairs and issues affecting developing countries, having worked as a correspondent in South Africa and reported from locations such as East Timor. He holds a Master of Arts degree in Political Philosophy, obtained from University College Dublin. He lives in Dublin with his wife and two children.

Also by Joe Humphreys

Foul Play: What's Wrong with Sport

The Story of Virtue: Universal Lessons on How to Live

Joe Humphreys

God's Entrepreneurs:

How Irish Missionaries Tried to Change the World

With additional reporting by
Ruadhán MacCormaic, Sarah MacDonald
and Brian O'Connell

GOD'S ENTREPRENEURS
First published 2010
by New Island
2 Brookside
Dundrum Road
Dublin 14

www.newisland.ie

ISBN 978-1-84840-076-4

British Library Cataloguing Data. A CIP catalogue record for this book is available from the British Library.

Book design by Inka Hagen

Front cover image: © Yolande De Kort/Trevillion Images
Back cover images, left to right: The Far East © Columban Archive; Fr Tony Byrne © Provincial Archives, Holy Ghost Fathers; Sr Orla Treacy © Sarah MacDonald; Fr Shay Cullen © David McNeill

Printed in the UK by CPI Antony Rowe, Chippenham, Wiltshire

10 9 8 7 6 5 4 3 2 1

In memory of Richard Macartan Humphreys,

a thinker as well as a doer

CONTENTS

ACKNOWLEDGEMENTS

Sincere thanks to the many missionaries who gave their time, and their trust, to speak to me for this book. Not one of them asked me whether I was Hindu, Muslim, Christian or atheist, and I suspect they'd have treated me just the same regardless. Inevitably, with a book such as this, one must do considerable editing of interviews. Just which missionary profiles, comments and quotes made the final cut were decided by me and me alone – and this should be borne in mind by readers. The narrative of this book inevitably reflects some of my own prejudices and opinions. Where mistakes have been made I take full responsibility for them.

A further disclaimer: not all missionary congregations got the same billing in the book, and this should not be seen as a slight against those which were relatively neglected. The book was written for a general readership and should not be seen as the last word on the history or contribution of particular missionary societies.

Among those to whom I'm particularly grateful are Fr Pat Raleigh, Fr Malachy Smyth and Fr Neil Collins, along with their Columban colleagues Fr Tommy Murphy, Fr Dan Fitzgerald, Fr Michael Healy, Fr Donie Hogan, Fr Allo Connaughton, Fr Liam O'Callaghan and Fr Shay Cullen. Fr Eamon Aylward, Ronan Barry and Fr Brian O'Toole of the Irish Missionary Union were exceedingly helpful, along with Sr Kathleen MacLennon, Sr Marian Moriarty, Sr Cyril Mooney and Sr Orla Treacy (Loretos); Sr Isabelle Smyth, Sr Dr Maura O'Donoghue and Sr Helen Ahern (MMMs); Sr Eileen Keane (Holy Rosary Sisters); Sr Miriam Duggan (Franciscan Missionary Sisters of Africa); Fr Michael Kelly and Fr

John Guiney (Jesuits); Sr Anne Ryan, Sr Kathleen Geaney, Sr Mary Dillon and Sr Sheila Crowe (Columban Sisters); Fr Donal Dorr (Kiltegans), Fr Ed Grimes and Jackie Pallas (World Missions Ireland); Fr Gerry O'Connor (Redemptorists); Brother Declan Power and Brother Michael Lynch (Christian Brothers); Sr Ailish O'Brien and Sr Angela Hartigan (Sisters of Mercy); Fr Jack Finucane (Spiritans); Sr Majella McCarron and Sr Kathleen McGarvey (Our Lady of Apostles); Fr Robbie MacCabe (Carmelites); and from South Africa Fr Kieran Creagh, Remigia Tloubatla, Sr Margaret Kelly OP, Fr Sean O'Leary and Sr Áine Hughes.

Many thanks also to Mike Greally and Denise O'Donovan (Misean Cara); Dr John Manton; Dr Joe Barnes and Dr Betty Barnes; Ruán Magan; Noel Gavin; David McNeill; the staff of NUI Maynooth Library and of Dublin's Dundrum Library; not forgetting my colleagues at *The Irish Times*, in particular Kevin O'Sullivan and the newsdesk team, as well as Patsy McGarry and Simon Carswell, for help in different ways. I'm very grateful also to Deirdre O'Neill, Edwin Higel and everyone else at New Island for their enthusiasm, support and assistance.

My co-authors, Ruadhán MacCormaic, Sarah MacDonald and Brian O'Connell, who provided reportage from Brazil, South Sudan and India respectively, cannot receive high enough praise. Ruadhán reported on Fr Jim Crowe in São Paulo, Sarah on Sr Orla Treacy in Rumbek, and Brian on Sr Cyril Mooney in Kolkata. Their dispatches have been incorporated into the overall narrative. All three writers went beyond the call of duty, giving their time and expertise generously, and in some instances critical advice at editing stage. On a personal note, thanks to Maura and Denis O'Brien, Niamh O'Brien, my mother Deirdre, brothers Richard, Mark and Frank – as well as their families – for their constant support but above all to Emer, Megan and Patrick: I promise to consult you fully before undertaking another 'minor project' like this.

PREFACE

I have seen missionaries doing extraordinary work, in some remote parts of the world, but none of them had the same sort of impression on me as the nun I once ran into at an embassy reception who was complaining of a sore tooth. The seventy-something Irishwoman was selecting a softish nibble from the canapé tray. 'The dentist says it needs a crown,' she explained, 'but there is no way I'm spending 2,000 rand (€200) on a tooth.' I munched away sheepishly on a vol-au-vent, neglecting to mention that I'd recently spent five times that on root-canal treatment. 'So I'm having it pulled out,' she continued breezily, as she surveyed the chicken dips, mini-tarts and other treats at the Irish ambassador to South Africa's hilltop residence in Pretoria. 'That money could go a long way for some people.'

A little later at the function – an annual bash held for Irish missionaries working in South Africa and neighbouring countries – the nun agreed to sit down with me to talk about her work. None of it was big picture stuff. None of it was glamorous. She spent her time with people on the margins of society: prostitutes, criminals, men and women dying of HIV and Aids. She visited them. She spoke to them. She counselled them and sometimes prayed with them too. Occasionally, she'd give them practical advice, help them to fill out a form or put an application together for an ID card.

Often she'd just sit with them and listen. She told me of a young man – a convicted murderer – whom she had recently befriended. She didn't dispute his guilt but lamented how predictable his crime had been in light of his upbringing: a childhood of repeated abuse and neglect. 'There is such a pattern,' she sighed, 'of someone who is oppressed going on to oppress others.'

The more she spoke the more I realised how difficult it was to define precisely her job. As a journalist, you are used to pigeon-holing. You categorise, and try to explain why people do the things they do. But, with this sprightly, defiantly upbeat pensioner, I didn't know where to start. How could I go about reporting accurately on her movements? How could I illustrate the relationships she has built up? And how could I estimate the value of her work? It was tempting to put her in a box, along with those of her ilk, and label it along the lines of: 'religious oddities – hopelessly idealistic and outdated'. But I'd met enough missionary priests and nuns by then, and I'd learnt enough about their work from headlines they'd made down the years, to know that – among their number – there are individuals of great depth, integrity and wisdom.

As the nun continued to speak, I also had a growing sense that I'd somehow met her before. It dawned on me suddenly, she reminded me of someone who is close to me: my mother. It wasn't just her dislike of spending money on herself, nor her unfussy, modest attire. Not *just* anyway. It was something in this woman's personality. Her practical-minded, unselfpitying character was at once both personally familiar and universally recognisable as a hallmark of the Irish Mammy.

This was somewhat unnerving for me because my mother once told me that she had in her early twenties contemplated becoming a nun. Luckily for me, the idea never took hold, but it would have been a very normal career choice for an Irish Catholic woman of her generation and I couldn't help thinking, as I continued my conversation on the embassy lawn, that had my mother's life taken a different course she could possibly have filled the shoes of the nun sitting across from me. Not just that but it would have fallen on someone else to sit where I was and listen to her story.

There were other personal connections which drew me to the missionary story. My father-in-law worked for a time in Nigeria as a teacher in a Kiltegan-run school. Some uncles and aunts had links with missionary, or related development, work. I went to a Holy Ghost Fathers' school, where every month or so we were presented with a copy of *Outlook*, the congregation's propaganda magazine. But the idea of writing a book on the Irish missionaries formed in my mind after meeting that nun, and other priests and sisters who seemed to be cut from the same cloth. My aim, only then articulating itself, was not to write an abstract history of the Irish missionary movement. Nor was it to concoct a hagiography on the lives of some of Ireland's 'finest exports'. Rather I wanted to capture somehow the Irish missionary spirit – a spirit that in different guises and despite the passing years was still very much alive.

Why, I wondered, did these men and women join the missions? What has motivated them? Do they have regrets? And do they still feel an attachment to Ireland? The more missionaries I met the more I sensed that something quite unique was disappearing before our eyes. Unknowingly, I felt, a generation of what were once Ireland's most idealistic young men and women was slipping away, largely unacknowledged. In 2008, the number of Irish missionaries fell below 2,000 for the first time. The average age among them that same year was over 70. In a decade or so, there will be only a few hundred Irish missionaries left.

Have we given these people proper recognition? Have we truly acknowledged what they have done for others, or indeed for us? Have we properly rewarded them for their influence on Ireland's reputation throughout the world? Sure, missionaries receive praise

– and not insubstantial amounts of money – from the Irish public. Individual priests and nuns have been presented with a myriad of awards. But how deep is our understanding of the movement to which they belong?

In truth, much that has been spoken about missionaries down the years has been either false or patronising. At one extreme, there is missionary propaganda: the self-congratulatory magazines, books and films produced by congregations themselves for a Catholic audience. At the other, there are tokenistic expressions of approval for missionary work. Celebrities, politicians and journalists – I'd been guilty of it too – dip their toes into the world of missionaries and pat them on the back from time to time without really engaging with them, or taking them seriously. There are those who label the priests and nuns – as, indeed, I had been tempted to do – as well-meaning but antiquated peculiarities. There are others who view missionaries as part of a failed and much flawed enterprise. And there are those – perhaps a growing number – who are actively suspicious of missionaries or openly hostile to them. The recent Church scandals have badly damaged the reputation of Church congregations, including those working overseas, and there is good reason to believe that not all of the abuses committed in the past have yet been uncovered.

There are a few problems with writing a book such as this. The first is that Catholic missionary societies – and there are more than eighty of them in Ireland – are independent of one another. Each has its own archive, and there is no central coordinating agency, other than the Irish Missionary Union (IMU), a modestly resourced umbrella group primarily set up to represent them in policy areas. For the most part, moreover, congregations have put little value on record-keeping or archiving. Generally, they regard assessing their legacy, or even documenting their history, as a secondary concern compared to immediate, pressing demands in the field. Extracting information from individual missionaries can be no less troublesome. Some are nervous of talking to the media, and perhaps understandably so. Others are stubbornly humble and unwilling to attract any publicity for themselves, regarding self-publicity as vaguely distasteful. A journalistic colleague in Africa once told me about an extraordinary day he spent travelling with an Irish nun through the high-security prison where she worked. The nun took him to meet prisoners on death row and spoke of her counselling duties and the small moments of satisfaction that came with them. Walking out of the prison gates, my friend believed he had a great feature story. Until, that is, the nun turned to him and said: 'Now, you know, you can't write about any of this. I don't want my name in the paper.'

Of all the pitfalls with writing a book such as this, however, perhaps the greatest is overlooking the diversity of missionaries. In their ranks you will find mavericks and pioneers, conformists, rebels, revolutionaries, conservatives and liberals. Each speaks of having his or her own particular 'charism', a term missionaries use to describe their spiritual orientation or the special purpose of their work. It is, indeed, a broad church. And it would be misleading to present it as otherwise – as though scores of individual biographies could be condensed into one.

A further caution: this book sets limits for itself in timeframe and scope. It takes as a rough starting point the 1916 Maynooth Mission to China. This was not by any means the first Irish missionary enterprise, but it was the acknowledged dawn of a new era in evangelisation. While missionary recruitment in Ireland had been accelerating from the mid-nineteenth century onwards, 1916 was a major turning point and it led to an explosion of religious activity to which today's missionaries can trace their roots. Second, Catholic missionaries dominate in this book. That is not to devalue the contribution of missionaries from other religious denominations, and it should be noted that Ireland's first missionaries in modern times came from the Protestant Churches. In 1714, the 'Irish Auxiliary' to the Society for the Propagation of the Gospel was founded, sending members to Africa, India, Japan and West Africa. Baptist, Methodist and Presbyterian missions followed suit, but their influence in Ireland declined in tandem with the rise of Roman Catholicism here.

It should be emphasised also that Ireland was relatively slow to join the modern missionary movement. Having no colonies, and having being colonised itself, Ireland was for many years in no position to mount any sort of foreign crusade – other than the weary exodus on Famine ships under the spectre of starvation. When Dr David Livingstone of the London Missionary Society set off to 'discover' Africa in 1840, the first potato crop was just about to fail – leading to a fall in Ireland's population by 2 million through death and emigration. It should be noted, furthermore, that Ireland is not the only country with a strong missionary tradition. In many locations overseas, Irish people replaced, or worked alongside, missionaries from countries such as Poland, Germany and France, while today the work of Irish missionaries is increasingly being transferred to African, Asian and other indigenous missionaries. Fr Eamon Aylward, IMU secretary general and a former missionary in Mozambique, expanded on this point when he said: 'It is a mistake to see mission as something that is inherently Irish ... Mission is a universal call from the Gospels to preach the Good News.' It could be added here that 'missionaries', in the broadest sense, are not exclusively religious. People of no faith have been shown to be capable of making extraordinary commitments in the service of others.

For all that, however, there is something peculiar and unique, or perhaps uniquely peculiar, about Irish Catholic missionaries. There is, in the best of them, an indefatigable, optimistic nature. There is also a spirit of compassion and frontiersmanship whose legacy is considerable. A disproportionate number of Catholic missionary societies operating today emerged from Ireland. Then, there are the informal knock-on effects of the missionary movement. Campaigning Irish priests and nuns have influenced people from rock star and lobbyist Bono to Africa's first female Nobel Peace Prize winner Wangari Maathai. Missionaries provided the impetus for, or helped to establish directly, some of the world's biggest overseas development agencies. And they played no small part in educating the Irish public about a world outside its national borders and about its responsibilities to those less fortunate. At various times in the history of the Irish state, missionaries acted as society's surrogate conscience. They reminded us – or, at least, they tried to remind us – of certain old-fashioned values. In the field of charity, Irish missionaries demonstrated how ingenuity and risk-taking could bring the best out of people, and in the process they set an example for countless religious and secular imitators. In a sense, missionaries taught us how to give. They showed us how to turn platitudes into practical assistance, how someone in Ballydehob can change a life in Burkina Faso. They broke the mould on philanthropy.

This book is divided into two parts. The first part traces the history of the movement, drawing on the testimony of key missionary figures. The second part is more thematic, examining the nature of missionaries today, their ideology, their legacy and their future. The Bible quotes that start each chapter are references that were either cited by missionaries in conversation or feature prominently in their publications. They are used here as a reminder that, for good or ill, missionaries are inescapably religious. It is tempting sometimes to portray the best of them as somehow divorced from the Church, or even secularised, but this would be a clear misrepresentation.

Finally, some readers, missionaries included, will take issue with conclusions that are drawn. There is always a risk of historical revisionism when scrutinising events that took place up to a century ago. What is beyond dispute, however, is that a robust, critical analysis of the Irish missionary movement is both necessary and urgent. The significant contribution of missionaries should be acknowledged, while also recognising that missionaries are not saints. They are human beings, with flaws, who are struggling sometimes to perform saintly acts. They annoy, they agitate, they push boundaries and they don't like resting on their laurels. They are no shrinking violets but, rather, they are men who sometimes stand between cocked rifles and their flock, and they are 'women on fire with the healing love of God', to quote one congregation's mission statement. They are, at heart, people of action, these worn-sandalled philanthropists. They are the Good News army. They are God's entrepreneurs.

Joe Humphreys,
Dublin, 2010

INTRODUCTION

It is autumn, and Shay Cullen is in Dublin to pick up another award. Three times nominated (and counting) for the Nobel Peace Prize, the Columban priest is this month being named as Ireland's Rehab International Person of the Year. In a few months' time, he will back for a humanitarian prize at the Meteor Ireland Music Awards – which carries a cheque for €100,000 to help fund his work in combating child prostitution and sex tourism in the Philippines.

Despite his nearly forty years overseas, he still feels very Irish. 'You have got roots, and it's good to remain close to them,' he says, relaxing at his family home in the south Dublin village of Glasthule. He has been watching the fallout from the abuse scandals in the Catholic Church and speaks of his disgust and depression at the revelations. Not that he is altogether surprised. He recalls in his autobiography suffering physical and verbal abuse himself at his local Christian Brothers school. Things got so bad his mother protested to the brother superior but 'all her complaints fell on deaf ears'.

Cullen worries about the Church but also about the way Irish society is going, and how 'it has abandoned very fundamental values and has exchanged them for a hedonistic lifestyle'. But, he sighs, 'that is other people's mission. I am not called to be a St Patrick, you know, for Ireland and engage in mission here.'

Cullen's home – a modest, compact house which he and his siblings inherited after their parents died – is rented out at present to immigrant lodgers. Cullen stays in a lightly furnished prefab that he built at the end of the back garden for whenever he flies in. The priest introduces himself with two business cards. One carries the name of his Filipino charity Preda (People's Recovery, Empowerment and Development Assistance Fund). The other is labelled 'Writer – Journalist – Photographer'. Among his many roles these days is occasional social-affairs columnist for *The Manila Times*.

Asked whether he should first be described as a missionary rather than a campaigner, he harrumphs. 'I don't think we should try to put a label on ourselves or anyone else. The question that interests me is how to be an authentic Christian disciple of Jesus of Nazareth … I am not going to invent a better lightbulb, I am not going to be a super engineer. But I am going to be a person who can engage with human beings in their direst circumstance, and challenge the system which oppresses them.' Patiently, he adds: 'I think I understand what I am doing.'

As a missionary, Cullen can trace a direct lineage back to a group of Maynooth priests who plotted their escape from Ireland in 1916, forming a new religious society in the name of the sixth-century saint Columban. But Cullen's line of work is radically different from his predecessors. Preda is a Filipino organisation, and he is its only Columban member. Over the years, he has shaped his own form of mission – which has sometimes led to clashes with his superiors. 'You don't own me,' he is fond of telling them.

Early missionaries would be horrified at Cullen's rebelliousness. They mightn't even recognise his form of activism as the work of the Church. On paper, missionaries a century ago had one aim – and one aim only – to convert pagans to Christianity. By any means possible, they said, the more the better: each baptised baby meant one less soul doused in the flames of purgatory. 'God, you had to stop all that. That was terrible teaching,' says Cullen, when asked about the early missionaries. 'You have to break away from the miracle-mania of Christianity: "Oh, just go to church, take the sacraments and you are saved, it is a miracle, it is magic." They allowed people to think it is magic, and they were the magicians with all the power. Oh wow!'

To see how missionary work has changed over the years imagine yourself in a village in central Uganda in the early part of the last century. People there had lived in relative harmony for centuries until, one day, a strange, pink-skinned woman turned up with her ideas and an axe. She held the latter as she argued with village elders about a sacred tree that lay on the site that she had earmarked for her first mission station. The woman was Mother Kevin, a County Wicklow woman, born Teresa Kearney in 1875, and the place was Nkokonjeru, or the Valley of the White Hen, described as an 'evil and sinister' place in missionary propaganda. The date was 17 September 1926, and it represented something of a high noon in the battle between indigenous, 'heathen' culture and 'civilising' Western Christianity.

The tree that stood in Mother Kevin's way had been struck by lightning some years previously and this, in native folklore, gave it supernatural powers. Legend had it that the white hen – a fiery creature that stalked the valley, destroying crops – had taken up residence in its crooked branches. The tree's reputation grew further still when some Mill Hill priests arrived in the village to try to set up a mission. The priests used the branches as a prop for building planks but a seasonal thunderstorm spewed forth another 'hammer of fire'. The tree was left unscathed but the planks were reduced to ashes. By the time Mother Kevin had arrived in the village the tree had gained the status of a full-blown shrine. Locals hung trinkets and jewellery from its branches, seeking favours from the white hen. On the morning of 17 September, Mother Kevin took up where the priests had left off and started building foundations for her planned convent. Suddenly and quite inexplicably, the Nkokonjeru tree crashed to the ground.

Mother Kevin was 'not over-concerned with omens', according to her in-house biographer in the Franciscan Missionary Sisters for Africa, the congregation which she went on to found. 'Having put her undertaking under the protection of St Thérèse she held that "impossibles" did not exist.' Yet the Wicklow woman must have been a little nervous as she stood before the tree that day, axe in hand. News of the shrine's collapse had spread to surrounding villages and within hours of the calamity a large crowd had gathered before the Irish nun. Construction work on the convent had stopped as villagers whispered to one another that further defiling the resting place of the white hen would be suicide. At that, Mother Kevin's patience ran out. She appealed for volunteers to chop up the branches, and when no one answered her call she grabbed the axe herself. In her blinding white vestments, she advanced on the tree, stepping over the offerings and gifts that villagers had placed around the shrine. Beads of sweat formed on her face, which was framed by her starched wimple and the yawning frill of her habit, as she set her stocky body before a branch and then swung the axe – and swung it again. The crowd watched with both horror and awe as she attacked the tree with increasing fury. Seeing no harm had come to her, a group of men stepped forward from the crowd and joined her in clearing the site.

The story has been told with fondness down the ages by Mother Kevin's followers. Embellished with a sense of danger and mystique, it has been used to illustrate the indomitable spirit of the early Irish missionaries. But as the years pass Mother Kevin emerges from the story in a somewhat less positive light. Her physical courage and sense of purpose can't be disputed but a contemporary audience will be struck by her presumptuousness, her attitude of 'I know best', her disregard for local custom. Like other Catholic campaigners of her generation, Mother Kevin was certain of the righteousness of her cause, and that certainty was reflected in uncompromising commitment and action. It was, in fact, the only life she knew, having been reared by nuns following the death of her parents before she was ten years old.

But an anecdote such as this doesn't sum up the entirety of Mother Kevin's character. During World War I, Kearney ran a field hospital for Allied troops in East Africa, earning an MBE for her courage under fire. In the more than thirty years she subsequently spent running hospitals and schools in the region, she won the respect of local governments and communities. Fondly known as 'Mama Kevina', she never lost her focus on evangelisation and she 'would have scoffed at the idea of being called a philanthropist', according to her biographer. But her work had an undisputed social dimension. She campaigned for nuns to have the right to work in medicine and midwifery and challenged the prevailing view in the Church that the missionary's job was merely to convert. Discussing Africa's high rate of infant mortality with a colleague on one occasion, she agreed it was 'a grace' to be able to baptise children before they died. 'But we won't build a living Church on dead babies,' she said. 'We must help the living.' After she herself died, the archbishop of Boston, Richard Cardinal Cushing remarked: 'Now, in some of the tongues of Africa, a *Kevin* or a *Kevina* means a hospital, a school, any institution of charity... Better still, *to do a kevina* is to perform an act of peerless generosity, of inestimable service to a neighbour, of perfect love.'

The truth is the missionary movement has always been evolving – and it's still in transition today. Missionaries moved from pure evangelism to something close to pure social work in a generation or two. They have lived through times of religious fervour and homogeneity and have coped – if not flourished – in more multicultural and secular settings. Throughout, however, some of the challenges faced by missionaries have remained constant: how to assimilate with alien cultures without compromising on core beliefs, how to intervene in people's lives without undermining their independence, how to promote certain Christian values without indoctrinating. The missionary movement has always lived with certain contradictions, and it also accommodated both the good and the bad.

The Murphy Report, published in November 2009, illustrated in just one particular context how this was so. It examined the cases of forty-six priests who served in the Archdiocese of Dublin and against whom allegations of child sexual abuse were made. Two of that sample study had strong links to missionary orders: Fr Patrick Maguire, a Columban who admitted that he might have been responsible for about 100 cases of abuse, and Fr Tom Naughton, who worked in Africa and the West Indies with the Kiltegan Fathers before he joined the Dublin Archdiocese where he serially abused altar boys. There were other priests named in the report who had spent time working in the missions. These included the pseudonymous Fr Laurentius, 'a promiscuous man' who confessed to a superior to having a sexual relationship with eight women in Africa and thirty-eight women in other countries, mainly Ireland. He said all his relationships were consensual and with adults but the report said he had attracted two complaints from teenaged girls in Ireland.

Just as these people brought shame onto the missionary movement, however, there were others who brought honour to it. Sandwiching the publication of the Murphy Report were two events which cast Irish priests in an entirely different light. On 11 October 2009, Fr Michael Sinnott – a 78-year-old Columban priest – was kidnapped in conflict-ridden Pagadian in the Philippines. He was released thirty-one days later, praising his captors for treating him so well, before returning to his work with special-needs children. Then, on 11 December 2009, Fr Jerry Roche, a 68-year-old

Kiltegan priest, was stabbed to death in a suspected botched robbery at his home in Kenya, where he had worked for more than forty years. Mourners at his funeral in Athea, County Limerick, remembered him as a gentle and unassuming man but – using an adjective that Roche himself liked to drop into conversation – 'mighty' nonetheless.

Who is more representative of the missionary movement? Sinnott and Roche? Or Maguire and those like him who abused positions of trust? The bad apples are few in number but they were allowed to go unchallenged for years and, in this, many people are implicated. Missionaries pride themselves on their spirit of free enterprise, but the system they've created for themselves is so decentralised and diverse it allows both good and evil to survive. Accountability is not a strong point among missionaries and, as a whole, Irish priests and nuns working abroad are not overly concerned with the finer points of law, be it state or Canon. They like their freedom, and they believe – with good reason – that they know what's best for their community more than any civil servant in Dublin or any cardinal in Rome.

Today missionary societies face some tough questions. Did they monitor their personnel closely enough? Did their regimes of training, or formation, cause some of the problems we see today? Did they send people abroad with the right intentions? Were they too arrogant or too presumptuous? Did they prioritise 'saving souls' over helping people in their daily lives?

For Cullen, there have always been two battles going on: one outside the Church and one within. He speaks of the 'infectious' faith of Fr Niall O'Brien, his Columban colleague who was imprisoned in the Philippines in the 1980s for defending the rights of the poor. But Cullen knows the radical theology that O'Brien promoted gained little traction under the last two popes. Cullen himself has been harassed and threatened by both criminals and police. His enemies have slandered him by accusing him of paedophilia.

At the same time, Cullen has been criticised and undermined by some members of his own congregation and of the wider Church. He says certain priests used to encourage him to move into a 'less political' area of work but his answer was always the same: 'What for? I would do the same mission wherever I was.' He recalls citing *Rerum Novarum*, Pope Leo XIII's encyclical on the condition of the working classes, to one clerical interrogator. 'What's that?' came the reply. He was told to leave his mission 'to the social workers', and besides, 'social work is socialism, isn't it? And that's close to communism.'

Cullen laughs giddily as he recollects these exchanges. His accent dips deeper into Filipino, with its elongated 'e's, and a lilt that turns every few sentences into a question, as he continues: 'Anyone who takes the gospel seriously has to remember this Jesus of Nazareth ended up with the death penalty, no?' He smiles. 'When you think of it, and look at that crucifix, you are looking at a criminal. We worship a man who was the son of God who ended up as a criminal hanging on a cross, and we have kind of forgotten that.'

It would be wrong to think of today's missionaries as entirely divorced from the past – as though one generation of priests and nuns was more progressive, or indeed better, than the last. As a whole, missionaries have always challenged the prevailing consensus. In whatever era they've lived, they've raised questions that no one else was asking and – like Cullen today – they've proposed unsettling and unexpected solutions to some of the big problems of their time. Asked whether he feels any attachment to the Church, given all its recent scandals, Cullen replies without flinching: 'My faith is in Jesus of Nazareth. I don't have faith in an institution and nobody wants that. That is not authentic faith.'

Part I

CHAPTER I: THE OTHER RISING

'Go then to all peoples everywhere and make them my disciples: baptise them in the name of the Father, the Son and the Holy Spirit, and teach them to obey everything I have commanded you.' (Matthew 28:19–20)

Autumn 1916: Europe was at war and Ireland was in political turmoil. The Easter Rising had brought a centuries-old struggle for Irish independence to a head. As the leaders of that rebellion were executed in quick succession, public opinion turned against British rule. By the time Roger Casement was hanged in August, a misguided and dangerous band of Republican rebels had been transformed into martyrs and visionaries. There was a whiff of revolution in the air. Even in conservative, insulated Ireland, it was clear the world – the entire world – was changing. And for those with their future ahead of them there was a stark choice: either be part of that change or a witness to it.

It was in this tumultuous season – in September, to be precise – that two young priests, Edward Galvin and John Blowick, met in a house in south County Dublin to organise a religious missionary expedition to China. Their proposal was as ambitious then as it is preposterous today. Groups of young Irish men, armed with nothing but the New Testament and a proselytising zeal, would travel 5,000 miles east to convert a pagan nation to Catholicism.

Galvin, a Corkman, had first travelled to China in 1912 and

spent four years there, trying to service the hotchpotch of Christian communities that had been set up by French Vincentians. Working largely alone in a vicariate with a population of '11,000,000 pagans', to use his own description, Galvin said Mass, heard confession and prepared people for baptism. But he was depressed by how 'ignorant, very ignorant sometimes' the locals were of their religion. 'The poor Chinese are only just converted; they have no such traditions of the Faith,' he wrote in one of a series of letters to the students of Maynooth College, Ireland's main training ground for priests.

Galvin had been ordained at the institution in 1909. With a glut of young priests in Ireland, he travelled to New York where he found work in a parish in Brooklyn. There, the tall, earnest Galvin met a Canadian missionary called John Fraser who persuaded him over dinner to take up a vacancy in China. Galvin had always yearned to travel, and he accepted the challenge of a very isolated posting with some pluck, as his letters home illustrated. There were stories of cramped living conditions, arduous physical labour and novel cultural encounters. In one letter, he described how he broke the ice with elder gentlemen by joining them in pipe-smoking – a popular pastime that left everyone 'enshrouded in cloudy happiness'. In another missive, laced with adventure and derring-do, he described how he trekked from dawn to dusk across a mountain and through marshlands to reach a sick parishioner. Halfway through the journey, he had to cross a river which had burst its banks under a dangerously strong current. 'Twelve miles further on there was a Catholic seriously ill and in need of the Sacraments. Something must be done…' And he, the letter made clear in breathless prose, was the man to do it. He commandeered a boat which then crashed into a river bank, nearly killing both Galvin and the boat's owner. The latter was not amused when the priest hastily fled the scene but, Galvin giggled, 'it takes a fleet Chinaman to catch a Cork rebel'.

Letters such as these weren't for amusement. Galvin was deadly serious about his work in bringing Christianity to China and was convinced that other Irish priests had a role to play. So while he wrote of much incident and hardship, he also wrote of the great sense of purpose and satisfaction he got from the job. 'I am never so happy as when on the missions, and though you sometimes meet with difficulties and trials, yet the consolations and joy you experience far out-number them. You are conscious of doing much good. You feel that a solid foundation is being laid slowly but surely, and that the seedling you now care for and nurture will one day blossom forth into a mighty tree.'

This was intoxicating stuff for the students of Maynooth. These were young men who were considered the most upstanding of their generation: bright sparks in school who had made their mothers proud by going into the priesthood. They were ambitious and idealistic but, due partly to their oversupply, they were about to be shipped off in their droves to America and Australia or wherever else the Irish diaspora had landed. Galvin offered his peers an alternative future. He held up the promise of colonising a new land: virgin territory that would form part of a new Catholic empire. Better still, it would be an Irish Catholic empire.

Among those who learnt of Galvin's adventures was John Blowick, a priest of the archdiocese of Tuam, ordained in 1913. Blowick was everything Galvin wasn't: an intellectual and an organiser, with proven administrative skills. An outstanding scholar, he was promoted to professor of dogmatic theology in Maynooth while still studying for his doctorate of divinity. But he was conflicted. He too had encountered John Fraser, the Canadian priest, and had come under the well-trained orator's spell. In 1911, Fraser addressed the students and staff of Maynooth College, describing how 'nauseated' he had been to see the Chinese people prostrating themselves before idols. Seizing the opportunity to mould some impressionable young minds, Fraser railed not only against non-

Christian faiths such as Buddhism, but also against Christian missionaries of other churches who were 'emissaries of Satan sowing the seed of perdition in this vast vineyard of the Lord'.

Blowick had been 'at once fascinated and appalled' by Fraser's accounts of China, according to one Church historian. 'He [Blowick] had never been able to forget, and when, as a professor of theology, he lectured his students about the universality of the Church, the question kept hammering in his mind: "Couldn't I be doing something about making the Church universal instead of just talking about it?"'[1]

Blowick's opportunity came when Galvin arrived back to Ireland to try to drum up support for his cause. The now bearded man of letters, best known to his peers as 'Ned' or later by his Chinese name 'Caw' (pronounced 'Ga-aw'), requested a meeting with the young professor of whom he had heard great things. A mutual friend, Father Thomas Ronayne, had informed Galvin of Blowick's interest in China. 'I saw immediately,' Galvin later wrote, 'that here might be the outstanding priest whom I had been hoping and praying that the Lord would provide.' Ahead of the meeting, Ronayne told Blowick exactly what Galvin was looking for. 'He wants a man of position, a man whom the bishops will support and back by practical approval, to come forward as head of the whole affair. This man will, so Galvin says, have to volunteer and give his life [*sic*] work for China... a Kitchener of the new army, so to speak.'

A date was set: 4 September 1916, 8 p.m., at Ronayne's house, 16 Longford Terrace, Monkstown. Galvin arrived early. 'I felt,' he wrote many years later, 'that this interview would be an important one for me and the mission, so I tried to put my ideas in order and I said a few prayers too.' Blowick joined him moments later on the doorstep. They stood there, each unaware of the other's identity, until Ronayne opened the door and introduced them to one another amid much nervous laughter. According to one account,

Ronayne's sister Maggie watched the three make their way up to the priest's quarters and then reported the scene to her mother: 'Father Blowick and a strange priest have gone up to Tommy's room and certainly there's some scheme afoot.'[2]

This encounter did not mark the start of the Irish missionary movement. Religious men and women had been leaving Ireland for decades, or centuries if you count Saint Columba of Iona and the 'Twelve Irish Apostles' who – in the early medieval period – kept Christianity alive across Europe. The dawn of the twentieth century saw some formidable new missionaries emerge, including Bishop Joseph Shanahan and Teresa 'Mother Kevin' Kearney, who helped to lay the foundations of the Catholic Church in central Africa. But 4 September 1916 does mark a beginning of sorts – the start of a recognisably modern missionary movement and a turning-point in terms of scale.

The combined efforts of Galvin and Blowick led not only to the founding of the Society of St Columban, an organisation which would send hundreds of Irishmen across the globe, but the establishment of at least four other influential missionary societies. More importantly, perhaps, they heralded a new era of missionary innovation and ideas. Priests and nuns branched into new fields, maternity care prominent among them, and into new territories. Influenced by social and demographic changes in the early twentieth century, the work of missionaries also grew massively in popularity. Missionaries were perceived as reconnecting the newly independent Irish Republic to its heritage as an Isle of Saints and Scholars. As an expression of a kind of proud, uncompromising Catholicism, becoming a missionary was seen as an outstanding – if not patriotic – thing for any young Irish man or woman to do.

The future was not so clear, however, when Galvin and Blowick first met in autumn 1916. They had no money. They had no recruits. They had no premises in which to base themselves. More problematic still, they had no supporters in the Catholic hierarchy in Ireland, or indeed the Vatican. The sanction of both would be needed for Galvin and Blowick's project to get off the ground, and Irish bishops were initially wary of the idea. They had overseen a number of missionary ventures in previous decades that had flopped. Priests and nuns had periodically gone to places in Asia and Africa with ambitious plans only to return sheepishly a few years later depressed by their failures. Chief among the sceptics in the Irish hierarchy was the deeply conservative Archbishop of Dublin William J. Walsh. He had a habit of refusing all priests' requests for transfers overseas and took grave offence at Galvin and Blowick's decision to start canvassing support for a missionary society without first personally notifying him. The 75-year-old archbishop believed the young priests were trying to establish a college 'in his diocese behind his back', and he sought to block the initiative at a meeting of the Standing Committee of the Roman Catholic Bishops in October 1916. Blowick was asked to appear before the bishops to explain himself, and all his diplomatic skills were needed to placate the archbishop and keep the plan for a Chinese mission alive. Aware of some hostility in the committee room, and conscious of the need to allow Walsh save face, Blowick asked for two things: permission to appeal to parishioners for funds and permission to found a missionary training college, the location of which would be agreed at a later date with the archbishop. This measured plea won the day, and Blowick and Galvin wasted no time in putting their plan into action.

On 22 October 1916, Galvin began a fundraising drive that would see him criss-cross the country over twelve months, preaching at Sunday Masses with a team of supporting priests. The group gave themselves a name: the Society of St Columban, in honour of the legendary Irish missionary. A magazine advocating its work, *The Far East*, was launched. Its idiosyncratic editor John Henaghan used the language of the crusade to appeal to readers. The priests and students volunteering for the mission were, he wrote, 'a bodyguard around the Person of Christ, an advance party to spy out the ground in this undying war to push the standard of the Cross into the farthest outposts of heathendom'. Archbishop Walsh of Dublin refused the Columbans a site for a training college, but the bishop of Galway was more welcoming, giving them the keys to Dalgan Park, an old Georgian building with a large farm twenty miles north of Galway city. At the same time, Blowick began lobbying for a territory of their own.

In those days, there were two ways of securing a missionary colony. The first was to negotiate a plot with the local bishop. He would usually greet the request by pointing the enthusiastic newcomer to a desolate or isolated parish that he had already given up on. This didn't appeal to the Maynooth men. They wanted an urban vicariate: a densely populated area with plenty of schools through which they could disseminate the Gospel. Their preference was for a city in which English – the commercial language of China – was commonly spoken. A city might also sustain a Catholic university, a pipe-dream of Galvin's at the outset. Such ambition meant turning to the second source of vicariates: the Vatican.

In 1917, the Columbans opened discussions with Rome about securing a territory in China. It would take three years before the negotiations were complete. In that era, land for evangelising was carved up by Rome with all the crude precision of a Western coloniser. The Vatican rolled out a map and argued the toss with the greedy applicants. Galvin set his sights on Eastern Hupeh, one of the most densely populous areas in China. Italian Franciscans were already located there, and the Vatican had records of 39,000 Catholics dwelling among a population of 16 million. Galvin and Blowick believed they could deliver a better return and made a case for being handed the ripest territory in Eastern Hupeh: the city of Hankow. Standing on the banks of the broad Yangtze River, at its intersection with the Han, Hankow was a thriving market town which still hosted colonial officers from Britain, France and Japan in the aftermath of World War I. The city was connected by bridges to Hanyang, to the south, and Wuchang, to the west – three conurbations that make up modern-day Wuhan, the most populous city in central China.

In bidding for the site, the Irish priests presented themselves as a highly professional and even modernistic outfit, boldly claiming that they would succeed where Catholic emissaries from other nationalities had failed. 'Galvin believed the French missionaries were stuck in a rut,' explained Neil Collins, an historian of the Columbans. 'When he was working with them during his early years in China, Galvin couldn't bring in new ideas – even down to riding a horse. "Jesus walked," I suppose, was their attitude.'

In contrast to the aloof, cerebral French, Galvin and his crew would be dwelling right in among the people – and here he borrowed from the Irish experience. 'Wherever missionaries go, there is an issue around how to access the people to preach the Gospel. You can't just walk into their houses,' said Collins. 'Schools, Galvin thought, were going to be their instrument.'

This was all well and good. However, the Columbans were an untried outfit, and self-confidence would only get them so far with the cardinals. The key argument used by Galvin and Blowick, then, was somewhat different. In an era before ecumenism, one of the chief concerns of the Vatican was the spread of Protestant missionaries to Asia. The then pope, Benedict XV, had himself described such preachers as 'the ministers of error', and he was receptive to any idea that might reduce their influence. Galvin and Blowick were happy to oblige, arguing somewhat cynically that the ongoing war in Europe made it an opportune time to push into

China. Across the globe, countless Protestant ministers had been called up to serve as chaplains in the British Army, leaving a void in their mission fields. Collins claimed the Columbans 'played up' the Protestant threat because they knew that was what the Vatican wished to hear. He said Galvin had been on good terms with Protestant missionaries in China and even consulted them over his planned new Catholic schools. But Rome heard none of this. Instead, the Columbans would base their sales pitch on what Galvin called 'our Protestant argument'. Their stated goal would be 'to counteract the influence of heretics'.

It was a message that went down well in Rome – even though at times the Columbans were seen as overly ambitious. 'You are dreadfully exclusive. You always ask for Hankow as if there were Protestants nowhere else. Why are you so exclusive?' one official in the Holy See asked. 'Not exclusive by any means,' Galvin and Blowick wrote back, with some bravado. 'We will take Shanghai or Canton, or Peking, or Tientsin. All we want is a city suitable for the work we are going out specially to do, and which you admit is the work which suits us especially, namely to counteract the influence of Protestantism, and Hankow is their citadel.'

There were other roadblocks in the negotiations. Blowick was on business in Ireland in May 1917 when he received notice to return to Rome immediately. A malicious rumour had spread that the Society of St Columban was merely a front for patriotic Irishmen who wanted to draft-dodge the British Army. Unfortunately for the Maynooth men, this claim had a credible ring to it. There were very real fears that the British government would introduce conscription in Ireland as the war continued, and the Catholic Church in Ireland had already seen a wave of hurried 'Lloyd George ordinations'. Now, the launch of the Columbans was being placed in this context. Blowick set off for the Vatican on a damage-limitation exercise. Of those speaking out against the mission, he recalled years later: 'They said we weren't genuine missionaries at all. We were a bunch of Sinn Féiners who were providing a decent front for priests that didn't want to go to the army.'

The Vatican might well have been picking up second-hand information from the British government, which had labelled Galvin and Blowick as nationalistic, anti-Protestant agitators. The Maynooth missionaries 'can be nothing but a menace to England in China', according to one British intelligence report. They were 'stirring up enthusiasm for the greatest cause on earth, i.e. Ireland'. A civil servant in London added a note in the margins saying 'the priests are probably Sinn Féiners'.

In November 1919, word finally came from Rome. It had 'consented to give us the city of Hanyang with a certain piece of country around it', Blowick relayed to one of his colleagues. The territory covered an area of 8,500 square miles (22,015 sq. km) and had a population of five million people. It was a less densely populated area than Hankow – which stared at it from across the River Han. Most of the men living there were illiterate farmers and fisherman. But it was a substantial colony, and it would be supplemented in time with two other vicariates from Rome. Nancheng, in southern China, and Huchow, near Shanghai, in the east, were to become the Columbans' second and third missionary territories. *The Far East* reported the breakthrough with typical restraint. 'At last the momentous word has come from Rome. An Irish vicariate has been established in China. The wire flashed across Europe the tidings that a definite field in the vast vineyard of Christ in China had been assigned to Irish missionaries. The reveille has sounded; the door has opened; out yonder is the battleground for Christ.'

Finally, after three years in planning, the first band of Maynooth missionaries left Dalgan Park for China. The group, which sailed from Ireland on 26 March 1920, was headed by Fathers Blowick and Galvin. The remainder included experienced and newly ordained priests, including two who had taken their vows just six weeks before their departure date. *The Irish Times* recorded the missionaries' adventure that week but only in the context of a curious incident before they had left. While the priests' luggage was sitting in Broadstone Railway Station, a contingent of British soldiers and police – purportedly acting on intelligence – surrounded the platform and ordered that the boxes of clothes, books and chalices be searched for ammunition. None was found.

There has been much debate in academia about the influence of the Rising on the missionary movement, and particularly the Maynooth Mission to China. Historian Edmund M. Hogan, a member of the Society of African Missions and author of *The Irish Missionary Movement: A Historical Survey, 1830–1980*, wrote of the 'smouldering emotionalism' that surfaced in the aftermath of 1916. This atmosphere was ripe for a missionary movement that blended the high ideals of Republicanism and Christian sacrifice.

What is certain is neither Blowick nor Galvin were afraid of playing the nationalist card. The latter's early letters from China appealed to a nascent spirit of independence. 'Have we not as strong a faith as the French, the Italians, the Belgians?' Galvin asked. 'Are we not quite as prepared to make sacrifices for God as they are? In the past, most of the priests Ireland could spare were sent to America and Australia… but now… Ireland is comparatively free to turn her attention to the heathen world. What glorious conquests await her!'

The Far East, which by 1920 had 60,000 subscribers in America alone, forced home the point with language that was 'a mixture of argument and exhortation, persuasion and encouragement. It was directed as much to the imagination as to the intellect.'[3] Priests and bishops spoke of a 'war for Christ in Africa and Asia' and of the need to 'enlarge the boundaries of Christ's kingdom'. In a paper entitled *Ireland's Destiny*, Dr Edward Leen – a Holy Ghost Father who was closely associated with the Nigerian missions – told students at Dalgan Park: 'There is something natural in the spirit of conquest… This tendency, being natural, is good if rightly directed.' In a revealing letter, Fr Edward J. McCarthy – a founder member of the Columbans – wrote to his classmate Fr Joseph P. O'Leary, who was fundraising for the China mission: 'If you want money move their hearts and you can only do that by praising up the Irish Faith, getting sentimental about "the wrongs of ould Ireland", putting a halo of glory and heroism about lads like you and Galvin, comparing your sacrifice to that of the patriots who died for Ireland.' A somewhat cynical strategy perhaps, but by the end of 1917 the Columbans had £40,000 in the kitty, along with seventeen priests and twelve student volunteers. It had also begun a relationship with the public, which would grow and deepen in the following decades. Mothers, widows and lowly paid workers were among those who began sending subscriptions to the society. Some were accompanied by letters, pleading for prayers or intercessions. 'I have a cancer lump in my breast and with God's help you'll do something for me,' wrote one woman to Blowick, enclosing a five-shilling order. Another woman arranged to meet the priest so she could give him five pounds – all the money she had. When Blowick protested she burst into tears. 'It is to God I give,' she told him, 'and you have no right to refuse.'

The influence of the Rising on the missionary movement can be overstated. But it did pave the way for a new form of Catholicism in Ireland: assertive, unapologetic, evangelising. Patrick Pearse, the 1916 leader, had himself drawn on Christian rhetoric in his speeches and, in the words of one historian, 'had transcended mundane Church teaching with a vision of morality which equated what he saw as Ireland's redemption with the work of the Redeemer himself.'[4] As he toured around Ireland raising support for his cause, Blowick read Pearse's account of Scoil Éanna, and he modelled Dalgan Park along similar lines – right down to using the Irish language in teaching. Pearse's school promoted brotherly fraternity and a spirit of self-sacrifice and loyalty. The Columbans tried to mimic that, establishing a code of familial obedience in their founding constitution. 'The same family spirit,' the constitution stated, 'demands that members should promptly carry out the will of the Superior not only when he gives an order but even when, as often happens, he merely recommends or lets his wishes be known.'

Reflecting on the influence of the Easter Rising years later, Blowick said it 'helped our work indirectly. I know for a fact that many of the young people of the country had been aroused into a state of heroism and zeal by the Rising of 1916 and by the manner in which the leaders met their death… And, accordingly, when we put our appeal before the young people of the country it fell on soil which was far better prepared to receive it than if there never had been an Easter week.'

Ninety years after it was founded, Dalgan Park is still producing Columbans, but few if any of the newcomers have even heard of the Rising. The last Irishman to be ordained in the society was in 1999, and all thirty-six of its seminarians in 2010 came from either South East Asia or South America. The society's headquarters moved in 1940 from County Mayo to an estate near the Hill of Tara in County Meath, where the name of the seminary was retained. Today, the corridors of the greystone building are whisperingly quiet as though it's a school permanently in holiday season. Large crowds gather a few times each year – for diamond and golden jubilees and funerals, as well as for an annual commemorative Mass for the families of deceased priests. But most days it is vacant but for the likes of a religious retreat, a workshop for returned missionaries or a visit from day-tripping school students. The latter generally come for the wildlife sanctuary, located in the park's 500 acres of woods, rather than the college itself, which houses a small museum detailing the history of the Columbans. Within the house, the high point of the day is lunchtime when visitors and priests – including those veterans who have long returned from the field and now reside in Dalgan Park – come down from their rooms and share a meal in the canteen. The talk is often of recently deceased colleagues.

Ferreted away in one corner of the building on a recent visit was the Columban historian Neil Collins. Surrounded by shelves of memorabilia – dog-eared, ancient copies of *The Far East*, early Dalgan lecture notes, correspondence from across the globe and piles of sepia-toned photographs – Collins was halfway through what promised to be the most thorough historical survey of the society to date. Having completed a PhD on the history of the society from 1916–1954, summarising his findings in a book *The Splendid Cause* (2008), Collins embarked on a second phase of research that would cover the intervening years. When asked how long he thought it would take to finish, the Derry man groaned: 'I'm not setting myself a deadline.'

As a Columban himself, ordained in 1962 and educated in Oxford, with close to twenty years' experience in the Philippines, he acknowledged the more you dug the more complex the past became. Take the relationship between Galvin and Blowick. While the society's official history suggested they were like-minded souls, 'in a whole lot of areas they were quite contradictory'. Blowick only spent a few months in China before returning to Ireland, and his focus was on creating a highly educated, superior missionary force. Galvin, who became the first bishop of Hanyang, wanted bodies in the field as quickly as possible, believing training was best done on the hoof. 'Galvin's idea was all the money should go to China, so building a seminary here was beyond his thinking,' noted Collins, 'whereas Blowick knew that if you want to produce students you need a decent place for them to live in.' This disagreement came to a head in 1924 when Galvin came home from China with the single objective of stopping Blowick from being re-elected as superior of the Columbans. While the dispute was unrecorded in official documents, Collins had it on oral record that Galvin regretted his intervention in later life. 'When he came home here in 1952, in a discussion in another house on these grounds, he said one of the mistakes that was made was getting Blowick out of office. And one of the other priests said, "That was your doing, Caw."'

Galvin died in 1956, the same year Collins joined the Columbans. Just over a half-century later, there were only a handful of old-timers at Dalgan who had direct recollections of the society's founder. They spoke of a determined, resilient man and leader: a man who wouldn't ask anyone to do something he hadn't done himself. No *bon vivant* but no dullard either. Someone with a deep, almost brooding faith.

Typically, Galvin never kept a diary, or wrote memoirs. 'He is the active missionary,' said Collins. 'John Blowick would have been into putting things on paper. Galvin was not into that.' What Galvin did do, however, was write letters – lots of urgent and sometimes unguarded letters – and these shed some light on his personality.

Probably the most revealing of these was written before he had planned the society's formation. After meeting Fraser in New York in 1912, and making the rather impulsive decision to travel with him on the next boat to China, Galvin sat down to pen a goodbye note to his mother. 'Don't grieve, don't cry,' he wrote. 'Mother, you know how this has always been on my mind. But I thought it was a foolish thought, a boyish whim; that it would pass away as I grew older. But it never passed, never, never, never. I can't write; I feel like a man going to the scaffold… I am leaving this morning,

28 February, for China. Oh, I hate that name. But I am going for Christ's sake and to save souls that are dearer to him than all the world.'

The psychological factors at play between Irish priests and their mothers calls for a book in itself but, suffice to say, Galvin was doted on by his mother in County Cork and their separation often played on his mind. 'I don't think you ever choose exile,' he once confided in a colleague. The worst was having to say goodbye, and each time he'd return to his mother's home in Newcestown, near Macroom, for a visit he would dread the final hugs and kisses before he would have to board a train and begin the lonely two-month journey back to China. On one return trip, in 1924, he slipped out of the family homestead without even saying goodbye. He'd left a message with his mother that he'd business to attend to in Dublin, and then he just kept going, until he was able to send word that he'd boarded a steamer for the Far East. Cutting the apron strings was all the more difficult because of the dangers involved in the missions. Any Irish priest going abroad in those days faced the real likelihood of never seeing their family again.

Galvin's strong bond with his mother perhaps explains why he was particularly saddened at the mistreatment of women in China. It was not uncommon among poor families for girls to be sold into slavery or otherwise disposed of when they were seen to be a drain on resources. As well as voicing concern on this, Galvin worried constantly about whether the Chinese parents whom he instructed would have a strong enough faith to pass it onto their children. Writing to the Maynooth students on this subject of indoctrination, he remarked: 'Think, for instance, of our own Irish mothers, and all we owe them.'

A review of the archived correspondence from Galvin and his peers also provides evidence that the Columbans undertook a very different type of mission to that pursued by their members today.

They had a rigid, almost colonial, religious mindset, and they showed little respect for other faiths. *The Far East* spoke unapologetically of 'the conversion of China by Ireland'. Even the internationalist, well-read Blowick uncritically endorsed the Vatican's teaching on unbelievers and argued against relaxing the Church's ban on celebrating Mass for a dead heretic. 'No one is saved outside the Church,' he wrote in an article, *Extra Ecclesiam Nemo Salvatur*, in September 1916. He depicted Jews and Muslims as 'primitives' in their faith but conceded they were better than atheists and pantheists who, he argued, through their own fault did not believe in God and would be punished in hell. 'If there be, then, bona fide atheists they shall never gaze upon the infinite beauty of God, face to face, but they will probably be the companions of those infants who die without the saving laver of regeneration.' Like many an Irish clergyman in the early twentieth century, Blowick had probably never met a 'bona fide atheist'. But he was nonetheless happy to condemn them to eternity in Limbo, along with children who had not been baptised (which meant most Chinese).

Doctrine such as this formed part of the rigid curriculum taught at Dalgan Park. The catechetical textbook, which was used there, and also typically in other seminaries, described Christians outside of Catholicism as 'adversaries'. Islam was worse still, with Mohammed accused of being 'aflame with the most foul lust in polygamy and adultery' and thus 'as the herald, not of the holy God, but of the evil devil'.

Thankfully, attitudes to women were somewhat more enlightened. Both Galvin and Blowick advocated the recruitment of women missionaries in China not only to help spread the gospel but also to try to challenge the low status afforded to women in the country. Acting on this plan, Blowick made a memorable appeal at Dublin's Mansion House in October 1917 'for a new congregation of nuns whose vow would be the medical care of the sick in pagan countries, whose members would be properly qualified in medicine, surgery and midwifery'.

It was memorable, at least, for one member of the audience. Lady Frances Moloney, widow of the former governor-general of Trinidad, was aged forty-four when she heard Blowick speak. Her husband had died four years previously and she had returned to Dublin to work with the city's poor, including neglected Belgian refugees who had been sent to Ireland when the war broke out. Blowick's appeal was quite radical at the time as the Church then prohibited nuns from working in medicine and especially midwifery. Specifically, it feared that were the nuns to have contact with young women who were having children, it might corrupt them morally or threaten their chastity. In 'Norms for the Approbation of New Institutes', issued by the Holy See in 1901 – and repeated in 1921 – the Church outlawed religious personnel from giving aid in childbirth and from attending women in maternity homes. The 'Code of Canon Law', published in 1917, further forbade the practice of medicine and surgery other than in exceptional circumstances. The Vatican was, in theory, able to issue a special dispensation but this was very rarely done.

Many women in the Church campaigned for change, and Blowick saw logic in their cause, albeit in rather sectarian terms. 'Protestant doctors and nurses are literally flocking to China – at the present moment there are 200 lady doctors in China, while we have not even one.' While Galvin broadly supported the move, he was less ambitious and also a little sceptical of women's ability. After returning to China, he recommended the Columbans try to recruit nuns with basic educational qualifications rather than medical specialists. 'Lady doctors are not, I think, practical,' he wrote. 'In practice men doctors do not want to work with lady doctors. To put it frankly, they cannot agree, so at least the doctor here assures me, and I have got the same view from a Protestant lady doctor.'

Moloney heard many such insults in the wake of Blowick's address at the Mansion House. Bishops told her not to defy God's will. Priests warned her not to get above her station. But a seed had been planted – another seed in a sprouting missionary movement. The well-connected society widow started recruiting women to her cause and together they would prove the patronising men in collars spectacularly wrong.

CHAPTER 2: NEW LEADERS

'The footsteps of those who bring good news are a welcome sound.'
(Romans 10:9–18)

Frances Moloney was just one of a string of impressive, pioneering women missionaries. If Galvin and Blowick thought they had it tough advancing new ideas in a conservative, inward-looking Church, at least they weren't the target of crippling, institutionalised gender discrimination. Moloney had it all to contend with as she planned to set up a new missionary congregation that would give women a role in medicine and midwifery. She was obstructed by bishops and underestimated even by well-intentioned priests like Galvin. In a comment that epitomised the casual chauvinism of the day, the founder of the Columban Fathers complained about American Protestant women missionaries because they were 'inclined to think for themselves'. Where nuns worked alongside priests in the 1920s, it was very much in a subordinate role. The priest's duty was to preach, to convert and to perform the sacraments. The nun's duty was to support him in whichever way he chose.

Moloney, however, didn't let such attitudes stand in her way. A few months after Blowick's appeal at the Mansion House, she approached some of her charity-oriented women friends and they agreed to petition Rome for permission to form a missionary society. While waiting for an answer, they arranged to get some nursing experience and medical training and hunted down a suitable location to establish their novitiate. The Columban Sisters was founded in 1922 but it would take another four years of bargaining, persuasion and fundraising before they were able dispatch their first team to China. Moloney – hailed by Blowick as 'the first live spark' to follow Galvin to the Far East – led the women's mission under her new name, Sister Mary Patrick.

In Hanyang, the sisters conveniently ignored canon law and established a medical dispensary. They also ran schools and orphanages and set up a centre for the training of catechists in what was a time of major political upheaval. Moloney, who used to ramble around streets bringing medicine to the ill and destitute, had a sense of her life turning full circle. As a child, her aristocratic father encouraged her to give a penny of her pocket money to a Christian charity for Chinese orphans – and here she was almost fifty years later looking after such children herself. As leader of the congregation, she demanded high standards and could be tough on her colleagues while showing a 'profound self-giving love' for the poor, her Columban biographer testified. 'She loved them and they loved her because they found in her the humility to love that had nothing to do with ostentation or condescension.'

In 1936, Moloney returned to Ireland and then undertook a series of overseas fundraising and field-inspection trips. Such travel was hazardous at times, and in 1940 Moloney found herself on board a transatlantic liner that was torpedoed by a German submarine. She was one of 152 survivors from the SS *Western Prince*, which sunk 400 miles north-west of Ireland. A newspaper obituary, which captured some of her personality, later recorded: 'The survivors spent many miserable, cold hours in lifeboats tossed about on the winter sea, and the Irish nun, although almost 70 years of age, reassured and raised the hopes of her fellow survivors by her cheerful confidence. They were found by a Scottish collier and were rescued from the lifeboats by the coal ship's coal-tubs, which were lowered over the side and then winched on to the deck. Mother Mary Patrick jokingly compared her experience of being pulled out of the sea in a bucket with St Paul's descent in a basket at the walls of Damascus.'[5]

One of Moloney's contemporaries – and another driven woman cut from the same missionary cloth – was Marie Martin. Like Moloney, she grew up in comfortable surroundings. Her grandfather built up a profitable shipping business, which imported timber, fireplaces, wallpaper and paint to Dublin, employing more than 100 people. Martin's father ran part of the company, and no doubt she inherited some of the family's entrepreneurial genes. As a sociable teenager, she was used to a life of parties, trips to race meetings and hunts. But she was far from a spoilt child, and when the war broke out she immediately applied to become a VAD (Voluntary Aid Detachment) for the British Army. In October 1915, she was deployed to Malta and bore the honour of being the only Irish VAD and the youngest nurse to sail there on the hospital ship *Oxfordshire*. In Malta, she served at the main medical post for soldiers evacuated from Gallipoli, working long hours tending to young men who had experienced horrendous burns and amputations, gangrene, scabies, dysentery or exposure to mustard gas. 'If Uncle Charlie saw these sores he would never kiss me again,' she wrote to her mother at the end of one arduous shift.

When the Armistice was signed on 11 November 1918, Martin returned home where she heard much talk about the missions. Fr Tom Ronayne, the man who facilitated Blowick's introduction to Galvin, had become the new parish priest at her church in Monkstown, and she became friends with him. She also met Frances Moloney and discussed the possibility of joining her in

China. Then in August 1919 she ran into Bishop Joseph Shanahan during one of his occasional trips home from Africa. Fr Ronayne arranged a further meeting between Shanahan and Martin the following summer, at which the aspiring medical missionary offered to go to Nigeria as a volunteer.

Even though Martin was then 'just' a lay person, Shanahan was wary of letting her do nursing in his jurisdiction. Mindful of the Church's doctrine on religious personnel staying out of medicine, he agreed to her travel plans only on the basis that she would perform the duties of a teacher rather than a nurse. In a Catholic solution to a Catholic problem, he did, however, permit her to give first aid whenever assistance was needed. With the deal done, Martin finished her nursing studies in February 1921 and two months later she received a cable from Shanahan: 'Urgently needed if you don't mind facing things alone.' Martin wired back: 'Will come. Have a companion' – in a reference to fellow nursing graduate Agnes Ryan, whom Martin had persuaded to travel too. Marie Martin spent four years in Calabar, and it was a taster for her future life's work. She was particularly struck by the suffering of women in rural communities, and she resolved while in Nigeria to set up a new type of humanitarian congregation. To be called the Medical Missionaries of Mary (MMM), it would break ranks with the schools-focused Irish missionary tradition. Care of the mother and child would be its unique mission statement.

It took many, many years, however, before her idea could be put into practice. Returning to Ireland from Nigeria, she had a handful of possible candidates but no money and little support in the hierarchy – not unlike Galvin and Blowick when they started out. A breakthrough came in fortuitous circumstances one afternoon when she bumped into her aunt while shopping on Grafton Street. In an exchange of gossip, Martin's elder relation conveyed the news that the Benedictine Abbey in Glenstal, County Limerick was having difficulty finding reliable housekeepers. Martin detected in this an opportunity of securing a religious sponsor. She would provide the monks with domestics, herself included, if they in turn supplied religious instruction to her fledging congregation.

'It is now we start in earnest the founding of MMM,' Martin wrote to her first recruits. 'We are called to be saints,' she proclaimed, and to create 'a school of saints, seeking and loving God in all things, learning His life and love, super-naturalising all our natural gifts (which are in our vocation to be used for God's glory) dying to self so as to remove all obstacles to the growth of the interior life of love and union.' It was an ambitious goal that would require much personal sacrifice. Martin's timetable for Glenstal 'housekeepers' recommended about fourteen hours of prayer and labour daily. Sisters were instructed to rise at 5.30 a.m. and end the day at 8 p.m. with the saying of the rosary and 'great silence'. At 10.30 a.m., Martin had generously pencilled into the schedule: 'Cup of tea (if necessary)'.

Martin was an untypical leader. A petite, gentle woman, she suffered from ill-health for much of her life. At times, misfortune seemed to stalk her. While in Glenstal, her right foot was badly crushed by a radiator that fell off a wall. Gangrene set in – so badly that a surgeon recommended amputation of the leg. She escaped instead with the loss of three toes. Martin's return to Africa was equally inauspicious. The Church ban on religious practising medicine was finally lifted in 1936 with the publication of the instruction *Constans ac Sedula*, and Martin wasted no time in setting sail for Nigeria. In January 1937, she docked in Calabar with two companions. Almost immediately, however, Martin contracted malaria and became seriously ill. She had a heart attack and the local monsignor James Moynagh gave her the last rights. On 4 April 1937, in a hastily arranged ceremony, Moynagh also inaugurated the MMMs. Its founder – now renamed Mother Mary – was put on a ship back to Ireland in more hope than expectation that she would make it there. As the English doctor who had treated her at the government hospital in Port Harcourt helped her on board he turned to Moynagh on the shore and said, 'Never let me see that woman in Africa again.' Moynagh later recalled: 'To us who saw Mother Mary on to the boat, her going seemed to be the end of any hope for the new venture. Indeed, it seemed doubtful if she could reach Ireland alive… From the human point of view the whole future of the new congregation seemed precarious in the extreme. The Mother Foundress was on her way to Ireland extremely ill. There were but two sisters on the mission – novices. There was no support, financial or otherwise, and the new congregation was unknown…' But the indefatigable Mother Mary had no such reservations. Moynagh noted, 'She left Nigeria not at all perturbed by the course of events but with that trustful smile on her face that only those who put their trust in God can have.' Sure enough, Martin arrived in Dublin a new woman. Her health much improved, she started to build a hospital in Drogheda that would train hundreds of Irish and foreign students in midwifery and general nursing.

There were other trailblazing women from that era. Anna Dengel, a lay doctor, travelled to Rome on six occasions to lobby against the Vatican's ban on religious medics. Agnes Ryan, who accompanied Mary Martin on her first trip to Nigeria in 1921, cofounded the adventurous Holy Rosary Sisters. Sr Charles Walker, an English-born member of the Irish Sisters of Charity, set up the congregation of the Handmaids of the Holy Child Jesus as a mainly indigenous congregation in Nigeria. There were pioneering men too, following in the footsteps of Galvin and Blowick. They included Pat 'PJ' Whitney, who set up a scheme with the ubiquitous Thomas Ronayne whereby diocesan priests could volunteer for a stint in Africa, with a view to making a permanent move out of

Ireland. This was the genesis of the St Patrick's Missionary Society, better known the Kiltegan Fathers. Among its first recruits was James Moynagh – Marie Martin's sponsor in Calabar – who had initially thought about going to China with the Columbans but felt it was too great a commitment.

The Kiltegans sold themselves as a more flexible set-up, but in practice they were highly disciplined and regimented, and this reflected the personality of their founder Whitney. He was ruthless at times in promoting the society and intolerant of dissent. The seminary he founded in County Wicklow made Marie Martin's convent seem positively lax. Priests who failed to march to meals in double line were sentenced to breaking stones in chain-gang fashion, and there was no mercy for transgressors. Two students who had a habit of sneaking out of their rooms in the evening to play cards with lay staff were thrown out of the seminary and sent home in disgrace. Whitney also organised a number of controversial fundraising initiatives, including the construction of a cinema in the seaside town of Bundoran that doubled up as a dance hall and was run on a commercial basis. 'He had none of the academic polish or indeed aspirations that goes with academic achievements,' wrote Moynagh in his memoirs. 'Father PJ would be typical of that [Maynooth] background, "pucks of brains", happy jolly personality, even cracking jokes, treating life as great fun, shrewd knowledge of men, deep *unshakeable* faith, but a rather ruthless strain to his character with a touch of craft which prompted him to *enjoy* getting what he wanted, or thought necessary for the work, by rather devious ways rather than by honest straightforward request...'

If Whitney epitomised one type of missionary – the cunning, charismatic manipulator – Edel Quinn represented another. An attractive young woman who swapped a comfortable life for a brief and ultimately fatal dose of hardship, she moulded herself in the fashion of Saint Thérèse of Lisieux, a French nun who died of tuberculosis in 1897, aged twenty-four. Like the 'Little Flower', whose relics still draw millions of followers around the world, Quinn has been revered by Catholics for her innocence and lightly worn piety. In the 1950s and 1960s, she did more probably than anyone else to popularise the work of missionaries – even though she was a 'mere' lay woman herself. People could relate to her because of her life story. It was one not just of personal courage and deep faith, but also of romance and unrequited love.

Born near Kanturk, County Cork on 14 September 1907, she belonged to a very middle-class family – not unlike Moloney and Martin, curiously. A vivacious, outdoorsy type, she had a carefree childhood and was captain of her school cricket team and an excellent tennis player, pianist and dancer. This tranquil existence was shattered, however, when she received a message one day at her boarding school in Cheshire, England telling her to return home immediately. It transpired her father, a bank manager, had racked up large gambling debts and was being threatened with prosecution by his employer for misappropriating funds. The family was in crisis and facing ruin. The teenaged Quinn did the only thing she thought she could do to help. She went to church and prayed, pledging that if her father was spared public disgrace she would devote her life to God. It was a holy pact, and Quinn resolved to see it through when her father was spared jail and instead redeployed – on a reduced salary – to a desk job at the bank's headquarters in College Green, Dublin.

After leaving school, Quinn worked for a French-owned tile factory in Dublin, where she developed a reputation as a firm and efficient office manager. Her employers were amazed at how she faced down angry trade unionists, and placated uncouth and unmannerly clients, with both tact and charm. Pierre Landrin, the company's boss, was particularly smitten, and in 1927 the Frenchman – every bit as dashing as she was pretty – proposed marriage.

'I knew her and I didn't know her at all,' Landrin confessed years later. On 1 September 1927, a date forever imprinted on his memory, the Frenchman had his proposal rebuffed with the painful news that Quinn had already been 'promised to God'. She informed him over lunch at Jury's Hotel in College Green that, while she was flattered by his offer, she had already made arrangements to enter the convent of the Poor Clares in Belfast. Landrin left the country heartbroken, and Quinn wrote to him in London six days later. 'Please do not say you are not worthy, Pierre, it is not true; you are far above me in every way. God knows that, and it is only His merciful love that could call me to serve him in religion, seeing what I am. Please pray for me that I may become a little less unworthy of Him.'

Thus began a lengthy, confessional correspondence between the pair, which would do much to create the legend of Edel Quinn. Her initial intention to write to Landrin was to encourage him to continue practising his religion. He had only just returned to the Church when he proposed to her and she feared he might 'lapse' due to the marriage refusal. In time, however, a deep friendship developed between the two, although the subtext of her refusal to marry him remained. She frequently referred to the writings of St Thérèse, who inspired awe for her self-effacing nature and celebration of small acts of kindness. When Landrin remarked in one letter of a resemblance between her and the saint, Quinn replied: 'You know you don't know me at all, if you could even for a moment think such a thing; you know the Little Flower was a saint; and I am not even on the first step of the ladder!'

Quinn wasn't the only missionary to be inspired by St Thérèse. Bishop Shanahan once made a special retreat to the grave of the Little Flower in Lisieux, while Mother Kevin talked about St Thérèse 'and to her, almost as if she were present', an American Jesuit recalled. 'One got the impression that they were close friends, and were constantly talking over problems together.'[6]

While preparing to join the Poor Clares, Quinn started working for the Legion of Mary, a religious organisation founded in 1921 by Dubliner Frank Duff. The Legion was made up of lay Catholics who would visit people in hospitals and slums, offering spiritual encouragement and practical assistance. It was organised along militaristic lines, with a strict hierarchy. The Legionary reported to the Praesidium, the Praesidium to the Curia, the Curia to the Senatus, and so on. Many different kinds of work were open to Legionaries, visiting houses, hospitals or prisons; bringing children to Mass; organising study circles; distributing Catholic literature; or caring for the Church. The only work forbidden to them was the giving of material aid. Apart from the fact that this would tread on the toes of the Society of St Vincent de Paul, which already did this sort of work, it was felt that giving money or food might result in stigmatising the homes to which they called. Stripped of their religious identity, Legionaries were essentially volunteer social workers – at a time when social work didn't really exist. They counselled and gave practical advice and encouragement to their clients, albeit with a religious twist, in circumstances where there were no other state supports.

One of the Legion's most noteworthy operations was the establishment of the Sancta Maria Hostel in Harcourt Street, where prostitutes could be housed and given a chance to get off the streets. At a time when a blind eye was being turned to the sex trade by both the state and the mainstream Church, Quinn spent long hours talking to girls at the halfway house. She arranged social activities, dances and theatre to give them a break – and even the hint of an escape route – from prostitution.

Quinn was scheduled to join the Poor Clares as a novice in 1932, but illness struck. Tests showed she was suffering from advanced tuberculosis, and she was placed in a sanatorium for eighteen months. When she emerged, she threw herself into her Legion work with added urgency and volunteered to help with the extension of the organisation to England and later Africa. Conscious of her fragile health, many in the Legion – including clergy – were opposed to her travelling to the 'dark continent'. But Duff supported her wishes, arguing that if she was going to die young she might as well be doing what she wanted. 'You don't hold an umbrella over someone who is already soaked,' he told his colleagues.

On 24 October 1936, Quinn left Ireland accompanied by a group of missionaries, including Holy Ghost priests and Loreto nuns. Her original plan was to alight in Egypt and then travel the full length of the continent – to South Africa – addressing people en route and helping to establish praesidia. She quickly discovered this was impractical, not least because she would have to spend months trekking across hostile Muslim land. Moreover, she had no language training and had only once ever addressed a public meeting before she sailed from Ireland.

What was certain in her mind was that she wouldn't be returning. 'I'm not putting the Concilium to the expense of sending me out only to come back after three years,' she told a friend, with a characteristic mixture of practicality and self-martyrdom. 'I'm not coming back. Missionaries don't come back.'

There is no denying the inherently evangelising nature of Quinn's work. In a letter to Frank Duff in January 1937, shortly after arriving in East Africa, she wrote about the establishment of a native praesidium. 'You will be glad to hear that one of the women, whose work was visitation of the native hospital, was able to baptise two persons, a woman and a baby, and both died. This is the first direct fruit…' Quinn saw her mission as spreading the word of God first, and humanitarianism second. But the latter became over time inextricably linked with the former. While extolling the merits of going to church and prayer, she also visited the sick and dying. She encouraged lepers to join the Legion and advocated a praesidium for both blacks and whites in racially segregated Kenya.

Quinn never made it as far as South Africa. She spent many years trying to extend the Legion into Uganda – under a somewhat sceptical Mother Kevin – before she died in Nairobi on 12 May 1944. Her death received little notice at a time of world upheaval. But Duff was keen to keep her memory alive and asked a Belgian bishop (and future cardinal) to write a biography. He agreed, and his book *Edel Quinn, A Heroine of the Apostolate*, published in 1953, drew international attention. It also started a long-running campaign in the Church for her canonisation.

Quinn had many admirers, including Marie Martin, who identified her pithily as 'very near to God'. Duff was more effusive, describing the impish, doe-eyed Quinn as 'terribly impressive… very girlish indeed but a very refreshing experience'. Like Landin, Duff recognised in Quinn something profoundly lovable. 'Her charm of manner was supreme but it went far deeper than the surface. There was nothing of the artificial in her. She attracted people very strongly. In trying to analyse this fact, one is thrown back on that suggestion which Chesterton makes about St Francis of Assisi: that the secret of the saint's power lay in the conviction which people gained that he was really interested in each one of them. I would say that anyone who spoke with Edel Quinn ended up with that same idea. As a consequence they loved her and wanted to do what she asked of them.'

Years later, Duff conceded that he had admired qualities in her beyond the religious. Asked about the nature of their relationship, he replied: 'I do not know what way my thoughts would have operated in regard to Edel Quinn if I had been up to marriage. I never was… But I have to admit that I was certainly impressed by Edel Quinn as a woman.' Quinn's biographer Desmond Forristal noted that both she and Duff had embraced a life of celibacy and, such was the strength of their faith, there was no chance of them going back on their commitment. 'Each of them had, in Newman's phrase, "a high severe idea of the intrinsic excellence of virginity". Neither of them was the kind to put a hand to the plough and then turn back. Their relationship was that of St Francis and St Clare, all the more fruitful in the spirit because it transcended the flesh.'[7]

Quinn, Martin, Moloney, Whitney, Galvin, Shanahan: these were but a few of the early missionaries. Their legacy can be measured in part by facts and figures – in the number of recruits they had or in the number of schools and hospitals they established. In January 1918, the Missionary Society of St Columban opened its doors and by 1979 it had 884 members, mostly Irish. The Missionary Sisters of St Columban, founded by Moloney, had 297 members by the mid-1950s, of whom nine were doctors and forty-two nurses. The MMMs, founded in 1937, had 450 members – all qualified medics – by the mid-1980s. The Franciscan Missionary Sisters for Africa, founded by Mother Kevin in 1952, had 251 members in 1973, seventy-four of them trained for medical work and the rest mostly for teaching.

In the early days, missionary congregations measured their success quite crudely against the number of baptisms they carried out each year. Under Vatican law, each parish had to report to its bishop a variety of statistics, not only christenings but also the number of confessions performed, the number of pupils under religious instruction, and so on. By these measures, the Maynooth mission to China was relatively ineffective. The number of Catholics in Hanyang rose from 14,000 in 1922 to 17,000 by 1930 but then started to decline due to the outbreak of war between communist and nationalist forces, and later the intervention of World War II. The schools fared particularly badly during the political turmoil. The number of boys attending Columban schools in Hanyang dropped from 3,886 in 1923–4 to 338 in 1927–8, and for the number of girls from 794 in 1922–3 to 105 in 1927–8. It was the same pattern in the Columbans' other territories. Mass attendances increased at times of peace and fell at times of war.

Like other Christian missionaries, the Columbans were seen as a threat by the communists, many of whom were organised around small 'bandit' gangs. In July 1929, Timothy Leonard – one of the first group of Columbans to go to China – was captured while saying Mass in his parish of Nanfeng, taken to the mountains and stabbed to death. At a show trial before his execution, his communist captors accused him of breaking the law, in that 'he had practised religion and that furthermore his church had "hooked on" with the Kuomintang [the Chinese Nationalist Party]'.

Leonard was the first of seventeen Columbans killed in China, the Philippines, Korea and Burma between 1929 and 1950. Dozens of other members of the society were assaulted, imprisoned or deported. Such persecution earned the Irish missionaries a reputation for great courage and loyalty to their people. 'A shepherd should stay with his flock' was the common refrain from those who put themselves in harm's way. Martyrs included Anthony Collier, James Maginn and Patrick Reilly who were shot dead by communists during the Korean War. John Henaghan, the colourful, original editor of *The Far East*, was killed by the Japanese army in the Philippines along with three colleagues, Patrick Kelly, Joseph Monaghan and Peter Fallon. Another Columban, Frank Douglas, was captured by Japanese soldiers and tortured for three days and three nights. One of the punishments he received was the 'water cure', where his stomach was forcibly filled with water and then emptied by having a board placed across his abdomen onto which pressure was applied. On the evening of 27 July 1945, Japanese soldiers threw his bloodied body into a truck and drove him away. He was never seen again.

In China, the Columbans' original mission territory, things took a turn for the worse around 1946, the very year Dan Fitzgerald – a young recruit from Cork city – arrived. 'When the communists took over,' he recalled, 'the whole atmosphere changed, and you discovered all of a sudden you had no rights at all.' He said Galvin was seen overnight as the leader of a group of 'reactionaries', and 'we were all under suspicion'. Fitzgerald's memory of that era still remained sharp as he sat down – approaching his ninety-fourth birthday – over a cup of tea at St Mary's parochial house in Nenagh, County Tipperary. Born in 1916, the missionary priest continued to celebrate 8 a.m. Mass in the parish daily, as well as hear confessions. A keen golfer in his day (he once played off a two handicap), he was showing signs of slowing down physically – his long limbed body was now supported by a walking stick – but as soon as the talk turned to Galvin, or 'the bishop' as Fitzgerald loyally called him, his eyes lit up.

Dan Fitzgerald joined the Columbans directly from school. 'I had this idea there are priests aplenty in Ireland, and not so many elsewhere,' he explained and, like Galvin, he was heavily influenced by his mother's deep devotion to the Church. 'She did not say too much but she said: *Remember this and don't ever forget it. 'Tis more important to lay treasure in heaven than put money in the bank*. That was one of the principles I got in economics.' In advance of travelling overseas, Fitzgerald had been told by Galvin to expect hardship. ('Think of anything. 'Tisn't here,' the bishop warned sagely from China.) Still, Fitzgerald was shocked by the desolation of his first posting: a parish 100 miles north of Hankow. There was little food, no water and no lighting. When darkness fell he could either sleep or pray. 'There was no such thing as a social life.' In any event, he had no prior language training to allow him converse with the locals. It was no wonder a Columban contemporary of his, who had lived with him in China and had been similarly prepared, suffered a nervous breakdown and was redeployed. 'In Ireland, there were consolations of a priest's life. But in China you had to pitch up where you could and for the first six months the only thing I could do was say the sacrament of the sick because it was in Latin,' said Fitzgerald. 'By working away at the catechism I was able to hear confessions after about nine months. But if anyone asked me after confession what was the price of eggs I wouldn't know what they were saying.'

Galvin's reassuring presence helped to sustain him through the hard times. 'You can only plan for normality,' the bishop once said, 'and since I came to this place we never had five consecutive normal years.' Another time, Galvin declared, 'Dan, unless you are prepared to be a fool, you have no business here.' Such advice had been 'quite helpful in the years since', Fitzgerald said. For those who stuck it out in China, the work became more satisfying as time passed. The Columbans became involved in health and education, and a sense of trust was built up with the local population. 'We started making a contact, getting their confidence. And when you got them to believe you could help them by curing their malaria, or whatever it was, then you could say, "I could do a bit for you in the other world too", and you could start to instruct them in the faith.' It was in this manner the Columbans developed a network of schools and parishes over thirty years – up until Mao Tse-tung's Red Army crossed the Yangtze River in April 1949. Diocesan property was then confiscated and churches were closed. As anti-religious sentiment strengthened, Catholics were rounded up and a great number of them were executed. The Columbans reacted by destroying their parish records, and telling Catholics to lie low. Eventually, in September 1952, the Columbans were expelled from the country. Fitzgerald was there at the bitter end.

He recalled the day the communists took over Galvin's final property in the city of Hankow, across the river from the bishop's then temporary home. 'I remember he said to me – and it was the first indication as to how he was feeling – "'Tis lonely work losing all you have." He was a great realist, of course, and I knew well I had no business saying anything – because pious platitudes did not go down well with him. So I said nothing and we walked and walked until we got back from Hankow… and I thought it was up to me at this stage to say something and I said, "I suppose, 'tis hard on everybody but it's particularly hard on yourself because you saw the start of it all." There was a crucifix on the wall and he pointed to it and said to me, "What else would you expect? Sure, look at himself. What had he at the end of his missionary career? The best of them denied him, the rest of them – except for one – ran away, and that's all he had left, apart from a handful of poor women." He had a wonderful gift of seeing the reproduction of the story of Christianity almost in the existence of the work.'

That said, being thrown out of China 'nearly broke' Galvin's heart, Fitzgerald added. Shortly after returning to Ireland, the bishop was diagnosed with leukaemia and he died in February 1956. Once asked by Fitzgerald how he had felt during his years in China, Galvin replied without a trace of self-pity: 'Utter helplessness.' His protégé recalled: 'I also asked him: If you knew at the beginning what you know now would you do things differently? He said, "I don't know. There was always a 50–50 chance that what you did was wrong. I'd probably have done the same again."'

Collins, the Columban historian, said Galvin and his contemporaries 'certainly thought they would have had more success than they did', which wasn't to say the Chinese mission was a flop. Chinese priests kept the faith alive despite persecution, and the Columbans found ways of supporting their former parishes through clandestine channels. In Hanyang, where it all began for the Columbans, there were an estimated 60,000 Catholics in 1995. How many of these were due to the Columban influence is open to debate but there is evidence of some sort of legacy. In recent years, an indigenous women's congregation originally founded by Galvin in 1939 had been re-formed. Collins said, when he visited the group in 2006, its superior told him 'the people know their grandparents were Catholics even though they don't know what that means… People wanted to be instructed and to know more.'

Whatever their achievements, or failures, it is clear the founding members of the Irish missionary movement were far from uniform. They were also far from perfect. Some of their schemes had a near-comical amateurishness, like Edel Quinn's planned trek from Cairo to Cape Town. Other activities were unnecessarily dangerous and foolhardy. Typically, these young Irish men and women adhered to conservative Catholic doctrine. They accepted hierarchical structures and sought to impose them in the areas where they worked. They adopted, initially at any rate, the 'gradualist' approach of other European missionaries whereby responsibility for running the church would remain in the hands of missionaries until a substantial number of indigenous members had been recruited. Initially too, there was a fixation on baptism. Progress was measured by the number of Catholics converted and the extent to which people understood their faith – or acted it out – was of secondary concern. Missionaries were not exempt from casual racism, and from today's vantage point their commitment to education and health might be seen as a cynical ploy aimed at shepherding people into Mass. But, in their day, the sort of work performed by the likes of Marie Martin, Ned Galvin and Teresa Kearney was closer to humanitarianism. They were development workers and social workers before such professions had been created.

Asked about the ideology of the early Columbans, Collins replied: 'They were pragmatic. They were: "Does it work? What works? OK, we will try an idea."' This meant trying to reach people through education, and if that didn't work trying health care or the Legion of Mary. Galvin once explained the approach thus:

'You have to build a bridge across which people can come to a knowledge of the truth but the bridge has to be built in material.' Helping people materially and helping them spiritually became one and the same activity, and in time this contributed to a rethink on evangelisation. It is noticeable that Columban rhetoric about 'conquering' pagan lands, and expanding 'empires' for Christ, all but disappeared within a few years of the society arriving in China. The shift in emphasis was expressed by Galvin himself in 1927 when he wrote to a colleague about his impending ordination as a bishop. While he said he didn't want a fuss to be created over the elevation, he was 'rather anxious' his motto of office would be *Fiat Voluntas Tua* ('Thy will be done'). 'I hope that might constantly remind us here in China that we are not here to convert China but to do God's will, and we don't know twenty-four hours ahead what that is.'[8]

This sense of realism spread to Galvin's missionary successors. When the superior general of the newly formed Kiltegans got a chance to promote the society on Radio Éireann in 1939, he confined himself to a few modest – if rather myopic – comments about the society's work in parishes in Africa. 'There is every reason to believe,' he proclaimed, 'that our missionaries will continue to go forth, year after year, to labour in pagan lands for the formation and preservation of happy Catholic homes like those we have in our own little island.'[9]

Perhaps the greatest influence the early missionaries had was on public opinion. They informed people – in crude terms admittedly – about human suffering in some very distant and alien places. They set an example, demonstrating the qualities that made an overseas missionary – what was then a new type of vocation. Self-confidence. Determination. Humility. A willingness to continue even when mistakes were made and when setbacks were suffered. A willingness to continue against reason sometimes. ('It is the will, the will, the will, that matters,' Edel Quinn was fond of saying.)

These were men and women unafraid of physical labour and accepting – almost welcoming – of hardship. They didn't spend endless hours on their knees in prayer. And they never occupied themselves greatly with theorising, not when there was work to be done. Galvin summed up the philosophy once in later life. As an ageing, overburdened bishop, facing an uncertain future in China, he was approached by the then new arrival Fitzgerald about a problem. 'Monsignor,' the younger man began, 'I cannot help thinking sometimes…'

The bishop interrupted him, gently but with emphasis. 'Dan, what good will thinking do? Put St Patrick in front of you, St Columban behind you, keep your head down and plough away.'

CHAPTER 3: THE RECRUITMENT DRIVE

'The good shepherd is one who lays down his life for his sheep. The hired man, since he is not the shepherd and the sheep do not belong to him, abandons the sheep and runs away as soon as he sees a wolf coming.'
(John 10:11–18)

The schoolgirls were hushed into silence as the lights went out and a film projector cranked into life. 'Ave Maria' – Jacques Arcadelt's chamber choir version – drifted across the classroom as the opening credits rolled. Then a plummy, male English accent interjected, telling the giddy young viewers that they were watching a bishop saying Mass in a church in Drogheda, the birthplace of the Medical Missionaries of Mary. 'Mass is universal to people throughout the world as members of the mystical body of Christ,' the narrator began. 'All over the globe, the mother Church pays homage to God in exactly the same way – whether, for instance, in Ireland…' The action on screen cut suddenly from one house of prayer to another. A white man in church robes could be seen raising the Eucharist to a crowd of black faces. '… or in Africa,' the narrator continued, 'where in this primitive church the same solemn glory is given to God.'

Watching these scenes intently sixty-odd years ago, amid the innocent gasps and sniggers of her classmates, was Maura O'Donoghue. She was in the penultimate year of her secondary-school education in Kilfenora, County Clare when the nuns in charge got hold of a copy of *Visitation*. After its premiere in 1948, the film had been passed from one school to another across Ireland like a religious relic. In an era before television, and just a few years after the end of World War II, it held out the promise of a new, exciting life for young Irish boys and girls. Especially girls. Captured on whirling spools of 35mm film were scenes of Irish women – then little older than O'Donoghue – doing their nursing rounds at a leprosy colony in Nigeria. At a time when most women in Ireland were chained to the kitchen sink, the MMMs could be seen taking charge of a hospital and administering life-saving treatment to women, children and men. The film ended with a scene in which bright-faced new members knelt before their superior, taking vows of 'chastity, poverty and obedience'.

This was radical stuff, at least for teenagers like O'Donoghue. After watching *Visitation*, she made contact with the MMMs and met its founder Marie Martin who immediately recruited her. The Clare woman went on to work in more than seventy countries, including Zimbabwe, Chechnya and Iraq. What was it about the film? What was it that moved her so? O'Donoghue was asked some six decades after *Visitation* was first shown to her. She grimaced slightly. A grey-haired woman now, she answered – in that understated manner typical of missionaries: 'I saw it and I thought, hmm, that's interesting.' And that was that. In such mysterious ways, Mother Mary recruited her 'messengers for Christ'.

Visitation was probably the single most effective piece of propaganda created by missionaries. The film was personally commissioned by Martin who ignored advice from within the Church that the project would be too costly and altogether too 'modern' for Catholic tastes. In fact, it became a box-office hit, playing to crammed picture-houses and parish halls – both commercial and Church-run – across Ireland and beyond.

Its first showing took place at the Abbey Cinema, fittingly in the MMMs' native Drogheda, in June 1948. Lines of people, two and three deep, stood on the street outside as foreign ambassadors and other dignitaries arrived for the premiere. The Primate of All Ireland Dr John D'Alton spoke from the stage inside, describing *Visitation* as 'a story that should make you proud of your faith and your country'. Missionaries, he said, had sought to extend 'the empire of Christ in pagan lands' and the MMMs in particular were 'a challenge to the materialism of the modern world'.

The film travelled to Dublin and then overseas. It got a nationwide run in the Odeon Cinemas in Britain before it arrived in the United States. By the end of its tour, it had put the MMMs on the map internationally, raised substantial amounts of money in fundraising and, more significantly perhaps, attracted a large number of new recruits. While the film glorified the work of the medical missionaries, it didn't sugar-coat their experience – and this gave it added impact. Nuns were depicted labouring in difficult conditions, performing unpleasant daily chores for their patients. They could be seen tending to people with physical deformities and cleaning and dressing ulcerated feet. Yet, throughout their duties, they carried an air of quiet satisfaction and peace. Speaking to its target audience of young women, *Visitation* concluded with the not-so-subtle plea: 'This story has no end. It will continue for as long as there is any suffering in the vast expanse of the world.' Reminding viewers of the scale of the task, the narrator proclaimed: 'The harvest is indeed great, but the labourers are few.'

Recalling her meeting with Marie Martin after watching the film, O'Donoghue said: 'She asked me what subjects I liked best. I mentioned maths and science. Then she asked what I wanted to do. I thought "pharmacy", and she said, "Why not medicine?"' O'Donoghue laughed at how simple – how uncomplicated – it sounded today. A short interview was all it took to change her life forever. For Irish people of O'Donoghue's generation, entering religious life was a very respectable career move. However, the medical missionaries were at the most radical end of the Catholic congregational spectrum. 'As MMMs, we were regarded as very much second-rate sisters. We didn't wear habits and we rode bicycles – ordinary push bikes,' said O'Donoghue, who trained at St Vincent's Hospital, Dublin and at the congregational headquarters, Our Lady of Lourdes Hospital, Drogheda. The common perception of a 'religious' in those days was a nun tucked up in a convent saying the rosary. O'Donoghue recalled once visiting her parents in civilian clothes – which was not unusual for an MMM – and walking into a local shop in County Clare with her father. 'The shopkeeper said to my father, "One of your daughters has 'entered', hasn't she?" He said, "Yes, this is her." And the shopkeeper said, "Oh! Has she left?"' O'Donoghue smiled at the memory. 'One of the reservations was the congregation was just 13 years old at the time. People would say, "Why doesn't she join a proper order?"'

After completing her medical and religious studies, O'Donoghue was assigned to Nigeria but then ordered to return prematurely. Martin had requested she join her central council and travel with her around the world as her personal assistant and medic. It was a high honour for someone so young. O'Donoghue, just 26 at the time, was put in charge of the health and welfare of the 67-year-old head of congregation, whom many then regarded as a saint. The world tour lasted the best part of two years. The pair stopped in eighteen countries, from Angola to Zimbabwe, taking in large parts of central and southern Africa, south-east Asia and the United States. The aim was to review the performance of mission projects worldwide, but O'Donoghue remembered the odyssey best for her superior's frequent health scares. Martin had an irregular pulse and heart problems and was instructed to travel with a doctor at all times. One incident stuck out: a night flight from Bangkok to Hong Kong. 'I was asleep on the plane,' said O'Donoghue, 'when I got a knock and then heard this voice, "I am not well." Her face was blue.' Martin's young assistant kept her heartrate under control and radioed ahead for assistance on the ground. An ambulance wasn't available, but they caught a taxi to hospital where she was able to recuperate.

O'Donoghue would not speculate as to why she specifically was chosen for the trip. 'I don't know what she saw in me,' she replied when pressed on the matter. But she was not so tongue-tied when it came to singing her mentor's praises. 'Part of it was her attitude to life, I think. Several times the doctors in Drogheda had to persuade her not to go travelling, but she would say, "I have to go."'

Courageous, charismatic, gentle, humane, intelligent: all these characteristics were associated with Marie Martin. But O'Donoghue reached for another epithet: 'very practical. I go back to the Benedictine spirituality which attracted her: *ora et labora*, prayer and work. That was the basis of her whole approach. The other thing that was so impressive about her was: no rigidity. You wouldn't know which way she would go. While she would obey Rome and all the rest of it, rules and regulations were not the end; they couldn't be the end in themselves. It was how to make people feel more human, how to make the environment more pleasant for people rather than rules and regulations. Those were very strong points that she kept emphasising. She used to say, "No rule will ever keep a Medical Missionary of Mary." Ordinarily you wouldn't get a superior saying things like that; instead they would be saying, "Stay in line."

'Her focus all the time was on people rather than institutions. While she wanted the institutions to work well, her big concern was how people are being treated, how the people are being served,' O'Donoghue continued. 'She would have been an excellent business person. She had great managerial skills. She was a very charismatic leader, of course, but that was combined with very business-minded, managerial principles.'

Measured against other congregational leaders, Martin had a more analytical mind and a longer-term view about what she wished to achieve as a missionary. While she could be a hard taskmaster, her instinct was to encourage people rather than put them down. 'Everyone felt they had a part to play,' said O'Donoghue. 'When I think at the age of 26, she put me on the general council. I was being introduced on tour, and she would say: "This is one of my general councillors." And the bishops would say: "And, what age is she?" I felt like crawling under the table; I mean, what had I to offer? That was a great aspect: she had great confidence in people, and trust.'

While the MMMs were trailblazers in terms of bringing nuns into health care, other congregations played their part. When Miriam Duggan approached the Franciscan Missionary Sisters of Africa to enquire about joining in the mid-1950s, they urged her to study medicine as part of her religious formation. 'I thought the study would be too much but it was something I grew to love – even though in my time I would not have chosen it. In the 1950s, women would not have done medicine,' recalled Duggan, who grew up in Limerick city – on South Circular Road, 'near the Redemptorists', she made a point of noting.

At the time when she studied medicine in Cork, it was prudent for women religious not to advertise what they were doing. Although Rome had lifted the ban in 1936 on nuns practising midwifery and gynaecology, some members of the hierarchy still opposed the practice and would try to keep the prohibition in place informally. Curmudgeonly bishops stopped some nuns from graduating in their studies. Others refused religious women much-desired transfers to the mission fields, ordering them to remain in often mundane diocesan jobs. While Martin's work was widely respected, there were plenty of men – clerical and otherwise – who thought a woman's place was firmly in domesticity. Moreover, there was still no doubt within the Church as to where the power lay. Before she could screen *Visitation*, Martin had to show the film to Archbishop of Dublin John Charles McQuaid who ordered three cuts, including one of a caesarean section operation in a mission hospital. That the state censor approved the film in its complete form didn't matter one bit. The MMMs' founder acceded to the archbishop's request, and indeed throughout her life she dutifully – or perhaps just pragmatically – obeyed orders from above.

Reflecting on the atmosphere of the time, Duggan said she was told by her superiors not to publicise the fact that she was a religious novice while studying medicine in university. 'We weren't allowed to wear the habits. But the "incognito" did not last long because other students would be asking us whether we were going to the dance, or the films, and we ran out of excuses. So eventually we told the other classmates who we really were, and it was something they honoured, and they were good to us. They would cover for us to get to Mass in the morning, and we would cover for them so they could get their pints in the evening.'

Another religious recruit from that time was Eileen Keane. Born in 1933, she was educated by the Mercy sisters in Doon, County Limerick and it was there she first got bitten by the missionary bug. They were tough times and she was a boarder in a remote school where the ice-cold dorms gave her chilblains. 'They would put the missions before us, and then sisters would come looking for postulants. I remember them saying to us, "If you can't go out to India, you can at least learn from the sisters who have been there." And I said to myself, "Why can't I go out to India?"' The seed was planted: a sense of 'Why?', or rather 'Why not?' Nourishment came from a diet of missionary newsletters. Keane heard all the folktales about Bishop Shanahan, who was instrumental in founding the Holy Rosary Sisters, the order which Keane eventually joined. Sixty years later, she still spoke of Shanahan intermittently in the present tense. 'Many other missionaries would not have his vision,' she said.

Like Duggan, Keane enjoyed college life, although she was conscious of missing out on some aspects of being a student in Dublin. 'There were about twenty girls in our class and eighty boys. My best friends were three fellas. We were interns in St Vincent's Hospital. But I used to be pure mad because we would come out of Vincent's after our ward rounds, and go up to our place, and they would go into The Singing Kettle for a cup of coffee and argue about the case we had that morning. So we missed that sort of a mix.' Life as a lay person was 'kind of getting attractive' towards the end of her studies, and she recalled telling herself it was 'now or never' if she was going to become a nun.

Like many recruits, Keane was posted overseas almost immediately after qualifying. She completed her surgical internship in Portlaoise in July 1961 and made her final profession the following month. In September, she started work at a hospital in Sierra Leone. It was described as a 'travelling scholarship'. But, within six months, the doctor with whom she worked returned home to Ireland. 'I was the only doctor in the hospital and had to do anything that came in. I was terrified of it, really very frightened. I had to do sections and hernias, everything.'

Keane discovered years later that another sister had been asked to take up the posting in Sierra Leone but refused it. Keane was young, and blind obedience was the order of the day. 'It certainly wouldn't be proposed to a young person today. It wasn't fair to myself and certainly not fair to the people. As if you can do some good for people without having the language or the culture. We were simply deployed as soon as we qualified. We didn't take time for training in language or culture, which was a mistake really.'

Coming under the spell of a Marie Martin or Bishop Shanahan was one explanation for joining the missions. Another was a sense of adventure. There were few enough ways to get out of Ireland and see a bit of the world in the depressed post-war era. The missionary life could satisfy a person's wanderlust. It also guaranteed more immediate responsibility and independence compared to a priest or nun who stayed at home. Due to a glut in ordinations, religious personnel could spend years hanging about in parishes or at congregational headquarters, waiting for a more senior member to die so they could get on to the first rung of the hierarchical ladder. By the end of the 1960s, the average age of appointment for parish priests in Ireland was 56. Reflecting on that era, Holy Ghost priest Richard Quinn wrote: 'The problem facing the aspiring priest is not… unemployment – he is assured of some task within the Church – but rather of underemployment or a lack of scope to utilise fully his talents and skills.' Quinn continued, 'It seems reasonable to suggest that many missionaries have left Ireland in order to escape from the kinds of situations' which were linked in academic studies to 'the migration of the highly educated, i.e. archaic structures, little chance of exercising initiative, no hope of promotion or autonomy until almost retirement age, and a general lack of challenging opportunities.'[10]

The spike in vocations in Ireland in the first half of the twentieth century was unparalleled internationally. While the Catholic population of the country remained static, the number of priests serving that population almost doubled from 3,436 in 1910 to 6,204 in 1970. The ratio of people to priests thus dropped from 963:1 to 564:1. During the same period, the number of religious sisters increased from 8,031 to 15,145 and the number of convents from 367 to 722. A study commissioned by the Catholic hierarchy in 1962 confirmed there were too many priests and nuns in Ireland. But still new recruits came forward, and there was always work for them overseas. By 1970, about one in five Irish people in religious life were in the missions, and typically they were among the best educated. A religious census in 1970 showed 40 per cent of missionaries were university graduates, holding mostly Arts degrees, followed by Science and Medicine.

In these conditions, Irish parents had mixed feelings about their children entering religious life. While it was usually a source of pride to have a son in the priesthood, or a daughter in the convent, the inevitable sense of separation and of lost opportunity had the potential to cause pain. This was all the more so when offspring were emigrating to dangerous foreign lands. Keane recalled that her father was less than enamoured when, as a young woman, she informed him of her career choice. His six uncles, two aunts and only brother had emigrated, mostly to the United States, and it bred in him a desire to stop his own children from leaving the country. Keane said: 'When I told him I wanted to go on the missions, he replied, "I never reared one of you for export." I said to him, "You'd think I was one of your prize heifers."' She laughed at the memory. 'But he also said to me, "I'll never come between you and God."' Those were sweet words which Keane carried through many difficult years in Africa. 'When I did have second thoughts it was connected with loneliness and being away from Ireland,' she said. 'I still do miss Ireland when I'm away.'

For those recruits in Keane's day who had an adventurous streak, risk was not a deterrent but an attraction. Africa was dubbed 'the white man's grave', and missionaries proudly vouched for this on their regular visits home. They spoke of the various diseases that failed to kill them and of the physical dangers they bravely overcame. For young Irish ears, this sort of bravado sounded rather heroic. As for dying in the mission field, it was portrayed as the ultimate act of courage, as well as a means of personal redemption and union with God. When Sr De Sales Duignan died in a ferry accident in Nigeria in 1949, the bishop of Calabar Thomas McGettrick (a Kiltegan man) reported home: 'The Medical Missionaries of Mary have now consecrated the soil of Nigeria with the pure body of their first martyr… She was ready to meet her spouse and lover.'

You might think premature deaths such as this would have been buried in the back pages of missionary publications for fear they would put off new recruits. On the contrary, news of 'glorious' deaths in the field was loudly trumpeted. Each congregation widely publicised lists of their 'martyrs'. At the Irish graveyard of the Missionary Sisters of Our Lady of Apostles a commemorative plaque was erected, the young age of its members highlighting what was once an extremely dangerous trade. Among the African deaths listed were: Cecelia Keating (26) died Ghana, 1922; Colman Keohane (27) died Ghana, 1927; Maura Higgins (24) died Nigeria, 1932; Ethnea Heaney (34) died Ghana, 1938; Fidelis Tuohy (26) died Nigeria, 1938; Annunciata O'Sullivan (29) died Nigeria, 1939.

While missionaries could be foolhardy at times, those priests and nuns who volunteered for dangerous postings had no death wish. They did their best to stay healthy, and out of harm's way, as evidenced by their eagerness to queue up in 1938 for a then untested vaccine developed against yellow fever. The disease had an 80 per cent mortality rate, and in the previous year – 1937 – it claimed the lives of three Irish missionaries in West Africa. Recalling in his memoirs how yellow fever, combined with malaria and blackwater fever, had tormented missionaries in the region, the Kiltegan bishop James Moynagh said: 'It was assumed that up to 50 per cent of men who went out would not survive.'

Personal security was a further concern for missionaries, and this was hard to guarantee in countries where violent crime or political turmoil was standard. In China, the rise of the communists in the late 1930s saw a direct threat to Columban life and limb.

Religious missionaries were labelled imperialist occupiers and were threatened with execution. Among those rounded up by the Red Army was Aedan McGrath, an inoffensive five-foot-three Dubliner, who joined the Columbans in 1923 aged just 17. In China, he was devoted to spreading the word of the Legion of Mary. His main role was visiting the sick, encouraging lapsed Catholics to return to the Church and teaching the catechism. But the communist party outlawed the Legion, claiming it was 'hostile to the whole nation' and seeking 'to overthrow the people's democratic state power of New China'. McGrath was thrown in jail and spent several months in solitary confinement in a cell the width of his arms. He kept himself sane by saying prayers and conversing with a bird on his windowsill which he befriended after feeding it a grain of rice. In April 1954, after two years and eight months in prison, McGrath was released. He was greeted on his return to Dublin by a huge reception at the National Stadium whose attendance included President Sean T. Ó Ceallaigh, Éamon de Valera, John A. Costello and Legion founder Frank Duff.

Publicity surrounding the persecution of McGrath and other Columbans in Asia had its part to play in attracting new recruits. 'There was all this stuff in the *Far East* and the newspaper about the missionaries being thrown out of China, and I wanted to go where the action was,' said Sheila Crowe, who joined the Missionary Sisters of St Columban in 1955. The County Limerick native developed a lifelong interest in China after making contact with the Columbans. Meeting for an interview more than a half-century after she joined the order, Crowe wore a red silk jacket stitched with an oriental pattern. By way of introduction, she jotted a couple of symbols on paper revealing her name in Mandarin: *Gao Shi Lan*, which translated as 'tall poetic orchid', she explained with a smile. Asked why she became a missionary, she replied: 'I felt we had a great heritage of Christianity and I wanted to share it.' But wasn't it a dangerous job? 'What about it? We were young and energetic,' she laughed. 'A lot of my classmates went to Africa; but I was going to China. Why wouldn't one want to have been involved in all that excitement?' It helped too that she had a brother who was a Columban priest. Many missionaries had a family connection – an uncle, aunt or cousin who would be fussed over and praised no end whenever he or she paid a visit home.

Others were recruited to the missions directly through Catholic schools. Josephine Ann Mooney, from Bray, County Wicklow, was taken under the wing of the Loreto Sisters from a young age. The daughter of a construction worker, she held the honour of being the first baby born at Wolfe Tone Square West, one of a number of local-authority housing estates that sprang up in the 1930s. Many of her peers quit school early and were put to work, but Mooney had done so well in her exams she was given a scholarship 'in the days when no scholarships were given to poor kids,' she said proudly. Speaking about it years later, she was still grateful to the nuns for the opportunity they gave her; however she cited another reason for entering religious life. It all went back to an incident at a school retreat when she was aged 13. Mooney still remembered the date: 3 November 1949. 'We were supposed to be silent but were spending most of the time writing "God bless you" notes and exchanging holy pictures. Then, I was hit by something the priest said: "Go therefore and teach all nations." They were Jesus's words to his disciples. I can't remember the context. I can't remember anything else from the talk – just that phrase. I sat there for an hour afterwards and thought about it. Then I raced home to my mother and told her what I wanted to be.'

O'Donoghue, Duggan, Keane, Crowe and Mooney: five women close to one another in age. Each worked in a different religious order, but all five shared an outlook on life. Reflecting years later on why they had become missionaries, they cited common reasons and also some very personal ones: the influence of a teacher, or a family member; a sense of adventure; a desire to get out of Ireland; the expectations that society – or their family – had placed on them; or what might be called a moment of religious inspiration. Usually motives were mixed. But what was clear from these, and other cases of recruitment, was that missionary propaganda played a vital role. The books, and magazines, and films, and letters home from cousins and uncles and aunties in the missions, were vital in promoting new vocations. Missionary congregations were well aware of this, and in time they became more sophisticated in the messages they communicated.

While early editions of the *Far East* and other missionary publications were laced with references to the 'war for Christ in Africa and Asia' and the Irish crusade to 'enlarge the boundaries of Christ's Kingdom', a softer editorial line later prevailed. Articles were published with a greater emphasis on adventure and human interest, with headlines like: 'A first journey to the bush', 'Christmas in Nairobi' and 'A lucky escape'. The magazines developed lifestyle sections, with cooking recipes, household advice, children's corners, puzzles and crosswords. *Outlook*, the magazine of the Holy Ghost Fathers, introduced an eight-page sports section 'edited by young people for young people'.

The Word, the magazine of the Divine Word Missionaries, which ceased publishing in December 2008, was typical of the genre. Setting out the magazine's objectives, the congregation's founder Arnold Janssen, a now canonised German priest, said, 'Firstly, it should be entertaining; secondly, impart general knowledge; and thirdly, be a source of spiritual instruction. It should be a *non-mission* magazine that will be able to bring the mission idea to circles which are not easy to reach.' Hence, alongside articles about missionary workers in the field, *The Word* published pieces on the work of the great artists, dispatches on international politics and interviews with

Irish writers and poets. It put an emphasis on photography and had a number of novelty features including a popular 'Saint of the Month' column. Its circulation peaked at 260,000 in 1970 – 170,000 in Ireland and Britain, 50,000 in the US, 30,000 in Australia and 10,000 elsewhere. Among *The Word*'s readers was a young Mary McAleese – the future President of Ireland – who was said by the magazine to have 'tramped the streets of West Belfast selling it' as a schoolgirl.[11]

Some congregations were reluctant to embrace new media, but the MMMs had no qualms. With *Visitation*, Mary Martin insisted on employing the best available technology. A noted producer of wartime documentaries and religious films, prominent London film-maker Andrew Buchanan was commissioned for the job and given considerable editorial freedom. But Martin's efforts didn't stop there. In 1957, the MMMs brought out *The Diary of a Medical Missionary of Mary*, a pocketbook costing two shillings and sixpence (little over ten 'new' pence) which was pitched at young readers used to a diet of *Treasure Island* and *The Famous Five*. The book was written by the late Sr Ruth Carey, the author also of a colourful 'official history' of the MMMs. Typically, for the ego-less missionary genre, however, the diary bore no by-line. Instead it told the story of a nameless new recruit to the MMMs, on the first year of her inaugural posting to Nigeria in 1953–4.

The cover illustration evoked the exotic: a picture taken from the seat of a light aircraft, looking out onto its wing above the clouds; there was a hint of the African jungle below. It promised excitement and no little amount of danger, and perfectly matched Sr Ruth's narrative. She wrote in a fresh pacy style, with very informal and sometimes irreverent detail, on life on the missions. Her cast of characters included stoic old nuns, stuffy colonial officials and exuberant – if somewhat superstitious and irrational – natives.

In a section on the climate of Nigeria, she reported, in characteristically florid style, 'While you are at morning Mass, the heat causes the candles on the altar to soften gradually until they droop and bow slowly and gracefully as if in adoration of the sacred mysteries taking place... One feels habitually conscious of this damp heat – always clammy, often quite sticky. Indeed it would not surprise me if the native clay of my mortal brow sprouted a crop of fungi overnight, and I were to wake up wearing a crown of fresh mushrooms!'

Other passages captured, with some innocence but also some insight, the routine of missionary life. About ten months into her posting, she recorded:

> *17 July*
> Life as usual.
> Rain, rain, rain.
>
> *18 July*
> Sunday.
> The rain is streaming down non-stop, the atmosphere so oppressive, so wet, so hot, so sticky.
> The rain makes you depressed, the sun makes you stupid.
> Blessed be God.
>
> *19 July*
> A beautiful sunny morning evaporates the blues – nurses, patients, everyone in much brighter form.
> Head clear. Work as usual...

Ultimately, of course, the diary was written for a purpose. Like *Visitation*, it was composed with an eye for new recruits. It was also a paean to the missionary life, arguing that there was 'nothing in the world quite like a missionary'. The author praised those veterans around her and the 'heroism' of the missionary priests under whose wing she had been taken. 'No words would be adequate to describe the life of a missionary,' she said, 'any more than they can describe the experience of a soldier when the battle is on. The story might be told in music, fully orchestrated.' She continued:

> 'A life without hardship is a miserable life,' a visiting missionary in Drogheda once told us. I can still hear him: 'Love hardship; work in hardship; that is part of the missions: hardship.' Well I must say our little band are thriving on it. And why not? Is not this missionary spirit the key to our whole vocation? It fulfils the same function, it seems to me, as poverty to the Franciscans, or silence to the Cistercians, or the Opus Dei to the Benedictines. It is the means by which the missionary soul makes the total sacrifice required for the gift of contemplation. It is the MMM way.

While couched in colourful language, such passages highlighted the austere nature of religious life at the time. Hardship, self-deprivation and self-punishment were expected of ordinary Catholics, and much more so of priests and nuns. In hindsight, one can see how this stored up problems for the future. Missionaries were not just expected to accept celibacy and the denial of all sorts of pleasures but, in some respects, to embrace pain. This could make priests and nuns harsh in their outlook and austere and authoritarian in their dealings with people. In less guarded moments, some missionaries would speak of their regrets. 'Looking back on it I dread the things we did because we had no formal language (training) and we did not get any of the acculturation that the Columbans do today,' said one Far-Eastern veteran. 'I shudder to think of the mistakes we made. We were trying to impose Irish traditions on Philippine culture. We had all the answers, God forgive us.' The risk of abuse rose within those congregations that were built upon a brutal training regime. Pat Whitney, the founder of the Kiltegans, admitted being 'just a little lonesome sometimes and much too cross with the people' during his early tours to southern Nigeria. One of his colleagues, Thomas McGettrick, who rose to the rank of prefect apostolic of Ogoja province, confessed to similar transgressions. 'He was rough with the people, failing to listen to their views and dealing out severe punishments to those who deviated from the straight path,' according to Kiltegan historian Fr Thomas Kiggins. 'It was a great temptation for a priest to adopt this line... The privileged position of a white man in a colonial set-up allowed great latitude in dealing with the local population. More to the point, where priests were concerned, the tradition of the people condoned great harshness in the exercise of authority.' The somewhat macho culture among Kiltegan priests could not have helped either. The society prided itself on its discipline, and members regarded themselves as the Navy Seals or crack commandos of the Irish missionary movement. They were boastful about the extent to which they embraced hardship. So much so that, as Kiggins noted, 'a luxury such as a radio was frowned on by many'.

Reflecting on how her predecessors in the MMMs operated, O'Donoghue accentuated the positives. 'One of the things that has impressed me over the years is the generosity, enthusiasm and dedication of our early members. They were prepared to go wherever, and it didn't matter what the difficulties were. The difficulties were there to be overcome.' But, she said, 'nobody gets everything 100 per cent right. The sisters took on so much they were overstretched. They developed fourteen hospitals in Nigeria alone.'

Echoing this view, Keane said: 'We spread too quickly. In the

1940s and 1950s we had a lot of people entering the congregation; we had big numbers and they were sent out to these missions as quickly as possible: Sierra Leone, Cameroon, Ethiopia, Kenya, Zambia and South Africa. It was too much.'

Had she personal regrets? 'Oh yes. For instance, I was trained in medicine, surgery – obs and gynae – so we had a therapeutic set-up for sick people. That was the emphasis. In hindsight, if I went back now, I wouldn't do anything in the hospital. I would get to know the people and their needs. I would get into public health.'

Missionaries could be their own harshest critics, and Keane was no exception. She said her motivation was 'to help' and 'that would be contrary to missiology today'. She added, 'We went out to give and never really averred to the fact that these people have a lot of resources themselves and have a lot to give to us, and we only really recognised that after living with them for a while. It evolved really… I don't think in the beginning we really absorbed all of Bishop Shanahan's vision of the resources in the people themselves – what they can do with so little.'

Bishop Shanahan's softly-softly approach with tribal leaders in Nigeria – an approach aimed at building up good relations and mutual respect – might draw plaudits from his followers decades later. But the passage of time cannot disguise an imperialist flavour to Shanahan's work. As an old-school Holy Ghost Father, his priority was getting more people into the Church. He encouraged his flock to 'learn book' but with the underlying motive of evangelisation. In a revealing comment, he once said: 'If we go from town to town talking only about God, we know from experience that much of our effort brings no result. But no one is opposed to a school.' Education was a means of soft-selling Catholicism. Ditto health care, as the medical missionary groups discovered. But were motivations the same across the board? And what emphasis did the missionaries put on conversion?

The MMM mission in Ogoja, Southern Nigeria is an interesting case study. The leprosy colony, which featured in the film *Visitation*, was run by the nuns in conjunction with the St Patrick's Missionary Society (the Kiltegans) and had the support of the British colonial administration in Nigeria. Nonetheless, it was infused with an overtly Catholic ethos. Each leprosy village had its own presidium of the Legion of Mary, and all patients were 'invited' to go to Mass. Everyone in the community reported up the chain to Thomas McGettrick, the sometimes harsh – by his own admission – prefect apostolic of Ogoja province. McGettrick, born in Killavil, County Sligo in 1905, had a strong sense of purpose, infused by a mixture of religiosity and Irish nationalism. He once turned down a posting to England on the basis it would no good 'explaining Christian doctrine to people who did not believe in God'. From his first visits to Ogoja, he had been struck by the plight of lepers, many of whom hung around outside churches where they 'held out their hands and beat their bellies hoping for a dash [of money] to buy food'. While in Ireland in 1939, and unable to travel because of the war, McGettrick raised £12,000 to get the leprosy project underway in conjunction with the MMMs. 'The lepers seemed to speak to the "soft centre" of Tom McGettrick,' Kiggins noted. 'This was an aspect of his personality which he tried to disguise by wearing the mask of a hard-boiled, impassive missionary.' Certainly, the Sligoman was held in high esteem by his parishioners. When McGettrick died in 1989, the head man of a leper village told priests who were recording a film on the bishop: 'For us, Mc Gettrick is next only to God.'

The sense that conversion was a high priority in Ogoja was underlined by *Visitation*, which climaxed with a scene where the leprosy patients, once treated, made their way to a church for prayer. 'Most of the lepers enter the village as pagans, but many, after experiencing the power of love and charity are eager to join the Church,' Buchanan narrated. 'A leper may be cured of his disease yet remain ill in soul, unenlightened and unChristian. And so his cure is incomplete until his soul and heart are awakened and he learns the meaning of a loving God.'

This commentary, while endorsed by the MMMs, was perhaps designed for a public audience rather than a congregational one and was not necessarily a true reflection of the society's priorities. Joe Barnes, a medical doctor who worked for Marie Martin in Ogoja and was featured in *Visitation*, said the Catholicism he and other people on the mission shared was 'assumed'. But 'it wasn't rammed down anybody's throats'. As a doctor working for the MMMs, 'the only religious thing I did was to attend Mass on Sundays. That was it.'

Barnes went to Nigeria in 1944 after meeting Martin on the way to a medical conference in Dundalk. The ever-persuasive MMM founder mentioned that she was opening a leprosy settlement, and Barnes replied that he had always been very interested in leprosy. 'So that was my appointment to the leprosy,' Barnes recalled with a chuckle. The doctor, who graduated from UCD, had previously done a three-year stint with the Holy Rosary Sisters in Emekuku in Nigeria. It had been a tough apprenticeship: the German doctors who had been working with him there were interned when the war broke out, leaving him with sole responsibility for a 200-bed hospital. Asked whether he felt it was too much for him, as he was then only in his mid-twenties, Barnes scoffed: 'No better time. Alexander conquered the world at that age.'

Interviewed at his home in Dublin at the age of 95, Barnes spoke lucidly on topics ranging from the history of leprosy treatment to the contemporary, atheistic writings of Richard Dawkins. 'I think the approach of the Church at that time was the Shanahan approach – schools, schools, schools. There was a school there and I presume they taught catechism there. But I never baptised anyone. I never belonged to any congregation. I went out to heal the sick and that was it. Even Dr Dawkins couldn't disapprove.'

Some orders would break for prayers, but the MMMs were 'very straightforward' and professional. Asked did Church teaching ever interfere with medical treatment, he replied, 'It never arose.' Did the nuns try to convert people? 'I never saw it anyhow.'

He said the nuns were merely responding to people's needs as they saw them, a point echoed by Barnes' wife, a fellow doctor who joined him in Nigeria after they were married. 'I never heard the bishop [McGettrick] preaching,' she said. 'They had catechists who taught people but they didn't seem very involved. These men were always talking about the price of a bag of cement, and a sheet of tin for the roof, and how much the petrol was costing.'

Her husband added, 'They might as well have been atheists, like Dawkins, as far as conversion went.' As for himself, Joe Barnes stressed, 'I was not a missionary doctor. I was a doctor employed by the missions.' The MMMs paid him a salary, albeit a meagre one, for his work, he explained. A few minutes later, as the conversation shifted to another topic, Dr Barnes suddenly stopped speaking; something had been playing on his mind. 'To be completely open about it,' he said, 'there was one single baptism I did, and this was a child – a newborn – and it looked as if it would die. In fact it may actually have been dead…' There was tenderness in his voice. '… and I poured a little water and said some words and that was it.'

Joe Barnes' free hand in the MMMs underlined the organisation's strong emphasis on patient care. The young doctor was allowed to experiment with the latest drug treatments, and this inadvertently led to a breakthrough in leprosy research. He had noticed similarities between tuberculosis and leprosy, or Hansen's disease, and carried out early trials on compounds that assisted in the development of clofazimine, which became one of the most successful treatments for leprosy (it still is to the present day).[12]

The MMMs were happy to facilitate his research and lobbied constantly for new treatments. John Manton, a medical historian who did a PhD at Nuffield College, Oxford on the Catholic mission in Ogoja, said the MMMs wrote regular begging letters to pharmaceutical companies, seeking free samples of different drugs. 'I don't think they were shy about anything,' he said. 'They really had to make things work on very little. They had to get by on improvisation and will.'

Compared to other missionary organisations, the MMMs had an 'unashamedly modern vision', said Manton. This included a relaxed, practical dress code, emphasis on best scientific practice and a willingness to work within existing health infrastructures in Ireland and in Nigeria, he explained. In promotional and fundraising literature, the MMMs made a great play of the fact that they were using the most up-to-date treatments and the most humane regime for patient care. There was, however, some ambiguity in this regard. Their blunt messages about 'unclean' lepers helped to loosen purse strings but did little to reduce stigma around the disease. Leprosy was a 'very useful propaganda tool', Manton noted, and the MMMs were not afraid to use a simplistic message in fundraising – even if their own understanding of the disease was more complex.

Whatever about disagreements over policy within the MMMs, there were frequent tensions between it and other religious bodies, especially the hierarchy. In Ogoja, and elsewhere, the bishops had the last word, and this created a potential for conflict. Martin had regular clashes with McGettrick over how best to deploy personnel. While the Kiltegan bishop was always seeking to expand, the MMM leader emphasised consolidation. She felt the society's hospitals needed to have a critical mass of nursing staff and administrators to run effectively. McGettrick was more impatient for results and tried to divert nuns in Ogoja to new mission stations.

Underlying the dispute was a traditional, hierarchical power struggle. 'The MMMs had to fight to stick to their mission,' said Manton. 'Sometimes they thought the Kiltegans were trying to turn them into secretaries because wherever they went the priest would try to have them doing the accounts for the diocese, that kind of thing.'

It is easy to forget the missionary movement was full of outsized egos and personality clashes. Harmony was not always guaranteed either within congregations or between them, and because those who went into the missions were so committed to the cause, when they fell out with one another they did so spectacularly. Bishop Shanahan was a prime example. There were few people whom he didn't antagonise in his forty years as a missionary. Before going to Nigeria, he worked for a short period at the Holy Ghost Rockwell College in County Tipperary where he once chartered a train at massive expense for the school's rugby team when its alternative transport to a fixture in Cork fell through. The decision was met with incredulity from the school management, and it hastened Shanahan's departure from Rockwell, but it was the same sort of single-minded arrogance that made Shanahan a success in the missions. He was the kind of man who wouldn't take no for an answer. He wouldn't let practicalities stand in the way of his belief, and that was a great strength and a huge weakness. Faced with the choice of either forfeiting defeat in the rugby game or undertaking a reckless expense which would leave the dean's fund in debt for years to come, it was – for Shanahan – a no-brainer.

The complexity of Shanahan's nature is reflected in his correspondence with colleagues and friends. They reveal especially how he struggled through life to retain loyalty from his followers. Marie Martin, whom he saw as a kindred spirit and a future leader of his brainchild, the Holy Rosary Sisters, left his company to form her own congregation. Fr Tom Ronayne, the 'introducer', who hooked the bishop up with Martin and badgered him with ideas for many years, was regarded by Shanahan to be 'the best, sincerest and most loyal man and priest on earth' but also a 'well-intentioned holy humbug'. Ronayne repaid the compliment by scheming behind Shanahan's back with Whitney in order to wrest the Society of Saint Patrick from the bishop's field of influence. In a letter to Ronayne, Whitney recommended, in Machiavellian style, 'We will use the old boy as long as he can help us, and ditch him when he becomes an obstacle.' The cruellest cut of all, however, came from the Holy Rosary Sisters, the order Shanahan helped to establish to work alongside the Holy Ghost Fathers in Nigeria. Keen to assert its independence when it became self-governing in 1934, the women's congregation suddenly cut the formal ties it had with Shanahan. Novices were warned by their superior of the bishop's 'very affectionate nature'. This might be a gift for the missions but 'it could be dangerous' for young and immature recruits. In an instruction laced with innuendo, nuns were told: 'Respect him, pray for him, show him due reverence at all times, but be careful of all that is too human and too natural.'

The episode highlighted the capacity for cruelty that lay within religious institutions. There was no evidence that the ageing Shanahan was anything more than a bit tactile, but he was ostracised nonetheless. It seems his brand of rambunctious personality fell out of fashion in the more pious, cloistered Ireland of the 1930s and 1940s. Sisters returning from Nigeria were told not to contact him. One of these young nuns recalled raising the matter with her superior who told her, using brutal logic: 'It does not matter if you are hurt or he is hurt or who is hurt. The important thing is, what does God want? And that we must do, no matter what it costs.' Shanahan was eventually banished from the convent and told to avoid any contact with the sisters. Heartbroken, he confided in a friend: 'A few of them think I don't know how to control my affections. Of course, I love the young nuns there very much, and I don't think God will ever be displeased with me for that.' Fifty years after Shanahan's death, the Holy Rosary Sisters admitted to having wrongly blackened the bishop's name, commissioning historian Desmond Forristal to write a book on their founder with 'nothing held back'. Forristal noted Shanahan's hurt at his exclusion 'remained with him to the end of his life. It has remained with the Holy Rosary Sisters to this day' and they wished to put the record straight 'as an act of filial piety, a righting of wrongs, an exorcism of ghosts, an acknowledgement of mistakes, a plea for forgiveness'.[13]

Shanahan was not alone in being eaten up, and spat out, by the very movement to which he gave his life. Pat Whitney, one of those ambitious priests who schemed behind the old bishop's back, himself ended up on the missionary scrap heap as soon as he had served his purpose. The founder of the Kiltegans fell ill in July 1938 while working near Ogoja. He was depressed and frequently disorientated. Eventually, his condition got so bad he was forced to return home and was admitted to the Mater Hospital in Dublin for six weeks. He received only one visit from a member of the Kiltegans in that time. In May 1939, he was ordered to resign from his senior position within the society, and he was offered no replacement role.

It was an extraordinarily hasty – not to mention heartless – demotion and reflected again the missionary's capacity for ruthlessness. Within the movement, there was no trading on reputation. If you were no longer useful you would be swept aside by a younger, more zealous replacement. The last correspondence Whitney received relating to official business was a curt, five-sentence letter from his new superior ordering him to hand over 'the names and addresses of benefactors which you have. Now that you no longer hold a position of responsibility I expect that you no longer need them.' The letter contained not a word of sympathy or thanks for his life's work with the Kiltegans. Whitney spent the next three years being moved from one convalescence home to another. Pitying his isolated state, Marie Martin offered him a room but it was members of Whitney's family who looked after him in his last days. He died on 17 July 1942 and was buried at the family plot in Carrick-on-Shannon. The Kiltegans made a somewhat cynical bid to have the burial switched to their headquarters, but failed. They never tried to establish the cause of Whitney's illness. Claims of alcoholism were widespread, and James Moynagh once wrote from Calabar: 'It is very difficult to prove that it is drink but if it is not drink it is mental and anyhow it is probably both.' However, Kiggins noted, there was 'no evidence' alcohol abuse was a factor. Martin, who saw Whitney towards the end, diagnosed Parkinson's disease, while a brain tumour and Multiple Sclerosis were also speculated as causes.

So much for the early missionaries. What of the generation that followed them? Were there any happy endings for those inspired by the likes of Shanahan, Martin and Whitney? Where exactly did the new recruits end up?

The volunteer Joe Barnes left Nigeria in June 1951. The *Nigerian Catholic Herald* reported that villagers marked the occasion by 'firing rifle shots – a token of grief'. The MMM employee became a dermatologist at the Mater Hospital in Dublin but punctuated many decades of treating warts and varicose veins with further adventures overseas. He worked as a doctor in the Congo in 1960, for the Red Cross in Biafra in 1968 and for the UN and other agencies in India-Pakistan, Thailand and Lebanon, up to 1983. In that time, he became a totem for volunteerism, and he won many honours, including a People of the Year award at the inaugural staging of the event in 1974. He also enjoyed a rich family life with his wife Betty. They had seven children.

Josephine Ann Mooney became forevermore Sr Cyril Mooney

after entering the Loretos from school. 'I picked Cyril as my religious name,' she said, 'because it was the only one I thought they couldn't make a nickname out of.' The Wicklow woman moved to Calcutta, India where she set up a string of housing, education and employment projects for street children and adults.

Sheila Crowe worked in education in the Philippines and Hong Kong before returning to the Columban Sisters' motherhouse in Magheramore, County Wicklow. There she was involved in a training programme for teachers who planned to work in China.

Eileen Keane went from Sierra Leone to Kenya and Nigeria, but spent most of her religious life in Zambia where she worked as a surgeon in a mission hospital before specialising in hospice care for victims of HIV. In 2006, she returned to Ireland and became a councillor with Spirasi, the support group for victims of torture.

Miriam Duggan went from medical college in Dublin to Uganda where she worked for fifteen years through coups and counter-coups under the despot Idi Amin. She became famous for her ability to remove bullets from different parts of the body and had to operate sometimes as mortars fell around her compound. 'It was more like a war-time surgery,' she recalled. She later became a prominent activist on HIV and Aids, before returning to Dublin to become congregational leader of the Franciscan Missionary Sisters of Africa and president of the Irish Missionary Union.

In the decades since she completed her round-the-world trip with Marie Martin, Maura O'Donoghue racked up the same flight miles many times over. In 1984, she helped to coordinate the Catholic Church's famine relief operations in Ethiopia, and travelled around Europe, the US and Canada lobbying governments for food aid. O'Donoghue subsequently worked with Muslim populations in Chechnya, Iraq, Bosnia, Serbia and Kosovo, and she said this taught her valuable lessons about diversity and how missionaries must 'take people as they are, from where they are'. She also worked with the Catholic aid agencies Cafod and Caritas ('but this is all about me,' she protested – with standard missionary humility – as she continued to detail her experiences). Later, she moved back to Dublin to coordinate a support group for women who were trafficked into Ireland.

Sixty-plus years after she saw *Visitation*, O'Donoghue rejected any suggestion that she had strayed off the course envisaged by her mentor. 'I do not see what I'm doing now as in anyway removed from the charism of Mother Mary. She wanted to address the big need in her day. Initially, it was maternity work, but then she broadened our charism over time. Her attitude would have been to ask: "What is the biggest need today?" She was always trying to address the poorest of the poor in every place. Plus, care of the mother and child was the big thing for her. That is intimately connected with anti-trafficking. I think if she were alive today she would say, "Get on with that."'

CHAPTER 4: FROM SACRAMENTAL TO SOCIAL WORK

'If anyone has two tunics he must share with the man who has none, and the one with something to eat must do the same.' (Luke 3:10)

Ask anyone aged under thirty today about Biafra and you are likely to get blank stares. Once, though, the failed breakaway province in south-east Nigeria was a byword for humanitarian disaster. Part post-colonial power struggle, part terrifying ethnic feud, the Biafran war represented a new type of conflict in the late 1960s – and it was observed by the world like no conflict before in a still-dawning TV age. Before Ethiopia, Rwanda and Darfur, there was Biafra. And at its centre was a group of aid-giving Irish priests and nuns. Prominent among them was Jack Finucane, a tall, strongly built Limerick man and Holy Ghost Father, who had been three years in Nigeria when the war broke out.

'It was away in the distance for a long time, and then it got closer and closer to me,' he recalled. 'Then, early one morning I heard a lot of noise outside my house and I went out and there were a few thousand refugees – what we now call displaced people – and they were running for safety from the Nigerian army which was closing in. Some were pretty malnourished and had been walking for a long time. So there was a very simple decision that had to be made – to close the schools and turn them into refugee camps. They were the first refugee camps I ever saw.'

Finucane has described this scene many times down the years because it captures a kind of birth of Irish overseas development work. In the days and weeks that followed his morning discovery in 1967, Finucane – aged just 30 – helped to purchase some of the first relief supplies for displaced Biafrans. Soon after, he was involved in raising publicity internationally about the unfolding humanitarian crisis. As the war intensified, he was put in charge of a covert relief programme, shipping aid through a makeshift airstrip at Uli in breach of a Nigerian government blockade. The medical and food supplies were funded by donations in Ireland under the banner of Africa Concern, the organisation which later became Concern Worldwide.

More than four decades on from that morning discovery in Biafra, Finucane reflected on how it had changed him and his missionary colleagues. Sitting in the living room of his apartment in Dublin, surrounded by carved wooden and ivory figurines, paintings and photos from his time in Africa, he spoke cautiously, pausing now and again to choose the right words. His reputation for not suffering fools gladly was plain to see. Asked if he agreed that priests had a lonelier existence than nuns because they missed the support of a community, he scoffed. 'Men and women are different. Sisters by their nature like to be together. Men are more odd. They are more independent.' He still travelled, played golf and had a wide circle of friends, he stressed. The latter was neatly illustrated when – mid-way through the interview – a neighbour called to his door with a plate of hot food to save him cooking that day.

One of seven children, three of whom chose religious life, Finucane was ordained in 1964 and shipped to Nigeria just weeks later. The Ireland he left behind was economically depressed and unashamedly religious. 'The missions were out there as an option,' he said. 'It was something you didn't analyse to a huge degree but as a young lad it was a great idea, and it impressed you.' There were various links in his family to the Holy Ghost Fathers, otherwise known as the Spiritans, and when his brother Aengus (Gus) signed up to the order a few years ahead of him, his fate was sealed. 'Nowadays we analyse these things,' he said. 'I don't think I even got into it. This was something – "respected" was not the word – but it was seen as the best thing to do at the time.'

There were nearly fifty other recruits to the Spiritans in the year he joined. Despite the pious atmosphere of the time, these young men were no quiet, contemplative waifs. They were muscular Irish Catholics in a novel sense: firm-handed and practical lads, sons of farm labourers and country doctors who formed physical bonds on the rugby field, a sporting altar worshipped with special reverence by the Holy Ghost Fathers. Among those who travelled to Nigeria around the same time as Jack Finucane was Dubliner Tony Byrne, who would – as the Biafran war developed – earn the nickname the 'Green Pimpernel' for his dangerous, blockade-breaching relief operations. In his memoirs, Byrne told of the giddy mood felt by his class of Holy Ghosts as they sailed for Port Harcourt in Nigeria on a steamer ship.

> We were full of enthusiasm, just recently ordained priests and keen to put into practice everything we had learnt, the Novice Master's admonition that we should be 'men for all seasons' fresh in our minds.[14]

A manly camaraderie was a hallmark of the Holy Ghost experience, and this bred loyalty, as well as obedience. 'If you were told to go to Timbuktu, you went there. You didn't ask why,' said Finucane. But, an incident on Byrne's sea journey to Africa suggested that independent thinking, and even a streak of rebellion, lay under the surface. Writing of how he detested having to wear the black suit, clerical collar and hat that was obligatory for priests under

Church law in Ireland, Byrne wondered whether his colleagues felt the same. He continued:

> One morning in the Bay of Biscay, Dick Brophy called us:
>
> 'I've had a peek outside, lads, and it looks like a great morning for a hat-throwing. Shall we say 9.30 after breakfast, upper deck, port side?'
>
> The bunk above me groaned as Gerry Smith, our gentle giant who was happier squeezing into the second row of a rugby scrum than this cramped berth, propped himself up on an elbow.
>
> 'They tell me the French like hats. They can have mine!'
>
> 'Anybody can have mine.'
>
> 'And mine.'
>
> Not another word seemed to be spoken about hats but, by 9.30, more than a dozen of us lined up on the upper deck. One by one, with great ceremony, we tossed our hats into the rough sea, in the direction of France.[15]

In terms of missionary work, the template for such priests was fellow Spiritan Joseph Shanahan, the charismatic and physically imposing bishop of southern Nigeria. Over thirty years in the region, he built up a close affinity with the Igbo tribe. He was just as happy to put his weight behind a shovel as preach from the altar and would sit for hours with local chiefs, sharing a glass of whiskey and discussing farming methods. One oft-heard story from his early days in Igbo country told how he saved a village from a rampaging bush-cow. Drawing on his experience herding cattle as a boy in County Tipperary, Shanahan smacked the animal on the tip of its nose – its tenderest spot – as it charged past him. The beast then turned on its heels and fled – much to the delight of the locals. For Jack Finucane and his peers, travelling to Africa in the 1950s and 1960s, the main responsibility was simply building on

Shanahan's legacy. 'We were following in a tradition. The world hadn't changed much since Bishop Shanahan's day.'

Almost immediately after his arrival, Finucane was appointed as a parish priest. His primary role was to visit thirty outstations, where he would perform christenings and administer the Eucharist, as well as check up on the Catholic schools. This would be the norm for six days of the week. The exception was Monday when he would leave the bush and travel to Port Harcourt for a round of golf – an unbreakable appointment – with his Holy Ghost peers. 'At that time, our work was very sacramental,' Finucane recalled. 'You had huge numbers going to confession, you had thousands being baptised. You were very much a sacramental priest. It was quite different to the guys who went to Brazil. They were working with the poor and trying to raise awareness about social issues, and didn't have the same emphasis on sacraments which we had in Africa.'

Asked whether he had tried to convert people to Catholicism, he shook his head. 'When I got to Nigeria the Church had been well established. You weren't really going out trying to beat the bushes looking for people, no… In many parishes, the Church was the only established institution. It was organised, and people like to be organised, and part of some kind of an institution.' He added: 'The biggest problem was trying to service the numbers in the church. They were pouring in. You might question that – how much they understood – but they were coming over the fences.'

How did he feel about his mission work now? Finucane smiled nervously as he considered a reply. 'I don't want to be accused of –' he began, and then his voice trailed off. 'When you look back now you say, "OK, it was all very strange." And would you do it the same? Probably not, probably not. But there was a great emphasis on education and a lot of parishes had schools attached to them, which was very positive.'

The Finucane brothers might not have had the same evangelising zeal as Bishop Shanahan but, in other ways, they seemed cut from the same cloth. In Biafra, the elder brother was once travelling in a convoy of aid vehicles when it was stopped by an armed raider. 'An indignant Fr Gus Finucane jumped out of a Peugeot 404 estate,' according to the official record, 'threw himself at the bandit and embraced him in a 19-stone rugby tackle.'[16] Bishop Shanahan would surely have done no different. And, over time, chiefly through their work with Concern, the Finucanes would help spawn a new branch of Spiritan folk memory. They even made the order seem cool for a while. 'Both strong and formidable characters, they put one in mind of a couple of tag-wrestlers,' journalist Kevin Myers – an unlikely cheerleader for things Catholic – once wrote of them.[17]

Plaudits such as this lay in the years ahead, however. Back in 1967, Jack Finucane and his colleagues were struggling to put together a relief operation for the people of Biafra. It was estimated that 6,000 children were dying every week due to a lack of food and medicine. 'Things are decided for you,' said Finucane, who was loath to give himself any credit for the charity initiative. 'You are not sitting there making big plans yourself. There is a school, and you have 1,000 refugees, so you move them in. That means the school closes, and you have to look after the people in some way. So it wasn't any great decisions on my part. It was decisions on their part, and you had to react to them.'

The images and reports of starving families had a particular resonance in Ireland, with its historical experience of famine. But what could be done? This was nearly eighteen years before Live Aid. And while the Biafran war spawned a number of new international aid agencies, notably Médicins Sans Frontières, a method for allowing the Irish public help a distant, suffering group of people like the Igbo had yet to be imagined. What the Holy Ghost Fathers had on their side was a huge network of parishes, perfectly designed for aid distribution. Along with other missionary orders, they also had a significant number of personnel on the ground. There were about 1,600 Irish Catholic missionaries in Nigeria at the time, including roughly 300 in Biafra. Their tentacles reached into the remotest parts of the country where the wasting disease of kwashiorkor was at its worst.

A few months after Finucane had his early morning wake-up call, a colleague, Fr Raymond Kennedy, returned to Ireland to raise awareness about Biafra. He challenged his brother John to do something, and this led to a meeting at the home of John and Kay O'Loughlin-Kennedy on 19 March 1968 at 82 Northumberland Road, Dublin. About forty people came, including two exiled Biafran chiefs. Africa Concern was thus born under a non-denominational banner. Its very diverse steering committee included the head of the Knights of Columbanus, a prominent freemason and a senior trade unionist. The charity launched a public appeal to 'Send One Ship' of aid supplies to Biafra. Newspapers were arm-twisted into giving free advertising space. County-by-county league tables were set up to encourage competition between donors. Within three months, £250,000 had been raised. A ship, SS *Columcille*, was purchased and, on 6 September 1968, she sailed for Sao Tome, a small island off the coast of West Africa. From here supplies were flown into Biafra under a now finely tuned smuggling operation spearheaded by Fr Tony Byrne.

The 'Green Pimpernel' had been involved in organising the very first airlifts of aid into Biafra in breach of the Nigerian government's blockade. When the different Christian denominations formed Joint Church Aid (JCA) to rapidly increase shipments, he was put in charge of the transport operation. Between 1968 and 1970, over 5,000 flights were made, usually at night to avoid detection. Landings had to be made on a roadway at Uli which had been converted into an airstrip after the capture of Biafra's only airport nearby. Propeller engines would be kept running on the ground to allow planes a quick escape. Crates were unloaded hastily and moved to a central deposit ten miles away. This was run by Jack Finucane, who was then head of Biafran operations for Caritas, the Catholic Church's humanitarian aid wing. It was difficult and dangerous work, with anti-aircraft fire a constant hazard. Nine JCA planes either were shot down or crashed during the war. Some 172 Biafran and thirty-five North American and European JCA workers, including seventeen pilots, were killed. The war claimed missionary casualties too, the first among them Sister Cecilia Thackaberry. A member of the Holy Rosary Convent, she was travelling in a car when a Nigerian jet plane swooped overhead and opened fire, killing her and wounding one of her colleagues, Elizabeth Murray.

The situation was complicated by the fact that Irish missionaries were working on both sides of the front. Those located behind federal lines were suspected of collaborating with the Biafrans and frequently harassed. Biafrans had their suspicions about the religious interlopers too, wary of the fact that Nigeria was supported by Western governments in the war. The fraught nature of the situation was highlighted in July 1967 when Ogoja was taken by federal troops. The soldiers swept through the streets just as the eleven o'clock bell was chiming over Bishop McGettrick's cathedral. They thought it was a signal to the Biafran troops and shot at the bishop's house in reprisal. One bullet missed McGettrick by inches; another grazed a lay volunteer who was staying with him. Subsequently, it was rumoured among Biafrans that the Kiltegan bishop had rung the bell to celebrate the arrival of the feds. One priest recalled local Catholics taunting him: 'You are a pikin [child] of that bishop who helped the Nigerian vandals to take Ogoja.' Another priest, Frank Morris, spoke of the terrible dilemmas the conflict created. Once, he discovered a man hiding in his house, and he felt he had no choice but to get the houseboys 'to take him out and put him on the road… I presume he didn't last too long… Although it was sending a man to certain death to put him out of the compound, yet there were in all sixteen of us, counting the cook's family, to be thought of, for anyone sheltering men was shot out of hand.'

Those priests and nuns who worked in Biafra had strong support from the Irish public. The Irish government was more ambivalent. Ireland had business links with Nigeria, centred on a large Guinness factory in Lagos. It was also under pressure from Britain to keep in line with the dominant international stance on Biafra. Nigeria had only gained independence from Britain in 1960, and there was widespread fear at the time that if the Biafrans succeeded in breaking away it would lead to a 'balkanisation' not just of Nigeria but of Africa. Irish government officials sometimes tried to influence missionaries, and their sympathisers, on the issue. In 1968, RTÉ's flagship current affairs programme *Seven Days* had planned to send a crew to Biafra, but the trip was cancelled by the station's management. *Seven Days* was taken off air shortly afterwards, and it was reported at the time that the government cited a range of objections to the series but 'the example most often quoted is the Biafran venture'.[18]

State papers released under the 30-year-rule show exactly how unimpressed the government was with the Biafran missionary position. In a letter marked 'secret' to the Department of External Affairs, the Irish Ambassador to Nigeria Paul Keating criticised comments that returned Irish priests had made about the Nigerian government. The 'lack of Holy Ghost discipline' in one case had resulted in three priests 'spending an uncomfortable and unnecessary time in prison', he reported. The ambassador further advised that a government policy of giving blank passports to Holy Ghost fathers to facilitate them in entering and leaving the country be revised. 'There is,' he said, 'the danger that the blank passports may be, in fact, abused by the less well-balanced members of the Holy Ghost Order if they get possession of them.'

Most pointed of all, Keating told the government in March 1970, two months after the war ended, that 'we in Ireland' think the missionaries were unjustly treated but 'Nigerian public opinion and large sections of the administration of Nigerian Catholicism, and even in some cases Irish missionaries, take a different point of view. They feel that the Holy Ghost fathers were impertinent busybodies from abroad who involved themselves in the internal affairs of Nigeria and, by their propaganda and aid and comfort to the Biafrans, unduly prolonged the war and caused great suffering to the Nigerian people.'

Asked whether the actions of the Holy Ghost Fathers indirectly prolonged the war, Finucane replied: 'That may be true but I would say also many more people would have died. So, OK, where do you go? We went out to work with these people – the Igbo. They were the ones who suffered during the war. There was, if you like, nothing else we could do. You either left Nigeria or you stayed and did your best for the people who were suffering. It was not a matter of taking sides.' He added, a touch defensively: 'The Irish government were down in Lagos, analysing it from a political situation. We were on the ground, and therefore it seemed natural for us to continue to work there.' Finucane admitted the missionaries made one major miscalculation. The genocide they had been predicting once the Biafran army had been overrun did not materialise. 'In actual fact, the Nigerian army behaved quite well. I have seen much worse afterwards in different countries.'

Finucane was arrested following the Biafran surrender and was found guilty of entering the country illegally. He was sentenced to six months in prison with a dozen other missionaries, but they were deported after just twelve days. 'They didn't know what to do with us really.' Later, the government blamed foreign missionaries like the Holy Ghosts for fermenting nationalist sentiment in Biafra. It was a charge the priests vehemently denied, albeit some of them – rather charitably – believed the Nigerian government was right to make them scapegoats to try to boost post-conflict reconciliation and national unity.

The impact of Biafra on the missionary movement was profound. Priests and nuns in Africa started spending less time on religious duties and more time on giving practical assistance to the poor. No longer would the Spiritans be known as the 'balcony fathers' due to their perceived detachment from the people. Helping the Third World became a new means of invigorating an old vocation. For the Spiritans, Biafra was an even more seismic event. In the first place, there was a practical issue arising from being barred from Nigeria. Some 200 Holy Ghost Fathers arrived back in Ireland, wondering where they would be sent next. Finucane recalled: 'The provincial and his team were convinced it would be a matter of a few months before we would be allowed to go back and then we would continue where we left off. So in the meantime, they gave us all, if you wish, a general absolution: "OK, lads go and find work where you can and we will give you a call in a few months time when the dust has settled." That was a defining moment, actually. The guys went to the four corners of the earth, and when the time came to call them back it was too late. They were involved in all sorts of different areas, different works. And that was the beginning in one sense of new initiatives, and new works.'

Some Holy Ghost priests retreated to the comfort zone of their private-school empire in Ireland. But many others started new missions, from the Kimmage Development Studies Centre in Dublin to Spirasi, Ireland's first – and only – treatment centre for victims of torture. Tony Byrne became one of Ireland's foremost experts in suicide prevention, while the Finucane brothers helped to turn

Concern into an organisation that, in 2010, was working in more than thirty countries, with a staff worldwide of more than 3,200. Gus Finucane worked as chief executive of the charity until he retired aged 65 (he died twelve years later, in October 2009), while Jack was, for decades, Concern's head of emergency operations.

Jack Finucane lamented that the Holy Ghost superiors had done very little analysis 'at the time – or since' about the way in which priests scattered after Biafra. 'I think they would rather forget what happened.' After the expulsion from Nigeria, 'rather, than sit down and plan where we go from here, it was almost "let it flow; wherever the Holy Spirit sends us". The Holy Spirit seems to have flown us in many different directions.' Asked if Irish Spiritans were now more united by camaraderie than a common sense of purpose, he replied with a hollow laugh, 'Probably.'

Looking back, Finucane believed Concern was a 'lost opportunity' for the order. 'Here was the possibility, or probability, of a new social arm of the Holy Ghost Fathers; it was on a plate. And without saying it, they didn't really know what to do with it. So they let it be. Not only did they let it be but I would say, maybe inadvertently, they distanced themselves from it, and they saw it as a work that was not the work of the Holy Ghost Fathers; this was going outside our traditional work.' The Spiritans had been asked to donate some land for an office for Concern but the request fell on deaf ears. ('They never wrote to say, "No",' Finucane sighed.) Instead, Concern became determinedly secular in its structure. One of those who supported this move was its then chairman Michael Fingleton, who went on to become chief executive of Irish Nationwide. While his business reputation had plummeted since the 2008 banking collapse, he was remembered by Finucane as 'a very good' chairman.

For Finucane, it was a 'pity' the Holy Ghost Fathers didn't get more involved with Concern, but he saw little difference between the missionary priests and the lay volunteers with whom he worked in more recent years. 'In the early days, I used to tell a lot of the volunteers – they didn't like to hear it – that if they had been born ten years earlier they would have been sisters or priests.' In this more secular age, Concern has chosen to play down its religious origins, but Finucane said history couldn't be rewritten. 'Concern would not be there were it not for the missions, because the missions inspired it, and the missionary ethos influenced Concern in a huge way… The way the organisation was set up and run was very much like how the Holy Ghost Fathers were organised in the missions.'

But what was the wider legacy of the missionaries' work in Biafra? In 1973, spurred in part by Concern's success, the Irish Catholic bishops set up Trócaire, which now operates in thirty-nine countries, from El Salvador to East Timor. In 1974, the Irish government launched its own overseas development wing, Irish Aid. From the outset, it was guided by the values and principles of Irish missionaries. Or, as former minister of state for overseas development Liz O'Donnell commented, 'The Irish missionary position is very much the template of the official Irish government approach to overseas development aid.'[19] This approach meant money was directed at the 'poorest of the poor', with few – if any – strings attached and in sympathy with local customs and conventions.

That, at least, was the theory. In practice, early missionary charity to the Third World was characterised by crude fundraising tactics and a presumption that developing countries had no coping mechanisms of their own. School children across Ireland were in the 1950s and 1960s urged to give a '*pingin agus paidir*', or 'penny and prayer', to the black babies in Africa. In one notorious fundraising scheme, common in Irish schools well into the 1970s, pupils were told by visiting priests and nuns that if they raised enough money for the missions they could have a child in the 'African bush' baptised in a name of their choice.

There was little nuance to such tactics. As Tim Pat Coogan once wrote: 'In my schooldays it never occurred to anyone that there could be anything even remotely patronising in the philosophy that lay behind those collections. We were brought up believing that Africans as a class were as much in need of the civilising influences of the Irish religious as parched earth was of water. It was an image propagated by the missionary magazines with their pictures of a big, beaming Irish priest, generally robed in white, surrounded by a group of adoring, chubby little black children.'[20] Congregations attached to the Pontifical Missions Society, which was charged with organising the annual Mission Sunday collection, came up with a particularly effective ruse: collection boxes designed for the counters of shops and pubs across the country. One such box was of a hungry-looking black child, typically christened 'Sambo' by clientele, that collected spare change through a hidden chute in its body. Another figurine had working parts: when coins dropped inside the child's body its head would spring into life, giving a grateful nod. Missionaries today cringe with embarrassment when such fundraising devices are mentioned, and it is easy from a modern vantage point to accuse the Church of being culturally insensitive. But attitudes in the Church towards the 'dark continent' of Africa forty or fifty years ago differed little from attitudes in society at large, and the missionaries' crude publicity campaigns at least focused people's minds on problems outside of Irish soil.

A more learned approach to the problems of Africa came in the wake of the Biafran conflict and the expulsion of the Holy Ghost Fathers from Nigeria. Trócaire, under its founding director Brian McKeown, a former member of the Legion of Mary, was among those who tried to set new standards of fundraising. 'Trócaire could collect much more money if we adopted a different policy… but this would not be in the interest of the Third World,' McKeown said, in an interview in 1974. 'The starving child may be a good fundraising gimmick, if your aim as an agency is the collection of the largest amount of money, irrespective of the underlying needs of the Third World or the feelings of people whose dignity is continually hurt by being shown on posters and appeals as wretched and starving. Such gimmicks can wound international reputations irreparably.'

The Biafran experience, and the upsurge in development work among missionaries, had a further legacy in that it accelerated progress in volunteerism. Lay people had played a role in the Irish missionary movement almost from its inception. The Legion of Mary, which was founded in 1921, produced notable figures – and martyrs – like Edel Quinn, who died in Nairobi in 1944, and Alfie Lambe, who died in Buenos Aires in 1959. A group of third-level students who were involved with the Legion set up Viatores Christi (Travellers for Christ) in 1960 after a stint working in parishes in the UK during their summer holidays. In its first eight years, the group sent over 200 people on assignments in twenty-five countries, most of them volunteering their skills for existing missionary programmes, and Viatores continues to operate today.

There were other lay voluntary organisations, including the Medical Missionary Society, founded in UCC in 1942 as a vehicle for supplying junior doctors to the MMMs. But the organisation that has probably survived best is the Volunteer Missionary Movement (VMM), founded by Englishwoman Edwina Gately in 1969 at the height of the Biafran war. Gately first went overseas in 1964 when she taught in a religious-run school in East Africa. She wrote, however, 'I soon discovered it was not easy to be a lay missionary in a Church that tended to see mission only in terms of priests and sisters. I was simply a "volunteer" *helping* the missions rather than being an intrinsic and full member of the missionary activity of the Church. I soon realised that it was not my calling to work within a religious structure into which I did not quite fit.' The

VMM emerged at a time when the Catholic Church was more open to the involvement of lay people, as articulated in Vatican II. It also built on the success of non-Catholic organisations, such as Voluntary Service Overseas (VSO), which was founded in the UK in 1958 after an English bishop's appeal for volunteers in the missions.

The value of these volunteering groups was recognised by the Irish government in April 1974 when Garret FitzGerald, then minister for foreign affairs, established the Agency for Personal Service Overseas (Apso). It was geared largely for university graduates who could not find work in Ireland, offering them job opportunities overseas with either religious or secular aid agencies. In the first year, 111 people signed up for postings lasting usually twenty-four months. By 1996, assignments through Apso reached a high of 1,396. Many people were drawn into a life-long commitment to the developing world through the agency, which was wound up in 2004. Today, the scope for volunteering overseas has never been easier. You can spend a week building houses in South Africa or several years teaching in South America, depending on the organisation you choose. Those volunteering with Catholic agencies typically work alongside long-embedded missionaries, but the duties they perform are almost identical to their counterparts in secular aid organisations. They have similar skills, make similar sacrifices and also face similar dangers. This was shown in 1993 when Niall McMenamin, a volunteer with VMM from Letterkenny, County Donegal, was shot dead during a robbery at the construction site where he was working in Kenya. He was aged just 22.

When assessing the impact of missionaries post-Biafra it should be noted that public awareness of the Third World had been improving even before religious orders began proselytising on our moral responsibilities to the poor. Yet Irish opinion would have evolved quite differently were it not for the missions, and particularly the visible commitment of individual priests and nuns. In June 1977, the sports journalist John O'Shea saw a BBC television interview with Fr Pat O'Mahony, a priest from Cork who was sending medical supplies in tea chests to various missionaries overseas. 'I was hugely impressed with this,' said O'Shea. He rang the priest and then started fundraising for a feeding programme in Calcutta, thereby launching a new international aid agency, Goal. Shortly after the Live Aid concert in July 1985, Bono of U2 travelled to Ethiopia to see the work that Jack Finucane and his colleagues in Concern were doing. He later said Finucane 'turned my life upside down', and the trip 'began my life as an activist'.[21]

Finucane also became good friends with Bob Geldof. The musician and Africa campaigner had gone to school at Blackrock College, Dublin, a Holy Ghost institution, albeit 'if you brought that up he would react very negatively to it', Finucane said with a smile. These were not simple cases of cause-and-effect. But, as Fr Dermod McCarthy, former editor of the RTÉ social affairs series *Radharc*, once remarked, 'Bono and Bob Geldof did not come out of a vacuum. They came from that culture of concern for the world's less fortunate; that tough, practical Christianity which was the hallmark of those missionaries.'[22]

McCarthy and his *Radharc* team played their part in popularising the missionaries in the aftermath of Biafra. Between 1962 and 1996, *Radharc* produced over 400 films on social and international affairs, reporting on the work of Irish priests and nuns across the globe. These films included 'Night Flight to Uli', which was broadcast in February 1968 and did much to raise awareness in Ireland about the Biafran conflict. Estimating the influence of the TV series, McCarthy said, 'Up to then, people here only knew about the Irish missionaries as such through the *Far East* magazine, or the box on the counter of a pub with a little black baby whose head bobbed every time you put a penny in it. But here were, in your own living room, full-blooded men and women from Ireland who were running huge pig farms like PJ McGlinty in Korea, health programmes, schools and colleges, digging wells, managing big hospitals in Nigeria and Kenya, as well as remote bush clinics, all across Africa, Asia and South America.'[23]

The two original producers of the series were Fr Desmond Forristal and Fr Joe Dunne, the former highly academic, the latter a populist communicator with a buccaneering air. In his memoirs, published twenty-five years after the founding of *Radharc*, Dunne recalled seeking permission from Archbishop John Charles McQuaid for his first trip to Africa in 1965. Fr Dunne spelt out the benefits of the trip from a Church viewpoint, mentioning he was looking forward to seeing 'real lions and tigers' himself. The archbishop replied in bullet-point style: 'I accept, in principle, the proposal of an African trip. You do not say who is to go. No tigers in Africa. And you may leave out the "perhaps" in your suggestion that the trip could reasonably "perhaps" be made in the holidays.' Dunne couldn't resist taking the 'No tigers in Africa' line as a title for his book.

While *Radharc* operated independently of RTÉ and was largely funded by the Catholic Church through its communications wing, it set a template for reporting on the developing world that was copied by the Irish media in general. *Radharc*'s focus on Irish personalities overseas, especially missionaries, was replicated by other TV and press coverage of foreign issues. Whenever Irish journalists found themselves in conflict zones they would tend to seek out their clerical compatriots and sometimes co-opt them as fixers, translators and even drivers during reporting assignments. This symbiotic relationship between the Irish media and missionaries – who were later to be complemented by NGOs – developed over several decades. For much of that time, there was little thought given as to whether the independence of the media was being compromised, and that lack of scrutiny was an inevitable consequence of the strength of the Church in Ireland. Up until the 1980s, and perhaps beyond, the vast majority of Irish journalists were Catholics. Some had brothers, sisters, aunts or uncles in the Church. In his memoirs, Dunne confessed to having had a number of prejudices that informed his reporting but there were plenty of lay journalists of his generation who would have been happy to sign a declaration of faith along similar lines as his. 'I am against the use of atomic energy in any form,' the priest wrote. 'I am for capitalism, I think, because my father was a shopkeeper and I haven't yet seen socialism work very well in the long term… I am anti-English and anti-Spanish because of what they did in their colonies. I generally support one political party, which I am too cute to tell you about. And I am for Jesus Christ.'[24]

Reflecting years later on the relationship between missionaries and the media, former RTÉ broadcaster Rodney Rice, who joined the station in 1968 and spent twenty-five years making radio programmes on Third World issues, said Irish journalists were typically 'a bit unquestioning of the Irish angle' in developing countries. Coming from a secular perspective, Rice was sceptical about the impact of the work of the Church and questioned why it focused on the symptoms rather than the causes of poverty. 'Gus Finucane said to one of his workers to be careful of me because I was a "Trócaire person",' he recalled. Rice said he didn't know of any stories relating to missionaries that were suppressed or censored in RTÉ, but a 'sympathetic approach' existed from the early days of Biafra. 'The Irish media totally bought the Holy Ghost view of Biafra, and in general the approach of RTÉ and the newspapers was to go along with what the missionaries or NGOs were saying. Journalists would go out [to cover a story overseas] with them and would tend to be uncritical of whatever they were doing.'

Within the missionary movement itself, reverberations and

ripples from the Biafran conflict were felt for years. Because of their wide distribution geographically, and the fact that they were living close to ordinary people, missionaries established what was effectively an early warning system for conflict across the globe. They also developed a reputation for staying in war zones long after aid agencies had left. Demonstrably in for the long haul, they provided a different dimension to emerging professional development workers. While primary health and education remained the mainstay of their work, some Irish missionaries took on highly specialised roles in areas ranging from animal husbandry to microfinance. They also became more active in campaigning on development and social justice issues. Not satisfied by their role as aid givers, they increasingly sought to tackle underlying causes of poverty and underdevelopment. One Irish priest in particular came to define this new type of politicised missionary. His name was Niall O'Brien.

CHAPTER 5: REBELS AND REVOLUTIONARIES

'Preach the message, insist upon proclaiming it, whether the time is right or not.' (2 Timothy 4:2)

The son of a high-ranking civil servant, Niall O'Brien had a comfortable upbringing in Dublin, going to private schools – Willow Park and Blackrock College – before joining the priesthood. He opted for the Columbans over his educators, the Holy Ghost Fathers, and on completing his formation was immediately assigned to the Philippines. It was 1964 and a time of great upheaval and uncertainty across the globe. The Beatles were touring America; the Vietnam War had still to reach its nadir; the civil rights movement in the US was gathering pace. In that same year, 1964, Nelson Mandela went on trial in apartheid South Africa, signalling the start of his twenty-seven-year incarceration. Neighbouring Northern Rhodesia, now renamed Zambia, gained independence from Britain. The Second Vatican Council was also in full swing, and this more than anything else made it a time of 'great excitement and optimism' in the eyes of the then 25-year-old Niall O'Brien.

Vatican II promised to change the face of the Church. Mass would no longer be said in Latin, but in the vernacular of the local community. Altars were to be turned around towards the people so that priest and parishioner prayed face to face. The Church itself was to be reinvented as a more compassionate and less sectarian entity. Social justice was proclaimed as a key priority. Already simmering with idealism, O'Brien was enthused and energised by Vatican II and the liberation theology that came in its wake. But, as time passed in his new parish in the Philippines, he began to realise reform wouldn't be easy. The prevailing attitude in the missions, he wrote, was 'why change the rules of the game when you are winning?' The Church was doing well, baptisms were on the up, churches were being built, so where was the need for reform?

Such conservative thinking made O'Brien's initial stint in Negros, a boot-shaped island of about two million people, frustrating and somewhat disappointing. Surrounded by dehumanising poverty and few political freedoms, O'Brien tried to empower Catholics by getting them to organise religious services without a priest. He gave the laity more involvement in decision-making and set up community cooperatives – based on the Israeli *kibbutz* – with a view to meeting people's basic needs. Along with other Columban missionaries, he also challenged the rules of the order which decreed that priests should move locations every couple of years. Astonished that one of his colleagues had been forced to move nine times in fifteen years, O'Brien argued that the credibility of missionaries would be strengthened if they put down deeper roots. He wanted to be seen as a traveller with the poor, rather than a do-gooder parachuted in for short tours of duty.

As the years passed, O'Brien made some progress with his superiors but still, he wrote, 'I was floundering. I was more and more convinced that the whole system was rotten. I could see that our religious response was inadequate and at times added to the problem.' He cited his local Catholic school by way of example. While it served the poorer people, and made no profit, 'it was being twisted from its original purpose'. All the textbooks had been rewritten to incorporate the 'new society' ideology of the ruling

Marcos regime. 'Our school had become part of the martial-law apparatus.' Moreover, he believed the school lacked a community ethos. Students were encouraged to see education as a means of 'escape' or self-promotion. They saw farming as 'second-class labour', and this deeply depressed O'Brien. The brightest students would seek their fortune elsewhere. This, in turn, undermined efforts to develop the community and to challenge the social order.

'It was the custom of the Columbans,' O'Brien wrote, 'to keep resolutely out of party politics and not to let the Church be used.' But there came a time when he felt he had to take a stand. He started to preach against political violence. He began to educate his parishioners about human rights, and he helped to organise demonstrations against the government, the military and the American-backed plantation owners who had committed people to a life of penury. O'Brien immersed himself in what he called the 'science' of non-violence. He was inspired by figures like Gandhi, Martin Luther King and Daniel Berrigan, the Irish-American anti-war priest who was once on the FBI's 'ten most wanted' list for vandalising military installations in the US. Another influence was Gene Sharp, whose *The Politics of Nonviolent Action* had become something of a bible for civil rights campaigners in the US. O'Brien said the book – published in 1973 – confirmed to him something which he had known instinctively for a long time: power comes from below not above. 'If the people withdraw their consent, the ruler can no longer rule,' O'Brien reasoned.

Buoyed by this outlook, Niall O'Brien became more adventurous in his pastoral role. He replaced the traditional Catholic renunciations in church services with more contemporary, politicised ones. Instead of asking his parishioners 'Do you renounce Satan? And all his works? And all his pomp?' O'Brien posed the questions: 'Do you renounce land-grabbing? Do you renounce militarisation? Do you renounce the use of torture?' As time passed, this 'Christian community experiment', as he called it, attracted the attention of the military. A government intelligence officer described it as 'the most dangerous form of threat from the religious radicals'. O'Brien and his fellow priests were harassed and threatened. They also came under pressure in their own community to support a fledgling armed rebellion against the authorities. O'Brien tried hard to stay above party politics, and he remained firm to his non-violent principles, despite a rising number of state-sponsored murders. It was a hard path to travel. Government soldiers wanted him to inform on the guerrillas, while the rebels looked to him for shelter and moral support. In response to increasing tension and intimidation from both sides, he organised mobile church services; people would walk together from village to village as a show of both strength and solidarity. He developed 'a sort of theology of walking' on the back of it. 'Many people were reborn to a sense of their own dignity on those long walks,' he wrote. 'And for myself, I was beginning to realise that the journey was as important as the destination.'

O'Brien's work broke new ground not only for the Church locally but for the Columbans, and by extension the Irish missionary enterprise. He tried to create a new relationship between the visiting priest and the people and believed both needed to work together to recapture the real meaning of Christianity. In their struggle against oppression, the poor were equated with Jesus's first followers – those early Christians who had to hide in caves to avoid persecution. He wrote, 'The poor people in the Christian communities, by confronting the authorities, had gone back not in symbol but in reality to the early Church. They were beginning to live again the days of the catacombs and the life of Jesus himself. Their penance and sacrifice were written in their lives. They had integrated their spirituality – precisely what we had been trying to do. We had thought to catechise them, and now they were evangelising us.'

Such thinking turned the missionary enterprise on its head. O'Brien decreed it was the missionary and not the people who benefited most from their interaction. He also set new and very exacting standards for missionary work, and any personal failing of his own was felt sharply. On one occasion, the Columban priest admonished himself for simply failing to say goodbye to a young man in his parish. The man, an orphan who regarded O'Brien as a surrogate father, was leaving his village to live elsewhere and had hoped to see the Irishman before he left. But O'Brien was unable to make an appointment. When the youth was found dead some time later, O'Brien complained, 'I was struggling so hard to help the people that I could no longer see the person. I was so intent on being a Christian that I had failed to be even human. I looked back over the years and all I could see was the same pattern. And I was filled with fear that somehow I was only a shell.'

At times, it seemed O'Brien demanded he himself be superhuman, or literally a saint. His predecessors, people like Galvin and Blowick, placed huge physical burdens on themselves, but O'Brien's burden was more mental. He was constantly troubled by a fear of failure and a fear that when put to the test he would ultimately place his own personal welfare ahead of that of his people. 'I would say to myself: "But what if at the last moment I were to panic? What if when the sentence had been proclaimed I lost my nerve? What if when I was on the brink of darkness I was to step back? How would I endure the shame?"... Then I remembered the words of Jesus in Saint Matthew: "When they deliver you up, do not be anxious how you are to speak or what you are to say; for what you are to say will be given to you in that hour."'

O'Brien's journey to a new sort of priesthood was at once both personal and universal. Vatican II unleashed new ideological struggles in the Catholic Church and destroyed old doctrinal certainties. Some missionaries responded by holding firmer to the papal line. Others drifted from the centre – some to the point of no return. For James Kennedy, a Columban contemporary of Niall O'Brien, 'everything started falling apart' after Vatican II. A farmer's son from Pallasgrean, County Limerick, Kennedy joined the Columbans at the age of 18 and, after several years working on the society's newsletter *The Far East*, he was posted to the Philippines in 1970. 'I thought I might change the world and go into the social justice side, but I never got the chance,' Kennedy recalled forty years later. At his parish in Zambales, he was 'so busy doing baptisms and funerals and all the magic I never got to grips with any real social issue'.

Vatican II, or more precisely how Rome responded to it, influenced Kennedy greatly. Like many of his peers, he saw the 1968 encyclical *Humanae Vitae* – on the ethics of birth control – as representative of a retreat into heightened clerical judgmentalism. Another retrograde step, he believed, was the silencing of dissenters in the Church. 'I remember my bishop coming back from Rome with a smirk on his face that he had put radicals like [Hans] Küng in their place. I realised then there was no place for me in this Church.'

Thousands of men and women joined Kennedy in leaving religious life in the period 1968–1978. The impact of this exodus was severe and far reaching. The Columbans alone lost 197 members, 'most… in a relatively short space of time immediately following the Second Vatican Council', according to a survey of former Columbans in March 2008. Confidential records show that celibacy was a key issue for the men who departed. Abuse of authority was another commonly cited complaint. 'There was a ruthlessness in some of the institutional bosses,' said Kennedy. 'Some of them were good but the majority of them were tough buggers. Once they considered you a traitor that was it.'

For Kennedy, the Church's attitude to sexual morality and its hierarchical structure were part of one and the same flaw. 'All the bishops went to Rome and voted in favour of celibacy and then came back and turned a blind eye to it. A survey in one parish in the Philippines showed 90 per cent of Filipino priests were living either openly or secretly with partners.' Leaving the priesthood to find a life companion had crossed Kennedy's mind on occasion, but he believed he could have stayed within the rules of the Church had he been able to keep faith with his superiors. 'The problem was leadership. That's what I wanted.'

Kennedy's denouement with the society arrived in 1977 when he discovered he was going to become a father. The previous year he met a Filipino nun, Vicenta 'Vising' Benavidez, with whom he worked on a community project in Candelaria. The couple fell in love and when Vising became pregnant they realised they had no option but to leave their respective religious orders and the Philippines. Before departing, they arranged to get married in Manila. Kennedy asked a few different priests to officiate but none agreed to do so, and 'two people were picked out of an office' as witnesses to the ceremony. The couple's first child, Patrick, was born in Dublin in 1978 and a year later they had a daughter, Noriana. Reflecting on the experience decades later at his family home in Lucan, Kennedy said he felt a mixture of pity and disappointment at his Columban peers. 'Religious never spoke about two things to one another. They never spoke about their interior spiritual life – they never shared on that – and they never shared on sex. They were the two big secrets that everyone carried around.' Asked why he had entered the priesthood in the first place, he replied: 'In 1952, when I signed up, joining the Church was the most respectable form of emigration. In hindsight, I should have gone to London and trained as a JCB driver because in the end one of the things that really bothered me was the way your whole sexuality was distorted, inhibited... I was nearly too old to have sex by the time I got over the hang ups there.'

When Kennedy returned to Ireland he had to start a new career from scratch. 'It was a big shock to me to wake up one day and find myself adrift. I had no more health care, no more pocket money.' He reckoned the only saleable skills at his disposal were from producing *The Far East*, so he joined a publishing company. His first was job was editing a glossy women's magazine. A friend of his who left the Columbans around the same time joined Concern and became one of the charity's field directors. Another contemporary went to work on peace and reconciliation in Northern Ireland. 'Most of those who left went into the caring professions, working in rehab, or with poor groups,' said Kennedy. Most also got married or started families. Of 123 ex-Columbans whose marital status could be obtained in 2008, 110 were married, six divorced or separated, five in gay relationships and two never married.

Celibacy had always been a double-edged sword for the Catholic Church. While it made unnatural and perhaps unreasonable demands of clergy, it also freed them of the responsibility that a spouse or indeed children would have brought. This freedom allowed missionaries to commit themselves to their work in the whole-hearted fashion of a Niall O'Brien. Kennedy said, 'Niall was a very good friend of mine. I made sure we crossed paths when he came home from his holidays, or in Manila. He was a courageous man.' But, Kennedy added, 'Niall was able to hack the celibacy thing. In many ways he was a loner. I was not a loner.'

For Niall O'Brien, and many of the other Columbans whom Kennedy left behind, personal commitment to social justice became stronger with each passing year. By the early 1980s, the political tension in the Philippines was at boiling point and Negros – labelled 'Island of Fear' in a *Newsweek* article – was an epicentre of protest. As anti-Marcos sentiment continued to spread, the Filipino government moved against O'Brien, charging him, along with two other priests – an Australian and a Filipino – and six lay workers, with the murder of the mayor of Kabankalan, Pablo Sola. The 'Negros Nine' gained international attention, and their seventeen-month trial led to widespread condemnation of the Marcos regime and its main backer, the United States.

Three days after their arrest, O'Brien and his fellow priests were moved to house arrest while the lay workers were left in Bacold City's foetid jail. The Columban took exception at this, and he arranged for the priests to 'break back into prison' – by first visiting their colleagues in jail and then refusing to leave. As their detention became more embarrassing for the government, Marcos offered the group a pardon but they turned it down as it implied guilt. Irish politicians and Church leaders, led by the Bishop of Galway Eamonn Casey, supported O'Brien's case. On his first foreign assignment for RTÉ, Charlie Bird interviewed O'Brien in his prison cell. Pressure mounted on the US during Ronald Reagan's visit to Ireland in June 1984. The following month, charges against the 'Negros Nine' were dropped on condition that the two foreign priests were deported. O'Brien returned to Ireland to a hero's welcome. Cardinal Tomás Ó Fiaich, Dr Casey and a smattering of government ministers were among those to greet him at Dublin Airport.

Niall O'Brien died in Pisa, Italy on 27 April 2003 while receiving treatment for a rare bone-marrow disease. He has lived on, however, in folk memory. For a time, he was one of the most famous Irishmen abroad, and still today he shapes many people's notion of what it means to be a missionary. The label 'turbulent priest' – which he carried through his life – was perhaps fitting as it captured something of his fighting spirit. O'Brien wrestled with himself and he wrestled with his Church. By tackling injustice wherever he saw it, he set the tone for a 1960s generation of missionary priests and nuns, and something of his spirit can be found dotted around the continents today. That said, O'Brien was more the exception than the rule. He shocked many of his peers by rebelling against the Church authorities. Politically, he was left of centre and highly critical of US policy in Asia. He was also an internationalist – in a contemporary sense. He saw the world as interconnected, believing what people did in rich countries affected those in poor. An obituary on his death said Niall O'Brien 'can be seen as a founding exemplar of the anti-globalisation movement'. But, looking at the great sweep of missionary history, just how representative was he? Despite his example, many priests and nuns chose to play it safe, and continue to do so today.

Missionaries themselves talk about a split along geographical lines: in Asia and South America, missionaries could push out the boundaries; the bishops there were more progressive and sympathetic to liberation theology. In Africa, it was a different story – that was reflected in the continent's very different history. In the 1960s, Africa was gripped not by Cold War politics but by the process of decolonisation and independence. After centuries of European domination, African countries were suddenly set free. Starting with Ghana in 1957, one state after another threw off the yoke of colonial rule. Apartheid South Africa held out longest, surrendering eventually in 1994.

In this African setting, Irish priests and nuns were engaged primarily with questions of political rather than economic justice. Instead of grappling with the relative merits of communism and capitalism, they saw themselves first and foremost as nation-builders. What's more, they believed themselves to be uniquely equipped for the task as they came from a country with its own history of colonisation. The prevailing culture of Irish Catholicism – patriotic and anti-Protestant – meant missionaries were particularly predisposed to Brit-bashing, and in several colonies they played a rather subversive role in educating indigenous political leaders. Irish Jesuits, for example, taught Robert Mugabe in Zimbabwe and Kenneth Kaunda in Zambia, both of whom went on to become presidents of their respective countries. The Jesuit Fr Michael

Kelly recalled that Kaunda had a particularly strong bond with his late colleague Fr Paddy Walsh, who helped to set up a multi-racial club in Lusaka. When Kaunda had been in prison, before becoming the country's first president, Walsh looked after his wife and helped put their children through school. 'I was at Kaunda's eighty-fourth birthday party and he said he could never forget what Paddy Walsh did for him,' said Fr Kelly. 'The respect was such that when Paddy got a heart attack and had to be evacuated it was the president and his cabinet who carried the stretcher to the plane. That was an extraordinary mark of respect.'

The close relationship between missionaries and certain politicians in Africa was not always a healthy one, however. When governments turned bad, friendships like that between the Jesuits and Mugabe suddenly became an embarrassment. Asked on a visit to Dublin in 1997 to explain his description of homosexuals as 'worse than dogs and pigs', the Zimbabwean dictator said he had the good fortune to go to school under Irish missionaries 'who taught me the Bible'. In fairness to the Jesuits, they were on the same learning curve as other 'well-intentioned' whites in Africa in the post-colonial era. Over time, they discovered independence was not the panacea for the continent's woes. They also found aligning themselves to a particular political regime carried physical, as well as moral, dangers. Governments toppled regularly in Africa, and missionaries didn't want to be on the wrong side of a purge – as they had been in Biafra.

South Africa was one of those countries which saw both the best and the worst of the Catholic Church and its missions. For decades, the hierarchy collaborated with apartheid. It kept silent on abuses and refused to call for the overthrow of a racist regime. But individual members of the Church, missionaries included, did resist. They fought their own bishops and cardinals and they helped – sometimes in significant ways – to bring about change.

Probably the most radical, and most influential, of these dissenters was Bishop Denis Hurley. He wasn't a missionary *per se* but he was someone with a toe in its tradition. His parents were from Skibbereen, west Cork, and they gave him what he called 'a strong Irish-Catholic faith'. In 1913, the newly married couple emigrated together to South Africa where Denis Hurley's father had already found work as a lighthouse keeper on Robben Island. The future priest was born in Cape Town and educated for a time in Ireland. When he returned to South Africa in 1940, he worked under a Catholic Church that submitted to the country's racial divisions. As time passed, however, the young priest began to question the Church's policy of appeasement, and with rare honesty also admitted to latent prejudices in himself. Step by step, he began to challenge the status quo. He took part in demonstrations and supported the Black Sash women's movement. Dubbed a rabble-rousing communist, his house was petrol bombed in 1976 and he was charged with subversive activities but later acquitted.

'He was ahead of his time; he was a prophet in the Church and in the country,' said Bishop Kevin Dowling of Rustenburg, who worked as a priest under Hurley and who has since become the liberal standard-bearer for the Catholic Church in South Africa. 'The vast majority of the bishops [during the apartheid era] were expatriates, and they were very concerned about the continued presence of the missionaries: would they be kicked out? Schools, hospitals, all of that, would be under threat if they took too strong a stance against apartheid. So they were slow in catching up to where he was. He had the intellectual and experiential discernment to see that this [apartheid] was not on.'

Denis Hurley was made Vicar Apostolic of Natal in 1947, the youngest bishop in the world at the age of 31. He was never made a cardinal, despite – or most likely because of – his high profile. He was, however, a representative for the African bishops at Vatican II, where he championed a more radical agenda than was agreed by the papal council. One of his foot soldiers on anti-apartheid campaigns was Margaret Kelly, a petite Dominican nun from Dun Laoghaire, County Dublin who went to South Africa in 1963 at the age of 20. Nearly a half-century later, now grey-haired but still youthful-looking, Kelly remembered her experiences in South Africa with enthusiasm and affection, charmingly slipping the occasional word of Afrikaans into conversation. A powerful persuader, whose political conscience was first pricked by her father – a Labour Party supporter – Kelly learnt the art of diplomacy during years of tricky campaigning. She recalled being sent by Hurley to the US to persuade the bishops there not to call for a lifting of sanctions against South Africa after negotiations had begun between the apartheid government and the ANC. 'It's very useful to have a sweet little nun, who has no real authority, and no one's ego is hurt,' Kelly said with a smile. But being a messenger girl for Hurley was just one of her responsibilities – and a minor one at that – during her thirty years in South Africa.

Kelly started out as a teacher in Port Elizabeth just as the black consciousness movement was taking off. The city was a hub of ANC activities and a base for Steve Biko's student movement. The Irish nun helped to start a Catholic peace and justice group in the city, of which she became chair. The schools in South Africa were an ideological battleground, and many missionaries were uneasy about their relationship with the state. The Bantu Education Act stipulated that churches had to either hand over the schools to the state or else implement Bantu education – a basic curriculum designed to train blacks as gardeners and housekeepers. The bishops felt handing over schools would have been suicidal to their mission and agreed to the curriculum – but as time passed they tried to bend the rules as much as possible. This softly-softly approach didn't appeal to everyone. A Church survey in 1975 found that religious sisters and brothers were heavily concentrated on teaching whites, with 70 per cent of the Church's education resources devoted to just 30 per cent of the school population. Seizing on this publication, Sr Kelly's order, the Cabra Dominicans, decided to act. The bishops had been considering issuing an instruction for white-only schools to start admitting blacks but the nuns believed enough talking had been done and they chose in January 1976 to admit eight coloured girls to Springfield Convent in suburban Cape Town. The move gained international attention and saw the weight of the apartheid regime mobilised against the renegade nuns. Even Hurley was unhappy with their defiance as he wanted the bishops to be on board prior to any opening up of schools. Now, 'both the government and the bishops had to respond to a situation that was no longer hypothetical,' as Hurley's biographer Paddy Kearney put it. 'Children of other races had been admitted to several Catholic schools registered as exclusively white. The law had definitely been flouted, but there was not much the government could do about it.'

Emboldened by the protest, the Holy Rosary Convent and St Dominic's Priory in Port Elizabeth enrolled thirty-three African pupils in January 1977. This 'open schools' movement gave the Church increased credibility among blacks. It also helped to further radicalise the local Church. 'In a way, it broke what might be called a "civil disobedience barrier",' wrote Kearney. 'Previously, the Church had been reluctant to break the law, but now it began to see such action as an important way of bringing about change in the face of government intransigence.'

Sr Kelly remembered it as a time of great uncertainty. The government tried to bully the nuns into reversing their decision. State subsidies were withdrawn. Forced closures were threatened. But the Dominicans ploughed ahead. They introduced 'African studies' on the curriculum. Latin was thrown off the course in favour of Xhosa. 'We didn't think of it as political, or in terms of protest,' she remarked. 'We said, "It is an open school; that's all we are declaring. And we feel pulled by the gospel to have the school open to everyone."' Politics was second to the needs of the pupils, and things had to be judged on a case-by-case basis. Insisting that a black child would turn out for the school sports team, for example, would usually mean the team forfeiting the game, and that might lead to the child feeling guilty or ostracised. The nuns' policy, then, was to move forward only with their pupils' consent. 'You were trying to progress things in a way that was fair to everyone and not using children as a political statement.'

Her school was subjected to harassment and she sometimes picked up the phone to hear heavy breathing. Once, a perimeter wall was daubed with the slogan: 'This school is run by a communist'. Sr Kelly said: 'I went into assembly next morning, and the kids looked at me, and I felt so sorry for them. I said "Good morning comrades," and then they collapsed laughing, and relaxed again.'

The dangers associated with the nuns' work were clear, however. In August 1977, the youth leader Steve Biko was arrested and beaten into a coma by police. The following month, he was thrown naked into a prison van and driven 1,200 kilometres to Pretoria where he died. It was just one of a growing catalogue of atrocities, and 'you had to be very careful' not to expose other people to danger, Sr Kelly recalled. Being 'white and foreign' offered the missionaries some personal protection, but the same didn't go for the African activists who worked alongside them. 'I remember one young man in our group who was detained, and when he came back to me he said, "Don't tell me anything you don't want the security police to know because they will torture me and I will tell them." He had been really badly tortured. So you could be very grandiose if you wanted to and think you were a big fellow but you weren't going to take the brunt of it.'

Between 1981 and 1985, Sr Kelly worked on the bishops' council in Cape Town, promoting the open schools concept. She travelled to rural areas with an outspoken local nun, Sr Bernard Ncube, to 'conscientise' sisters elsewhere. They taught fellow religious, who were cut off from politics due to state censorship, about the ANC and about the scriptural basis for opposing apartheid. 'I think when Bernie switched into Zulu she was a bit more radical than she was in English but I didn't enquire into that,' Sr Kelly laughed.

As time passed, the Church shifted more behind the liberation struggle. Some priests and nuns operated an informal network of 'safe houses' for activists and it was no surprise that Donald Woods, the 'banned' editor of the East London *Daily Dispatch* who exposed the circumstances of Biko's murder, was smuggled out of the country on a priest's passport. Bishop Hurley gave his blessing to this sort of radicalism, and he led various campaigns of civil disobedience. Gradually, he enjoyed increased support from his hierarchical peers. Sr Kelly recalled the bishop of Port Elizabeth, JP Murphy, a Mayo man, to be one of a number of helpful clergy. 'He pretended to have nothing to do with these radicals – and then would issue a statement when you needed it.'

The repercussions weren't slow in coming. In September 1988, South African special forces fire-bombed Khanya House in Pretoria, a religious residence and the headquarters of the South African Catholic Bishops' Conference, which was overseen by Hurley. The building went up in flames as people inside slept in their beds. 'Again, you would feel guilty,' Sr Kelly said, thinking of the victims of the attack. It was around the time of an election – a white-only poll against which the bishops were campaigning, 'and you wondered, "Did you bring it upon others?"' By then Sr Kelly was secretary general of the South African Peace and Justice Commission, a post she held until the first multi-racial elections in 1994. Throughout her time campaigning, she avoided imprisonment, something she put down to being 'very lucky, or very cowardly'.

The first group of Columbans to go to Hanyang, China in 1920.
Front: M. McHugh, E.J. (Ned) Galvin, J. Blowick, J. Dawson.
Second row: T. Quinlan, O. MacPoilin, R. Ranaghan, E.J. O'Doherty, J.P. O'Brien, C. Tierney, T. Leonard, M. Dolan.
Rear: J. Crossan, A. Ferguson, A. McGuinness, W. O'Flynn, M. Mee.
(Photo: Columban Archives)

The first Missionary Sisters of St Columban to go to China in 1926. Mother Patrick Moloney is seated furthest right. Columban joint-founder John Blowick is standing second from the left.
(Photo: Columban Archives)

Vol. III., No. 11. NOVEMBER, 1920. Price Twopence

The Far East.

St. Columbanus
St. Gall
St. Kilian
St. Fergilius

"The harvest indeed is great but the labourers are few"

Peregrinari pro Christo

Cum glóire Dé agus onóra na h-Éireann.

Jos Tierney, Dublin

Nihil Obstat:
Censor Theol. Deputatus
Patritius Cleary, D.D

Imprimatur: ✠ Thomas
Episcopus Galviensis

The Far East: Appealed for recruits and donations for the Columbans with 'a stirring mixture of Irish nationalism and Catholic crusade'.

(Photo: Columban Archives)

Bishop Joseph Shanahan, the burly Holy Ghost priest who saw education as a means of spreading the church in Nigeria. 'No one is opposed to a school,' he said.

(Photo: Provincial Archives, Holy Ghost Fathers Ireland)

Marie Martin, known as Mother Mary by her followers, overcame chauvinism in the church to found the Medical Missionaries of Mary.
(Photo: MMM Image Library)

Trail-blazing volunteer Dr Joe Barnes with a Holy Rosary Sister in Nigeria, circa 1940.

Sr Cyril Mooney, who decided to become a missionary nun after a religious experience on a school retreat.

A collection box modelled on an African child, dating from the 1950s/1960s, that was used for raising money for the Irish missions. Some of the boxes were spring-loaded so the child's head would nod when a coin dropped inside.

Fr Jim Crowe, who has worked for 23 years in the Brazilian favela of Jardim Ângela which was once declared by the United Nations as the most dangerous place in the world. (Photo: Noel Gavin/Allpix for Misean Cara)

Fr Kieran Creagh returns to Leratong, South Africa, in November 2007, just seven months after he was shot and left for dead during a burglary at the hospice.

Kenyan environmentalist Wangari Maathai, the first African woman to win the Nobel Peace Prize, with her former Loreto teacher Sr Columbière Kelly in Nairobi, March 2008. 'After my education by the nuns,' said Maathai, 'I emerged as a person who believed that society is inherently good and that people generally act for the best.'

Uganda-based nun Helen Ahern on a trip home to the MMM 'mother-house' in Drogheda, Co Louth. The congregation's founder Mother Mary Martin is depicted in a painting in the canteen: she is shown sitting at the end of the table, being introduced by the Virgin Mary to Jesus Christ.

Fr Shay Cullen, campaigner against child trafficking in the Philippines: 'My faith is in Jesus of Nazareth. I don't have faith in an institution.' (Photo: David McNeill)

Sr Orla Treacy with her schoolgirls in Rumbek, South Sudan. When a missionary nun visited her Loreto school in Bray, Co Wicklow, she said, 'I began to realise that you could in fact be young, youthful, vibrant, maybe a bit half-crazy as well, and be a Sister.' (Photo: Sarah MacDonald)

Fr Tony Byrne, 'The Green Pimpernel', who ran a daring airlift operation into Biafra. He was expelled from Nigeria with other Holy Ghost priests when the Biafran war ended.

(Photo: Provincial Archives, Holy Ghost Fathers Ireland)

James Kennedy, a former missionary in the Philippines, with his wife Vising at their home in Lucan, Co Dublin. Kennedy was one of 197 Columbans who left the priesthood in the aftermath of Vatican II.

She recalled being asked to go on a banned march in Cape Town but said she 'couldn't do it' because she had booked a flight back to Ireland to see her mother for the first time in years. 'So I got out of the country and a few months later the state of emergency was declared. The first thing I did when I got back to South Africa was to try to get people out of jail.'

Sr Kelly got to know many figures in the ANC leadership, including Thabo Mbeki, a future president of South Africa who was one of the chief negotiators in the transition period. When the ANC asked for a meeting with representatives of all the churches in South Africa, Kelly was selected to attend for the Catholics. (Ironically, 'the other group to send a woman was the Anglicans, the two groups who don't go in for women at all,' she laughed.) Describing it as one of her 'really privileged moments' as a missionary, she recalled ANC leader Nelson Mandela telling them, 'You must only do one thing: you are the Church; you take the mandate from the gospel. You tell the truth; no politician wants to be told the truth so you keep telling it.'

On the same occasion Mandela paid tribute to one of Sr Kelly's compatriots: Fr Brendan Long, a native of Scariff, County Clare who spent twenty-five years as a chaplain in Robben Island. Mandela claimed Fr Long put snippets of news from the outside world in the prayers that were said in prison services but, speaking from his home in County Tipperary, where he was living in retirement, Long suggested the ANC leader had a false memory in this regard. 'Ah, no, you couldn't have brought news in,' the priest said. 'It was all prohibited.' Long did recall, however, that Mandela was an enthusiastic participant in his services. 'He was not a Catholic but he was a very religious man. He would read the Bible for me. Nelson loved to read from the Bible.' Whatever the reason for it, Mandela did become more religious over the course of his incarceration. On leaving prison, the ANC leader preached reconciliation and forgiveness, and moved away from political extremes or ideologies – something that wasn't universally welcomed. Criticising Mandela and his colleagues for adopting economically conservative policies once they were in power, the left-wing commentator John Pilger wrote, 'Although there were those who had flirted with radical change, it was mission Christianity, not Marxism, that left the most indelible mark on the ANC elite in exile and prison.'[25]

South Africa was a political issue like no other in the 1980s. But, from a Catholic missionary perspective, there were shared features between it and other struggles. One pattern was that the best of priests and nuns from Nairobi to Natal worked against the mainstream Church, rather than with it. This said much about the conservatism of the Catholic hierarchy in Africa at the time and the success that the Vatican had in stopping the spread of liberation theology in the developing world. The Vatican's *modus operandi* was not to rock the boat, which usually meant cosying up to the state, whether in Ireland for much of the twentieth century or in Africa for the latter part of it.

Fr Padraig Ó Máille, a Kiltegan priest from Louisburgh, County Mayo, saw this during his years as a teacher and university lecturer in Malawi. When the country gained its independence in 1964, the Catholic Church seamlessly – and somewhat cynically – switched loyalties from the British, colonial administration to the new, indigenous government headed by Hastings Banda. The man who declared himself 'President for Life' started out as a relatively benign, if incompetent, ruler but over time persecution of political dissidents increased. Horrified by the detention of some of his academic colleagues in 1976, Ó Máille became involved in the pro-democracy movement. He collaborated with Amnesty International and fed news of human rights abuses to the international media, often communicating sensitive information in the Irish language to avoid government censors. As the clamour for elections grew, Ó Máille persuaded the country's bishops to issue a pastoral letter calling for freedom of speech, opinion and association. He also helped to print the letter and distribute it through a network of parish activists, without the knowledge of police informers. 'Over the years people had accepted that the churches were no different from any other group or individual,' Ó Máille recalled. 'Ordinary Christians had long since ceased to expect radical leadership from them on social issues.'[26] Thus, when the Lenten Pastoral *Living Our Faith* was released on 8 March 1992 people stood up and took notice. The statement was highly critical of the government and condemned police brutality. Within a few days of it being read out on altars across the country, students were in open revolt, and mass street demonstrations were mounted. Ó Máille was deported with other missionary 'agitators' on 18 April 1992, and they were exiled for the toppling of Banda's regime the following year.

Another missionary dissident who made his mark on Sub-Saharan Africa was Bishop Donal Lamont (1911–2003). The former superior of the Carmelite mission in Rhodesia, he was once nominated for the Nobel Peace Prize and had a commemorative stamp issued by the Kenyan government in recognition of his solidarity with Africa. From Ballycastle, County Antrim, Lamont was appalled by the level of brutality Rhodesia's white-only government was willing to use to stay in power. After the execution of guerrilla fighters in 1972, in an episode with resonances of the Irish freedom struggle, he wrote to Ian Smith's government: 'Conscience compels me to state that your administration, by its clearly racial and oppressive policies and by its stubborn refusal to change, is largely responsible for the injustices which have provoked the present disorder and it must in that measure be considered guilty of whatever misery and bloodshed may follow.' This and other acts of defiance saw Lamont being charged with helping terrorists who had sought food and medical attention from his priests and nuns. At his trial, he pleaded guilty to prevent other people from incriminating themselves by testifying on his behalf. He was sentenced to ten years in prison, but after a period of house arrest was stripped of his Rhodesian citizenship and deported.

Lamont's expulsion from Rhodesia had a bitter footnote in 2008 when Fr Michael Bennett, a Kiltegan priest from Ardee, County Louth, was refused permission to stay in Zimbabwe. Irish missionaries thus found themselves in conflict with both pre- and post-independence regimes. Between 2004 and 2008, the number of Irish missionaries in Zimbabwe dropped from ninety-six to fifty-five amid tightened residency rules. Those who remained – mainly Carmelites, Presentation Sisters and members of the Little Company of Mary and Franciscan Missionaries of Divine Motherhood – continued to act as a bush telegraph for human rights abuses under Mugabe.

A common trait among these gentle revolutionaries has been a willingness to put their personal welfare on the line. Some have made the ultimate sacrifice. Joan Sawyer, a Columban sister from County Antrim who was active in liberation theology in Peru, was killed on a prison visit in Lurigancho in 1983. Felim McAllister, a Holy Ghost Father from Donabate, County Dublin was murdered by armed rebels in Sierra Leone in 1994 while trying to protect villagers and aid workers from attack. Fr Rufus Halley, a pioneer in inter-faith dialogue between Muslims and Christians in the Philippines, was shot dead during a failed kidnap in 2001. Bishop Michael Courtney, a tenacious peace-broker in Africa's Great Lakes region, was murdered in Burundi in 2003.

Other missionaries can count themselves lucky they avoided the same fate. In August 2000, Fr Brendan Forde, a Franciscan priest and outspoken critic of US security policy in Colombia, was ordered out of his parish of La Union by right-wing paramilitaries.

Six men in the village had been murdered and he was told he'd be the next to die if he didn't leave immediately. But Forde stood his ground and redoubled his efforts at drawing attention to the pitfalls of the 'war against drugs' in Colombia. As *Irish Times* columnist Breda O'Brien wrote at the time, it was 'not a very Celtic Tiger thing to do'.[27]

Another priest cut from the same cloth is Nicky Hennity, a resilient, no-nonsense County Down man who has tried to navigate the fraught ethnic minefield that is Rwanda. Hennity arrived in the country in December 1994, just months after the genocide that left an estimated 800,000 dead. His predecessor, a Tutsi priest, had been hacked to death in front of his hilltop chapel at Cyanika, near Gikongoro. Since then, Hennity has helped to rebuild a sense of trust in the community, as well as rehabilitate a Church whose reputation has been badly damaged by the slaughter. In 2001, a Belgian court convicted two Rwandan nuns of genocide crimes, and as many as twenty priests were charged with crimes before either the local judiciary or the International Criminal Court for Rwanda.

In nearby Kenya, Sr Mary Killeen, a Sister of Mercy from Phibsboro, Dublin, has become a fearless campaigner for the rights of children, exposing abuse within the Church locally and attacking paedophilia more widely in the city of Nairobi. In 1985 she helped to set up – along with a group of Irish Christian Brothers and Marianist priests – the Mukuru Promotion Centre, which educates thousands of slum children each year. Killeen has received death threats for seeking to have child sex offenders prosecuted but she is not easily intimidated, and her work is strongly supported by parents in her community – so much so that Killeen and her colleagues in the Sisters of Mercy are now among the first ports of call for people seeking to report child abuse in the slums. 'We have eight social workers, three men and five women, and they alert us to what is going on,' explained Sr Angela Hartigan, who runs a school at Mukuru. 'There is a chain of action that takes place. You get the child medical attention, and we have access to women's lawyers who will take the case. The police are nobody's friend.'

The Mukuru centre, which is funded by the EU and other international donors, has expanded in recent years to include adult education and vocational courses in computers, catering and hairdressing. Hartigan, who went to Kenya on a 'two-year loan' from a secondary school in Tullow, County Carlow in 1989 and has been there ever since, helped to set up a secondary school in the slum in 2008. Designed to cater for the large number of children who had nowhere to go after they completed their primary education, the school is holding its first graduation ceremony in 2011. 'The next problem is how to help a percentage of them move forward,' said Hartigan. 'Their parents in the slum say we want our own university now; that's the joke.'

Another Irish nun, similarly occupied by the needs of those on the margins of Kenyan society, is Clare Tobin. The Ursuline sister, whose thirty-year career in the region has taken her from the remote desert of Turkana to the refugee camps of Tanzania in the aftermath of the Rwandan genocide, helped to set up a school in Kitui, near Nairobi, for girls who were unable to access mainstream education. In 2007, the fiftieth anniversary of the arrival of the Ursulines in Kenya, Tobin handed over the leadership of the society to a Kenyan, Sr Pamela Kiraithe, and a Kenyan leadership team. Many activists talk about working themselves out of a job, but Tobin has done it: passing on responsibility while continuing the fight at grass roots for better education and health services. Perhaps the best compliment for Irish nuns in Kenya has been the emergence of indigenous leaders, people like Sr Ephigenia Gachiri, a Kenyan Loreto sister who is one of the country's most prominent campaigners against female genital mutilation.

Among Irish missionaries in Kenya, the most outspoken is Fr

Gabriel Dolan, a Kiltegan priest who has organised a string of demonstrations against corruption and police brutality. In August 2005, he was arrested and charged with 'incitement to violence' for leading a campaign to help squatters regain their right to public land, which had been assigned to the cronies of former Kenyan president Daniel Arap Moi. He was released following an international outcry, including a campaign by human rights group Amnesty International. 'I wish he would teach people how to fight their own battles instead of doing it for them,' his superior, the Cork-born Bishop of Kitale Maurice Crowley, once said.[28] But Dolan has refused to compromise, despite obvious risks to his safety. In 1997, Brother Larry Timmons, an Irish Franciscan, was shot dead in the Rift Valley in controversial circumstances. In 2000, Fr John Kaiser, an American priest, was assassinated in Naivasha in a killing that was linked to his work as a civil rights campaigner. Dolan has taken some security precautions and describes himself as 'no hero' but it was noticeable that in January 2008, when a wave of political violence erupted in Kenya, he was one of the first people to publicly call for a new power-sharing government – a subversive proposal at the time. One of his roles these days is regular columnist with Kenya's *Daily Nation* where he has railed against the state 'kleptocracy' and in particular 'the rich' who 'in most cases… have been made wealthy due to inheritance, theft, appalling labour laws and legal protection; rarely due to the sweat of their own brows'.[29]

While Dolan has used his high national profile in Kenya to his advantage, other missionaries regard any sort of attention as unwelcome. This is especially so in sensitive interface areas between Christians and Muslims, or in countries like Burma (Myanmar) where a handful of Columban Sisters today operate anonymously under difficult political conditions. In Pakistan, the logic of a low profile has been highlighted by periodic attacks by religious extremists on

Christian churches. In 2008, the Taliban destroyed a school belonging to Irish Presentation sisters in the Swat valley.

Columban priest Fr Liam O'Callaghan, who saw such sectarianism at first hand in the nine years he spent in Pakistan, said 'it is a case of the militant minority holding the majority – including the majority of Muslims – to ransom.' While his own church in Lahore had to be put under a 24-hour police watch during the 2006 riots over the Danish Muhammad cartoons controversy, O'Callaghan was optimistic about the future of Christian–Muslim relations in the region. The soft-spoken County Waterford man described Rufus Halley, who hailed from a village just six miles away from O'Callaghan's Butlerstown home, as 'a hero of interfaith dialogue', recalling sorrowfully too, 'I met him in the July before he was killed.' O'Callaghan said the key was getting Christians and Muslims working together on common goals, be it health, education or social justice. He described it as a 'kind of humanist, social acting for people of goodwill, or working for a common good, coming first, and the fact that we are Christian or Muslim coming second… To get locked into doctrinal stuff is going nowhere. It is like the dialogue of the deaf.'

O'Callaghan's arguing for more 'social interaction' and less 'theological debates' between different faiths might be seen as further evidence that Irish missionaries are out of step with Church norms. If Catholicism is to be judged by the rigid doctrine of the Vatican, these 'turbulent' priests and nuns appear closer to being outside the Church than in it. Just as it is hard to reconcile the grandeur of Rome with the unpretentious, frugal life of the mission field, it is hard to see how the same organisation can produce the likes of, say, Cardinal Joseph Ratzinger and Sr Majella McCarron. A stocky, pugnacious County Fermanagh woman ('everyone knows I would be a real contrary person', she beamed), McCarron was recruited into the Sisters of Our Lady of Apostles while only in her teens. With little formal education (and, she admitted, little appreciation of 'what I was getting myself in for'), she was assigned to Nigeria in 1964 where she spent thirty years, mainly teaching science in secondary schools.

'Liberation theology made no impression on Africa at all,' she said, as she tried to justify her lack of political *nous* as a young woman. 'We were very traditional missionaries. We had our schools and our parishes, and that was it, because we transferred the Irish model hook, line and sinker to Africa and our bishops came from that model too, and that was a very Rome-support type of model.'

It wasn't until 1990 that she first heard talk of a 'justice dimension' to missionary work. An instruction came down from the Vatican that different religious institutions should get involved. Before she had time to make excuses, she was named contact person for Nigeria on the Africa Faith and Justice Network (AFJN), an international umbrella group representing Catholic missionaries. 'Why was I asked after twenty-something years to go into this area I really don't know.' Her wish had been to do pastoral work, but this was refused. Somewhat bitterly, she described how she had since discovered there were 'hundreds of institutes who never bothered' branching into advocacy and campaigning. 'It passed them by, and those of us who did try had a ferocious struggle with it... If I had three years to study justice and peace I would be pretty efficient at it, but most of us had no training.'

Not one for taking things lightly, McCarron decided that she needed a serious issue – or rather a serious injustice – on which to campaign. She bought every newspaper that she could get her hands on and started cutting out articles on controversies in Nigeria. She was looking for an issue 'that met the requirements' of the AFJN. At the end of her research she had six bundles of clippings. 'One was to do with some village that had to move because of a game park, another was about a rubber plantation, another was to do with a dam but, this pile, on Ogoni, just grew and grew.'

By chance, a colleague at university had a phone number for Ken Saro Wiwa, a novelist and poet who was leading the Movement for the Survival of the Ogoni People (Mosop). She rang him and he immediately invited her to a protest rally that he was planning in Ogoniland, a ten-hour journey by road. 'I went to them to learn,' McCarron said. 'I would have seen myself as apprenticing myself to the Mosop movement.'

That was March 1993 and within weeks Saro Wiwa was in detention, in the first of a series of prison sentences until he was hanged by the state in November 1995. Prior to his execution, Saro Wiwa wrote regularly to the Irish nun and she was one of the Ogoni people's few 'international' friends. As her involvement deepened with the cause, she became isolated in the Church in Nigeria and, feeling the strain and fearing she might be putting colleagues at risk, she took sabbatical leave to return to Ireland. 'I sensed my congregations in Nigeria were relieved… I don't know what pressures they were under, and I don't want to know.'

Once home, she continued campaigning. No one told her to stop and 'they couldn't because there was a mandate coming right down from the top'. McCarron hooked up with the Ogoni's support group in London, as well as Trócaire, which was also highlighting the issue. In January 1995, she got hold of a leaked Nigerian military document which suggested it was collaborating with Shell on a security clampdown in the region. She had it circulated in the Irish media and helped to organise a campaign to boycott Shell petrol stations. Ironically, the AFJN – which had been responsible for turning her into an activist in the first place – responded with 'dead silence' to her work, McCarron said. This was despite the fact that the Ogoni struggle was a 'top class' issue by its criteria. 'It was probably the first problematic issue that went that far… I was totally alone, and trusted my instincts and trusted

I was right, and this was what was meant by justice work. I appreciate the fact that it was tolerated – but it wasn't supported.'

Some fifteen years later, McCarron could still be found badgering Shell Oil, this time in relation to its exploration of the Corrib gas fields in County Mayo. Her activism still had an amateur quality to it, and she remained a marginalised figure in the Church, but by now she was used to the criticism and the isolation that came with taking an unpopular stand. 'I think what the Church fears desperately is publicity,' she said. 'The Philippines perhaps is an exception; it's a plus there to be a campaigner. But in Ireland, or Nigeria, it's not a plus, even if the mandate comes from within the Church.' Asked to characterise the Church's social teaching, she replied: 'Limp. The Church is good at producing documents. They give you a document to act on, and then you act on it, and that creates a huge dilemma. There are a number of people who did act on the mandates, but they stand out like sore thumbs.'

Part II

CHAPTER 6:
MISSIONARIES TODAY – WHERE DO THEY BELONG?

'By the grace of God, I am what I am.' (I Corinthians 15:10)

It's the sort of humid spring morning that casts a flatteringly peaceful air over Jardim Ângela. A few miles from central São Paulo – the throbbing, overworked heart of Brazilian capitalism – the *favela* is languorous and still, and the proximity of the great smoky metropolis that imposes itself on the skyline might as well be a trick of the light. In the parochial house, the gregarious Fr Jim Crowe is cradling his pipe and projecting his boundless energy across the room.

Almost forty years have passed since he first arrived in Brazil, and Jardim Ângela has been his home for much of that time. When he trawls the back roads of a lifetime's memory and tries to put order on the inchoate jumble of recollections, the story of this, one of São Paulo's toughest neighbourhoods, comes to him through the faces he knew and the friends he lost and glimmers of light that push him on.

He remembers two brothers, Sergio and Mosa. Sergio, a 21-year-old crack addict, was shot not far from the parochial house and it was not long afterwards that Crowe came across the scene. It was no more than seven years ago. 'Mosa, he was 16, and he was going down the same sort of line. Sergio's body was being taken away, and Mosa was beside me. I said to him, "Mosa, you'd better pull your socks up. The same is going to happen to you if you don't."

'The following day, in the graveyard, I was just after doing the funeral, and Mosa, looking at his brother in the coffin, he says, "Look at him now, Jim, isn't he better off than me? What am I living for?" I'll never forget it. For a young fella of 16 years of age to say, what am I living for, in front of his brother's body. I buried Mosa in the same place, a day less than a year afterwards. He was shot too. To have to tell someone that age that life is worth living…' Crowe shakes his head and lets his voice trail off.

To many paulistanos, the name Jardim Ângela instantly evokes the depth of their city's turmoil and yet, for an incorrigible optimist such as Crowe, it also offers a seductive corrective to the assumption that the city's troubles are entirely intractable. In 1996, the United Nations confirmed what Jardim Ângela's 300,000 inhabitants had long suspected and declared it to be the most dangerous place in the world. 'When that declaration was made by the UN,' Crowe recalls, 'we said, "It's not enough to stay praying about it; this isn't going to solve the problem." So we got a bit of a movement going.'

That movement began on 2 November 1996 – All Soul's Day – when 5,000 people – mothers, sisters and brothers of the dead – turned up for an evening 'march for life and peace' through the cemetery. Crowe remembers standing on the street that evening with Fr Eddie McGettrick, another Kiltegan father living in the city, wondering whether they would be alone on that first march. 'But in the last ten minutes, people flew in from every corner.' Five thousand showed up, all dressed in white shirts.

In the organisers' analysis, the spiralling violence was due not only to the growth in the drugs trade but to the abandonment of the area by public authorities. There was a lack of schools and clinics, and the police had pulled out long ago. The marches continued and resulted, among other things, in the creation of Brazil's first community police force, which is still in place today. The murder rate fell from about 120 per 100,000 in 1996 to 25 per 100,000 in 2009. 'It was a success,' Crowe says, 'but like everything, it's not all sunshine.' To emphasise the point, he hears later that day of the death of a 13-year-old girl, who had fallen for a 38-year-old drug dealer. After telling the man she wanted to end the relationship, she was raped, had her throat slit and her body was thrown in the local reservoir.

The missionaries were widely acclaimed for their efforts in organising the march and Crowe gained a high profile in the city as a result. Some thirteen years after that first gathering, the 'forum for the defence of life' still meets every month in Jardim Ângela, and the parish now also has a centre for vulnerable young people and a shelter for victims of domestic violence.

At the last count there were 114 Irish Catholic missionaries working in Brazil, most having spent the greater part of their adult lives here. Words come quicker to many of them in Portuguese than in English, and at thirty or forty years' distance, contemporary Ireland might as well be a foreign country. Looking from the outside in, they seem somewhat peculiar too. Ministering at an imperceptible remove from the people (Fr Crowe rarely wears the priest's collar), they don't speak, or move, or dress like religious in Ireland. Instead they are shaped by an altogether different physical environment.

If you were to drive from Jardim Ângela to the far side of São Paulo, the first of the gleaming office towers and condominium complexes that make a bar chart of the skyline would come into view within half an hour. With 20 million people spread over 3,000 square miles, São Paulo is Brazil's banking and commercial centre and the capital of the country's richest state. It's also a place of staggering inequality. Befitting its status as a regional powerhouse, the greener parts of town boast a choice of designer chocolate shops and Japanese cuisine to rival New York's, served in garden restaurants guarded by men with earpieces. And thanks to one of the largest populations of helicopters in any city, those who can afford it need never come into contact with the millions of ultra-poor who populate the *favela*s that run along the city's endless periphery.

Like most of the shantytowns, Jardim Ângela arose out of wasteland, when the rapid industrialisation of post-war Brazil brought thousands of migrants to the city from the poorer states of the northeast. With nowhere to live and no money for rent, they erected their own homes – flimsy huts made of a jumble of wood, dry brick, cardboard and cloth. Padre Jaime, as Fr Crowe is known, has been here long enough to have seen São Paulo's population quadruple. He has also seen the drug gangs gain almost total control of some parts of the city and has had a close-up view of the human suffering that has ensued.

Jim Crowe joined the Kiltegan Fathers in the early 1960s, at the age of 17. He could never see himself as an Irish parish priest, he says, but in school he knew about the missionaries' overseas work and, after sitting his Leaving Cert, the choice was between going to university or 'going to Kiltegan'. Spurred by the appeal of working in Africa and 'an urge to do something for other people', he made his decision at the last minute. The Kiltegan Fathers had begun to work in Brazil in 1962, the same year that Pope John XXIII made a special appeal – driven by fear of the spread of communism, Crowe says – for all missionary societies to expand their work to Latin America. Today, Crowe doesn't necessarily toe the Vatican line. As well as embracing liberation theology, he has taken issue with certain statements from Rome, and in 2007 he spoke out against a papal declaration labelling marriages after divorce a 'scourge'. Almost three-quarters of families are led by a single parent in Jardim Ângela, so 'here, we see any stable family unit as a blessing', Crowe remarks evenly. 'I mean, 72 per cent of my parishioners are single-parent families. What can I say? How do I handle that situation? My father and my mother, God be good to them, and all my brothers and sisters are happily married, and I'm a strong family person – I'm part of a family, and I believe in the family. But you're in a different situation [here].'

Does it put missionaries in a difficult position, defying the Vatican so publicly? 'Very much so.' Then he adds, with a smile, 'The Vatican is a long way away from Brazil, you know… We have to take what Rome has said, and we have to adapt it to our reality.'

Crowe has been voted Person of the Year by a Brazilian national magazine and has been honoured by the University of São Paulo for his 'concrete action' in defence of human rights, justice and peace, but his job description remains somewhat vague. Every second year, he is asked to fill out a survey for the Irish Missionary Union (IMU), the umbrella group representing Catholic congregations, and is given a choice between identifying his work as 'pastoral' or 'community development/social work'. Neither adequately describes what he does, and the same problem applies to the nearly 2,000 other Irish missionaries worldwide. Because they tend to work in out-of-the-way places, far off the radar of the international media, missionaries can be underreported, or even unreported. What they do isn't really news and, as a general rule, they only ever enter the public consciousness when one of them is kidnapped, shot or killed.

The latest IMU census shows there were 1,976 Irish missionaries overseas in December 2008. More than 60 per cent of them (1,199) were in Africa, 19 per cent (385) in Asia or Oceania, 18 per cent (356) in Latin America or the Caribbean and the remainder

(36) in the Middle East or Eastern Europe. Across all continents, 41 per cent listed pastoral work as their core activity, 16 per cent education and 8 per cent health. Some 7 per cent worked in each of administration, formation/renewal and community development/social work, while 4 per cent were in other ministries and 9 per cent retired. The distribution of activities was fairly evenly spread across all regions, albeit more missionaries in Latin America said they were involved in pastoral work compared to Africa or Asia (61 per cent versus 38 per cent and 34 per cent respectively), a reflection perhaps of the way in which the Church is more integrated in social services in countries like Brazil, Peru and Chile. Another disparity was the fact that only 2 per cent of missionaries in Asia said they were involved in community and social work, compared to 8 per cent in both Latin America and Africa. Here political and religious sensitivities are thought to be a factor, as the scope for campaigning by Irish missionaries is limited in countries that are predominantly Muslim, or where civil liberties are routinely denied.

Wherever missionaries have gone they have adapted to local needs, or more precisely perhaps the local population's greatest need. Where prostitution is endemic, they've become social workers. Where unemployment is high, they've taught. A prime example of such adaptation can be found in Africa where a number of Irish medical sisters went into the specialist area of fistula repair, having seen at first hand the devastating impact of vaginal fistula on young women. Common in the poorest parts of Africa, the condition is associated mainly with obstructed labour but can also be caused by rape. Sufferers are unable to control bodily discharge, which can lead to serious infections, as well as ostracism within the community. Sr Dr Lucy O'Brien, a member of the Missionary Sisters of the Holy Rosary who spent twenty-five years as a gynaecologist in Zambia, was among those to first highlight the condition internationally. As well as setting up a treatment centre for vaginal fistula, the Galway woman recognised the stigma attached to childless women within communities and thus set up an extraordinary sideline in advising couples on fertility. 'Whatever Lucy could do with them she would have a baby within a year,' said one her contemporaries cheerfully. Her success in the field was confirmed by the large number of girls named Lucy and boys named Brian in the town of Monze where she was based.

Lucy O'Brien died in 2006, aged 83, and was buried at a cemetery near Monze at her request. Building on her legacy today is Sr Dr Maura Lynch who has set up an internationally acclaimed training centre for fistula repair in Uganda. From Youghal, County Cork, she worked for seventeen years as a doctor in Angola before returning to Ireland to retrain as a surgeon. In 1987 she was assigned to Kitovu Hospital, 120 kilometres from Kampala, where she carried out over a thousand fistula repairs between 1993 and 2007. Dozens of doctors and nurses have been trained at the hospital in fistula repair surgery and care management for the condition. Lynch has attracted funding from a range of international donors, including the US government's official aid arm. She has also received a string of awards, including a 'Certificate of Residency for Life' from the Ugandan government: a not-so-subtle plea for her to stay put for as long as possible.

Probably the best example of missionary adaptation today, however, can be found in the large number of Irish priests and nuns who work in the field of HIV and Aids. A 2007 Misean Cara report found that no less than fifty different Irish missionary congregations were operating projects in this single area.[30] The range of disciplines – which were found across thirty-seven countries – included HIV prevention and education; medical and curative services like anti-retroviral treatment; palliative care for the terminally ill; advocacy on gender rights; nutrition and food security programmes; and water and sanitation. Mary Myaya, a UK-based development specialist, says missionaries were particularly 'well placed' to deal with the unfolding HIV and Aids crisis in the mid-1980s when there was no treatment in sight and people were dying in large numbers. 'It really was their niche: care and support of the dying, and making sure people died with dignity.'

It might surprise people that so many Irish missionaries are working to combat HIV and Aids, and in so many different ways. The Vatican's doctrinaire stance against artificial contraception has created an impression that the Catholic Church's main weapon against the pandemic is sermonising from on high. In fact, scores of priests and nuns are fighting a ground-level war against HIV in their communities and, what's more, many of them are using tactics which stray far from Church doctrine.

One such dissident is Fr Michael Kelly, a septuagenarian former school principal who says he is 'absolutely convinced there is a role for the condom' in combating the virus. Despite failing eyesight and an increasingly stooped physique, Kelly is a formidable campaigner and jets across the world to share his knowledge as an educationalist and a mathematician who has forensically studied policy responses to the HIV and Aids crisis. 'Between now and Christmas I have to go twice to Botswana, twice to Dublin, once to Paris, once to Pretoria, once to Lesotho and I think once to Kampala,' he says, sitting down for a breathless mid-summer interview in Dublin. 'It is a lot in four to five months because they all involve talking, and that all involves preparation, because I never like to give the same talk twice.'

Kelly, a silver-haired Jesuit with a toothy grin that he flashes frequently as he speaks, was born in Tullamore, County Offaly in 1929. But when asked for his nationality these days, 'I say I am Zambian' (and he has the passport to prove it). He moved to the sub-Saharan state more than fifty years ago, armed with a first-class honours BA and a licentiate in philosophy. The Jesuits in Zambia were, at the time, 'looking for maths teachers and I had a degree in maths,' he explains. After working as a school headmaster for many years, he joined the University of Zambia as a lecturer and later professor, and then deputy vice chancellor – the first 'non-Zambian' to hold such a post. Among his academic duties was helping to set the curriculum for schools across Zambia, and he wrote extensively on educational psychology and school reform. That was until the late 1980s when the Aids issue 'became my life'.

A few things happened at once. He fell ill with an unknown disease, and the doctors tested him for HIV. 'I didn't have it but it turned my mind to it.' Around the same time, Zambia's then president Kenneth Kaunda announced one of his sons had died of Aids, a 'very courageous' thing for an African politician to do at the time. From his work in education, Kelly started to notice how teachers were at high risk of infection, how this would have a devastating effect on schooling and also how the crisis would produce a huge number of Aids orphans. 'Being mathematical, I have a kind of analytic mind, and could analyse the way it was going.'

Long before the international community put together a plan, Fr Kelly was publishing research papers on how to stop the spread of HIV infection and lobbying politicians. He recalls addressing a group of African educationalists in the early 1990s. 'They were joking about when the next meeting would be, and I said, "From what I can see some of you won't be at it because you'll be dead." They were shocked but they took on the message very well.' Since then, the Irish priest has worked on projects for Unesco, Unicef and the World Bank, and has advised governments from the West Indies to Australia on the links between education and HIV and Aids. He was also ahead of the curve in highlighting the 'feminisation' of the crisis – how women were suffering both from infections and as primary care-givers to those infected. Often swimming against the tide, he says his philosophy is 'putting the facts and figures together and hoping the right people will hear them.'

His attitude to condoms is similarly guided by statistics. Describing as 'irresponsible' attempts to ban them, Fr Kelly has argued: 'Condom use is an integral part of the effort to overcome HIV/Aids. Hence the use of condoms should be advocated or, at the very least, should not be opposed.' Moreover, he says, 'to say that the condom is morally wrong conflicts with Catholic moral principles and is not supported by any explicit Church teaching.' At the same time, he warns against focusing solely on 'end-game interventions', adding that 'we have to put more emphasis on high ideals, and abstinence is one of those high ideals'. He adds: 'This may sound very un-Catholic but if all the young people had sex just with one another this disease would die out in a few years because none of them are infected. There is much more promiscuity among young people in the US than in Zambia or in other African countries. The problem in Africa is trans-age, intergenerational activity is going on.'

Underlying issues such as poverty, cultural values and 'most of all perhaps the subordinate status of women' need to be addressed to really tackle the crisis, he argues. A story he likes to tell is of Fr Joseph Moreau, the first Jesuit to arrive in Zambia in 1905 and the man credited with introducing the plough to the country. As the story goes, Fr Moreau demonstrated the new technology to a village elder who then shook his head and said 'but my wife wouldn't be able to carry that'. Kelly's face wrinkles with laughter as he recalls some of his own efforts to highlight the patriarchal nature of African society. He once wrote a book on schooling in Zambia that was originally called *The Education of Girls in a System Designed for Boys* (the publishers insisted on a less offensive title). 'Women are second-class citizens in African societies… and in the Catholic Church.' He smirks and then leans towards the dictaphone on the table in front of him. 'You heard me!'

Fr Michael Kelly is widely respected by his missionary peers, but they don't all agree with him. One of his main sparring partners on HIV and Aids is Sr Miriam Duggan, superior general of the Franciscan Missionary Sisters of Africa, who spent more than thirty years working in Uganda. When Aids was identified in the mid-1980s as a serious public health risk for the country 'no one wanted to know about it,' the Limerick woman says, 'but we made a decision to make it an option, and drop a lot of our work to concentrate on that.' Duggan, who worked as a doctor during Uganda's civil war, was made a member of the government-backed Ugandan Aids Commission. One of its first initiatives was a public faithfulness campaign built around the crude but effective slogan 'zero grazing'. Through her lobbying, Duggan became friendly with Ugandan president Yoweri Museveni, and she praises him for speaking openly about the Aids crisis at a time when it was still taboo. 'The main message of the president was abstinence. The main difference with Uganda was the government and the churches were speaking the same language on it,' she says.

The efficacy of Museveni's policies are hotly debated in scientific literature. While the HIV infection rate in Uganda dropped from 30 per cent to 10 per cent over the course of a decade, analysts have different opinions on just what exactly caused it. Was it changed sexual behaviour? Or was it greater condom use, combined with premature death among those infected in the early years? Sr Duggan insists that abstinence was the key, and she accuses liberal opponents of being blinded by ideology. She has since collaborated on research in this field with Edward C. Green of the Harvard School of Public Health who has dissented from mainstream development thinking and argues that condoms create 'risk compensation', or a potentially fatal sense of security in promiscuous individuals.

'If you ask me about using a condom as a last resort, I would say, "Yes", but the medical research is 85 per cent for the condom, and that is a 15 per cent failure rate for a disease that kills,' says

Duggan, who also a former president of the IMU. 'I can only share my medical knowledge and say, "If it was me, this is what I would do." A condom will give you some protection but if you really want to stay alive abstain until you meet the right person and then be faithful. I have stood at too many bedsides of too many young people who relied on condoms, and it's not easy to die young.'

But what about those consciously engaging in risky sexual behaviour? What about sex workers? 'I have worked with prostitutes,' she replies. 'It is one of the greatest works that I have enjoyed. And people say, "You must give condoms to prostitutes," but I say, "No, you must pull them out of that slavery." They are in it through poverty, and I want to pull them out of that, and to restore their dignity. Today I can walk through Kampala and meet people in high places who once worked on the streets as prostitutes.' Her voice hardens. 'To me, if I am giving out condoms to prostitutes I am only disposing of them [the women] with the condom. That is quick work and you feel good. But it takes a lot of work to pull them out of poverty, find them alternative work. And which should I be doing as a Christian, or as a doctor?'

Ironically, given the Church's traditional antipathy towards sex education, Duggan has gained the imprimatur of African bishops for a youth-based teaching programme that proclaims to 'give clear and consistent facts' about sexual issues in a 'non-judging' fashion. The 'Education for Life' programme, developed with Sr Kay Lawlor, a Kenya-based Medical Missionary of Mary, seeks to bring about behavioural change through a series of workshops and lectures, typically over three or five days. Described by one development specialist as a 'Tupperware party' for sexually active youths, Educate for Life is now running in schools and parishes across fourteen African countries. For this, and similar work, Duggan was honoured by the Ugandan parliament in March 2008. The inscription on the award reads: 'In appreciation of the illustrious, selfless, unprecedented and pivotal contribution in the fight against HIV and Aids.'

Not everyone is so impressed, however. While trainers, or facilitators, on Education for Life are instructed to give 'information and not their own opinions or choices' there is no guarantee that this happens in practice. Some aid workers believe that, by emphasising abstinence at the expense of other interventions, the programme muddies the water on prevention, and they cite the Catholic Church's long record of contradicting public health messages across sub-Saharan Africa. Whereas governments tend to promote the ABC approach of 'abstain, be faithful and use a condom', the Church advises 'abstain, be faithful and character formation'.

Mary Myaya, who has worked for a number of international aid agencies, including the BBC charity Comic Relief, says missionaries are not unique in having to grapple with ethical issues over HIV. A question like 'What practical advice should you give someone who is infected and wishes to start a family?' is a challenge to everyone in the development sector. But, by virtue of their membership of the Church, missionaries are put in a particular 'ethical dilemma', and consequently many of them opt to stay out of the area of prevention, says Myaya. In contrast, the field of patient care is 'a natural match'.

To see how this is so one might travel to the township of Atteridgeville, near the South African capital Pretoria, where Belfast-born priest Father Kieran Creagh has established a hospice for the care of people dying of Aids-related illnesses. Driving through the centre of the informal settlement, weaving between street traders and taxi cabs that lurch towards would-be passengers without notice, the Leratong hospice appears unmistakably on the horizon. Built on a hilltop site above Atteridgeville's warren of tin shacks in a bid to bring Aids sufferers 'out of the shadows', Leratong has broken new ground metaphorically and literally. Today, it is recognised by the South African health authorities as a standard-setter in hospice care.

Creagh, a mildly hyperactive man with a wiry body and a mischievous smile, first came here as a parish priest. One of his predecessors had fled the township after being beaten up in a car hijacking but Creagh – who grew up in the Ardoyne area of Belfast during the worst of the Troubles – wasn't put off. 'I came straight from the airport to here – and it struck me in the face,' he recalls, 'it' being the depth of poverty and the scale of the Aids crisis. Close to 40 per cent of people aged 18 to 40 in Atteridgeville were reckoned to be HIV positive, and Creagh saw his own church congregation devastated by the virus. Not one for half measures, Creagh began speaking out against both state and Church policy on HIV, arguing that it was 'morally wrong not to condomise' if engaging in risky sexual behaviour. He also laid his body on the line, becoming in 2003 the first person in Africa to take part in an Aids vaccine trial. A solution containing a weakened equine drug and a harmless gene from a common strain of HIV was injected into his bloodstream by doctors at the Chris Hani Baragwanath Hospital in Soweto. Creagh's sexual status – 'sexual partners zero' – made him the perfect candidate for the vaccine. 'One jab for man, hope for mankind,' *The Star* of Johannesburg proclaimed the next day.

Seven years later, now aged 47, Creagh is still suffering no ill effects from the experiment, although he is a touch disappointed there was no breakthrough from the trials. Leratong is also still going strong and, as he walks through its clean, sunlit wards, he greets patients cheerfully in Sotho before slipping back into English to explain the rationale behind the hospice. 'Palliative care is not a luxury. When people come into the world as babies they are cared for in a proper, sterilised and caring environment. People need to exit the world in the same way, with the same quality of care.' From the outset, Creagh put a premium on the quality of nursing care and arranged for some of his staff to travel to Ireland to train under health professionals there. He also put much thought into the design of Leratong. A walled garden provides a shaded place for celebrations and sing-songs. Exterior balconies grant patients the best view in the township. Creagh volunteered a name for the place: 'Lerato', translating as 'love' in the local dialect. This was amended to 'Leratong' ('where the love is') on the advice of hospice matron Remigia Tloubatla, a former nurse who came out of retirement to become the Irish priest's trusted lieutenant.

The relationship between Fr Kieran and Remigia – the youthful priest from Belfast and the unflappable, experienced carer who is old enough to be his mother (and is sweetly protective of him, like a mother too) – has formed the linchpin for Leratong. Their partnership also underlines a broader truth about missionary work: nothing can be achieved unless you form real bonds with the local population. A parishioner at the local St George's church, Tloubatla first met Creagh after Mass one Sunday. She shared his concern about the quality of healthcare in the township, and especially for those dying of Aids. The pair started an ad hoc outreach service, calling to people in their shacks and offering them some comfort in their final hours. 'Kieran used to come into my home – he wouldn't even ring ahead – and he would say, "There is a patient: Just come and tell me what to do,"' the mother of three recalls, and then breaks into a smile. 'He said he had experience from a hospice in Dublin but, in those days, it didn't look like he had.'

With Tloubatla, Creagh visited the sick at dangerous hours of the night, bringing food, blankets and prayer. Once he even brought the mattress from his own bed to give to a dying patient. Of all the people whom they visited in those early days one sticks out. 'Ronald Mokwene,' Creagh recalls the name. He was 50 years old and had been left to die of Aids in the tiny box of corrugated iron he called home. The man's wife – herself gravely ill – crouched next to him. It was stifling hot and, typical for such a township shack, there was no running water and no electricity. Ronald asked Fr Kieran for a cigarette and 'luckily I had one', the priest recalled. 'I blessed him, and I remember thinking, "Where is Mother Teresa when you need her?"' Describing it as a 'moment of grace', he said: 'Sitting with Ronald, it formed in my mind. I saw it. It was just a sense I had – that it's not right for someone to be left to die like that.' This was in March 2001, close to St Patrick's Day. While Creagh's native peers were thousands of miles away, relaxing on a day off work, or perhaps enjoying a festive drink in the pub, he was witnessing a stranger's slow and painful death. And he was wondering – or 'fighting with myself' – what to do about it. 'I asked myself, "Why can't people be cared for here as well as they would be cared for anywhere else?"'

Leratong, which opened in June 2004, was the first hospice in a catchment area of 500,000 people. As well as serving an immediate community need, it established a model of palliative care that could be copied across South Africa. 'It was a struggle for us even to put up the burglar bars on the windows,' Tloubatla recalls. 'Kieran didn't want them because he wanted the place to be as open as possible. He was so trusting. Love makes you trust.'

A serious blow to Creagh's trust came in the early hours of 1 March 2007. Armed men broke into the hospice looking for money and shot the Irish priest twice at point-blank range. Creagh was left for dead on the lawn outside his living quarters. Bleeding heavily, he crawled to a balcony and sounded the alarm by banging some cutlery against the railings. Surgeons said it was a 'miracle' he survived, as one of the bullets ricocheted inside his body away from vital organs.

In the days and months after the event, Creagh was haunted by the fact that staff members who were on duty at the time fled the scene rather than coming to his aid. He felt alone, and even a little betrayed. 'I was a long time waiting for help so I said my prayers,' he recalls. 'I said an Act of Contrition, and it worked. I'm alive today.' The experience points towards an unpalatable truth for missionaries: that despite all the bonds they have created locally, they are ultimately on their own. By straddling two different worlds, missionaries appear to belong to neither, notwithstanding the individual friendships which they enjoy. Tloubatla rushed from her home to the scene of Creagh's shooting as soon as she heard of it. She also travelled in the ambulance to the hospital. 'I could not even pray,' she recalls. 'I could not even say "Our Father". I just held his hand and said, "Please, just make it".'

The shooting also highlighted what is a potential weakness in the development work of missionaries. Were Creagh to have been killed, or incapacitated, what would have happened to Leratong? There was, in the days and weeks after the attack, a very real fear that the hospice would collapse. A particular concern was that staff – who volunteered their services for a small stipend – would be afraid to return. Similar uncertainty is felt by missionaries who have been running their own projects in isolation for decades. So much of the developmental work carried out by missionaries is dependant on the personal dynamism and energy of a particular individual that it comes under threat whenever his or her health fails. A particular spectre which haunts many elderly priests and nuns is that their work will die with them: the school they run will close; the hospital will collapse; the people they feed and house will return to the streets and starve. It is a real concern and probably the greatest challenge facing the Irish missionary movement today: how to make their work sustainable and to guarantee a legacy.

At Leratong, a key ingredient is partnership with local stakeholders. Creagh always stressed that the hospice belonged to the community, not him, and in the immediate aftermath of his shooting – while he lay in hospital awaiting surgery – Tloubatla contacted donors, and the local health ministry, to reassure them of the situation. 'We had a staff meeting and everyone agreed that Leratong would go on, with or without Kieran,' she says. Six months after the attack, with Creagh recuperating back in Ireland, a large group of staff and supporters marched through Atteridgeville in a heavy rain storm, flanked by performing artists and musicians, to remind people that they planned to soldier on, no matter what. It was, says Tloubatla, a 'breakthrough event'.

Creagh returned to Leratong just seven months after the shooting. On his first day back, he said Mass for a jubilant gathering of local residents, patients and assorted fans who flocked to the hospice to welcome him back. Amending the Gospel for the occasion, he proclaimed from a makeshift altar in the brightly lit reception hall: 'Happy are those when people persecute you, and shoot you, and speak all types of calumny against you.' With a broad smile, he assured the congregation: 'God wants us to be happy.' Since he returned to Leratong, the hospice has expanded further, although Creagh has delegated many of his duties to a board of directors made up of community representatives, sponsors and other supporters. A new church has been built on the site, along with a crèche for fifty children – due to rise to 100 – and a health clinic dispensing anti-retroviral drugs to 1,000 people with HIV. Most of these patients either are too poor to afford the fees at public hospitals or are public health workers who can't go elsewhere in case they are identified and then stigmatised as a result. In 2009, South Africa's health regulators awarded Leratong a five-star 'compliance' rating (an 80 per cent grade is considered top class; Leratong scored 98 per cent). Creagh has since decided to make a clean break and return to Ireland – to study first and then perhaps embark on a new challenge. 'I am not very good at maintaining things,' he claims. 'I get them to a level and then move on.'

The shooting had a part to play in the decision. He was diagnosed with post-traumatic stress disorder, for which he has received counselling. He also realised that moving on would be no bad thing for Leratong. A 'wise' friend recently told him that hospice staff wanted him to go because they'd then cease to feel responsible for him and thus stop fretting about his welfare, a verdict that was 'probably right', Creagh says. Tloubatla – without whom, Creagh adds, Leratong 'would not have happened' – is also planning to step down from her post but she has made handover plans too. Creagh says the advice of his superiors in the Passionists down the years has prepared him for this transition. 'They would say to me, "What would happen if you left?" They didn't force me but they always made me aware that the project must stand on its own. It has to be bigger than the person.'

While it hasn't been easy to extricate himself from Leratong, Creagh is lucky that he can share some of his workload with others. For many missionaries there is no handover plan. Creagh is probably in a minority too in welcoming the chance of a return to Ireland. For a significant proportion of missionaries, the thought of 'coming home' is anathema. There are 105 retired missionaries in South Africa alone and none appears to have any inclination to leave a place where they feel respected and have made many friends.

Back in the humid head of São Paulo, Jim Crowe confirms he has no plans to relocate. On a recent visit to Ireland, he met with a group of priests who spoke to him about the shortage of clergy in the country and suggested it might be time for him to move back. But the decline in vocations doesn't worry him, he says. On that evening with his colleagues, he argued that perhaps the shortage was a good thing, that it might be time for the priest to step off the 'pedestal' he has occupied for so long and that maybe it would open up the Church to greater lay involvement. 'I think the whole concept of priesthood – especially celibate priests – will have to change anyway,' he adds.

Crowe had another reason for declining the invitation of a return to Ireland. After forty years, Brazil has become home. His accent remains, but he sounds more comfortable in Portuguese than in English and seems thoroughly absorbed in his parish, among his people. Though he returns to his family in Ireland regularly, he admits to understanding Ireland less and less with every passing year, and says that every day in Jardim Ângela brings reminders of how much work he still has to do.

São Paulo's murder rate may have fallen in recent years, but with the consolidation of the drugs trade by large syndicates the business has become more organised and the supply lines more difficult to disrupt. Despite some improvements, crime rates remain stubbornly high and the income gap has been slow to narrow. In parts of the city, HIV and illiteracy rates are worryingly static. And yet Jim Crowe feels no temptation to despair. 'I wouldn't call it depressed, but there are times when the going is tough, when you ask, is it all worthwhile? Naturally we all ask ourselves those questions. Where is it all going to? I don't regret it. I'm forty years in Brazil this year. I'd say to myself it's worthwhile.'

What pleases him most is the sense of community and the spirit of belonging that the people of Jardim Ângela have managed to hold on to, despite the violence and the poverty and the daily hardships of life in the *favela*. 'I know there's no hard barometer you can put up and say it's this high or this low. But there is a sense of belonging, a sense of realisation, a sense of saying, this is my place.'

CHAPTER 7: EVALUATING THE WORK, ASSESSING THE LEGACY

'If one part of the body suffers, all the other parts suffer with it; if one part is praised, all the other parts share its happiness.' (1 Cor. 12:26)

When Wangari Maathai returned home from Oslo in 2004 as the first African woman to win the Nobel Peace Prize she was brought to a special reception by friends in Nairobi. There was wild applause as speakers queued up to pay tribute to her work as an environmentalist. But one of the biggest cheers of the day was reserved for another woman: the slight figure of Kathleen 'Columbière' Kelly who had been standing discreetly in the audience. Maathai rose to tell the crowd how the Kilkenny woman and her Loreto colleagues had had a formative influence on her life, not only inspiring a love of science and nature but inculcating in her a spirit of social responsibility. 'After my education by the nuns,' Maathai later wrote, 'I emerged as a person who believed that society is inherently good and that people generally act for the best.'[31]

When Maathai entered Loreto-Limuru in 1956 it was the only Catholic secondary school in Kenya for African girls, and it drew students from all over the country. Its headmistress at the time was Sister Joseph Teresa O'Sullivan, something of a political activist in her own right. A former member of Cumann na mBan, she served a sentence in Kilmainham Jail for Republican activities in the Irish Civil War. On arriving in Kenya, she went about toppling the male-only education system, as well as challenging class and racial divides. Sr Columbière – who celebrated her ninetieth birthday in 2009 – described her late colleague as a 'pioneer feminist' who 'wasn't afraid of anything'.[32]

In her biography *Unbowed*, Maathai recalled how the Loreto Sisters ran an all-white school for the children of European settlers near her own school in Nairobi but 'nobody, least of all the nuns, discussed it', and the young Kenyan said she felt no discrimination. Quite the opposite, the school prided itself on its egalitarian Mary Ward ethos. The instructive slogan of the Loreto founder, 'Be agents of positive change', was emblazoned on the walls and reaffirmed daily in the classroom.

Maathai once said she 'admired certain aspects of nunhood' and 'would probably have become one if I had been raised as a Catholic' rather than a Protestant. However, she felt the pull of another cause, the protection of the natural environment which grew into a larger campaign of citizenship activism under her Green Belt Movement. She abandoned her Christian name, Mary Jo, in favour of her native, birth name. However, her sense of gratitude – and affection – for the Loreto Sisters never left her. Nor her admiration for how they had given up 'the pleasures of the world' to serve God. She wrote, 'I was impressed that these nuns would leave their own homes and their families to travel to a strange country to educate us complete strangers. Since childhood, I have wanted to emulate these women because they were not only beautiful, smart and kind, but also because they showed me what it meant to dedicate your life to something greater than yourself.'[33]

Maathai continues to keep in contact with Mother Columbière and the Loretos in Limuru and, while they mightn't brag about it, most missionaries can relate to their sense of being valued. Across the world, missionaries confess to being 'smothered with kindness' by former pupils, patients or parishioners. They tell of lasting friendships and bonds of mutual respect, and down the years they've collected many honours from their host countries. In Brazil, Sister Kate Nolan, a Wexford woman and member of the Religious of the Sacred Heart of Mary, won the Paulo Freire trophy in 2007, the country's highest educational award, for a literacy project in the *favela*s of Paraiba. In South Africa, Sister Ethel Normoyle, a member of the Little Company of Mary from County Clare, received the Order of the Baobab from the South African government in 2009 for setting up a rural school and resource centre which has been adapted to cater for people with HIV. In Kenya, Corkman Colm O'Connell has been declared a national hero for coaching no less than twenty athletics world champions, and three Olympic gold-medal winners, at the Rift Valley Patrician Brothers school where he has worked for more than thirty-five years. Names such as these mean little to people in Ireland, but in the towns and villages where they live the public recognition is instant and tinged with emotion. When Mary Doyle, a member of the St Joseph of Cluny order, died in North India in October 2009, her surviving brothers in Ireland were stunned to receive a letter of tribute from the Queen Mother of Bhutan. The royal family member had been a former pupil of Doyle's at a school in Kalimpong where the Wicklow woman taught for over sixty years, and she described the Irish nun, better known locally as Sister Mary Tarcisus, as 'a wonderful human being whose only aim in life was to spread joy and happiness'.[34] Doyle had previously received a number of awards from the Indian government for what it described as her 'legendary' service to teaching, including the Bharat Ghurav award, which had previously been presented to just one other religious recipient – Mother Teresa of Calcutta.

But how typical are these examples? Not everyone shares the same level of satisfaction with individual priests and nuns, and some believe that – over the course of their history – missionaries have done more harm than good. Prof Don Akenson, a noted historian of the Irish diaspora, has argued that Irish missionaries were little more than Western imperialists – and devastating ones at that. Irish religious and educational institutions, both Catholic and Protestant, were more effective in breaking down indigenous cultures than were 'entire regiments of the armies of the British empire or of the various American government [sic],' he once remarked.[35] As well as undermining native value systems and beliefs, missionaries engaged in 'criminal' levels of physical and sexual abuse. 'Not all clerics and teachers participated in these activities, but it would have been a rare institution in which the activities did not occur.' Akenson made these comments over a decade ago, and recent revelations of clerical child sexual abuse give them added credence.

What can't be ignored is that Irish missionaries sprung from the broader enterprise of Christian empire-building which, in turn, was allied to the colonisation and exploitation of entire continents. As European tradesmen scrambled for resources in Africa and Asia, clergymen of different cloths turned up in the colonies peddling religious salvation. In truth, many of these missionaries were as much interested in material conquest as spiritual. 'When the white missionaries came to Africa they had the Bible, and we had the land,' South African Archbishop Desmond Tutu once remarked. 'They said, "Let us pray." We closed our eyes. When we opened them we had the Bible and they had the land.' Clearly, some missionaries sold a version of Christianity that bore no resemblance to the life of Christ. Prominent African theologian Jean-Marc Ela damningly critiqued European Christianity, describing it as 'an effort to swindle a mass of mystified blacks'. Ela argued that 'liberation of the oppressed' should be the cornerstone of the Church and advocated Catholic independence in Africa from Roman rule. His plea for a distinctly African religious voice had echoes in the writings of Chinua Achebe, the celebrated Nigerian author. His novel *Things Fall Apart*, probably Africa's best-known work of literature, explored exactly this question of how a white man's religion damages indigenous culture. Interviewed a half-century after the book's publication, Achebe said the British missionaries who populated his homeland undeniably brought some good things but they also brought racism and attempted 'to narrow goodness into things of the Church'.[36]

Maathai too has mixed feelings about European missionaries who 'taught the local people that God did not dwell on Mount Kenya, but rather in heaven, a place above the clouds'. People from her own tribe, the Kikuyus, were greatly influenced by such teachings, and 'within two generations they lost respect for their own beliefs and traditions', she wrote in her autobiography. At the time of Maathai's birth in 1940, Kikuyus was the name given to 'those who had not embraced Christianity, who still held on to and advocated for local customs', while those who had converted through the missionaries were called *athomi*. This translated as 'people who read', and Maathai noted dryly, 'The book they read was the Bible.'

Unfortunately, no systematic critical examination of the role of Irish missionaries from the African, Latin American or Asian perspective exists. Furthermore, independent research into the impact of missionaries on development and poverty reduction is noticeable by its absence. We are left instead with fragmented opinions like those above – opinions which are inevitably selective, biased or contradictory. Some African commentators, for example, can be highly critical of the missionary movement while holding great affection for individual priests, nuns and brothers. Even strong critics of religious imperialism are capable of acknowledging certain benefits that came with the missionaries.

Desmond Tutu was a product of a European Christian education, and he was inspired and mentored in his early years by the Anglican missionary and anti-apartheid campaigner Trevor Huddleston. Ela worked as a Catholic missionary within Cameroon, while Achebe also went to a mission school and then experienced a Western-style, third-level education. Maathai likewise benefited from the Europeans' educational outreach, and this tempered her criticism of those early missionaries who helped to colonise Kenya. The first wave of Christians 'would generally do their work by visiting villages and attending to peoples' health needs', she noted. Praising their 'patience and ingenuity' in the face of a hostile environment and language barriers, she concluded: 'They did their work well.'[37]

The paucity of authentic African, or 'Southern', voices in the records of the Irish missionary congregations is a serious impediment to assessing their legacy. What we can say is that the work of priests and nuns differed depending on the continent on which they landed, and the era in which they lived. The mindset and priorities of missionaries shifted over time, and so too, critically, did the attitude of those people with whom they lived and for whom they proclaimed to work.

As evangelisers, Irish missionaries were relatively successful. Wherever in the world they have been free to preach, they've left Catholic communities in a healthier, or more corpulent, state than they found them. In Africa, evangelising giants like Bishop Joseph Shanahan and Teresa 'Mother Kevin' Kearney helped to turn large tracts of land Catholic, rivalling the impact of their Anglican and other Christian counterparts. It is estimated that in 1900 there were about four million Christians in Africa out of a population of 100 million; by 1980 there were 150 million Christians out of a population of 470 million. In terms of a specific Irish input, Nigeria stands out above all other African countries. In the sixty years between Shanahan's arrival in Igboland and the Biafran war, the

Catholic population of Nigeria grew from 2,000 to 2 million. In the late 1960s, 500 of the country's 850 priests were Irish, and the Irish church ran primary schools catering for more than 500,000 pupils. Today, the Igbo account for 70 per cent of Nigeria's baptised Catholics, and Nigeria itself produces more priests than any other African country, with the exception of the Democratic Republic of Congo.

Worldwide, the Catholic population rose about three-fold in the last century, to an estimated 1 billion people. Irish missionaries can take some credit – if that's the right word – for this explosion. For a time Ireland had more Catholic missionaries overseas than any other European country. In 1965, Ireland had 7,085 priests, sisters, brothers and laity working in developing countries in Africa, Asia and South and Central America.[38] This meant the Irish missionary corps was roughly equivalent in size to the Garda Síochána and had almost as many members as the Irish Army in the late 1960s. It was perhaps bigger than either of these organisations once the hundreds of religious and lay people, who were engaged in providing support services to the missions from home, were taken into account.[39]

Just what form of Christianity was 'successfully' exported from Ireland is a matter for some debate. Behind the numbers were disparate Catholic communities which did not necessarily embrace the teachings of the white-skinned men and women with their thick Irish accents and strange ideas. One early reminder for the Holy Ghost Fathers in Nigeria that the Igbo had, in fact, minds of their own came in 1923 when Bishop Shanahan discovered that, despite all his preaching, parishioners in Calabar were living double lives, some as polygamists and others as idol-worshippers. Everyone in the town knew about it except the missionaries – which would have been comical only for the inquisition that followed. Marie Martin was one of those commandeered by the bishop to interview the women of the town about the state of their morals, a task which she performed dutifully but with no great relish. An old Nigerian hand who worked in the region thirty years later admitted attitudes had changed little in the interim, noting, 'They did not understand our ideas towards sex. They did not take us seriously. We had planes and motorcars and drugs so they took us seriously on that front, but certainly not in relation to sexual morality; they thought we were weird.'

Looking at the quality of religious instruction in the missions, it is hazardous to speculate on cause and effect. Was Maathai's social conscience really pricked by the Irish nuns or would she have become a campaigner anyway? Would someone like Mira Nair, a film director and celebrated former pupil of Loreto Shimla in India, have gone on to make the movie *Salaam Bombay* to highlight the plight of street children in her homeland had she been educated in a government-run school instead? And should such cases be weighed against the graduates of Irish missionary schools who went on to become corrupt state officials or exploitative company bosses?

A further issue that warrants attention is the impact of missionaries on the Catholic faith in Ireland. While the focus of the missionary movement was evangelising overseas, it had the indirect effect of boosting, or even salvaging, the reputation of the Irish Church at times of clerical scandal and controversy. While a more in-depth exploration of the subject is necessary, it could be argued that missionaries – and especially those working in social justice and poverty – helped to keep alive the flames of Catholic faith in Ireland through the 1980s and 1990s by demonstrating there were, after all, some good people in the Church. In a revealing television interview with Gay Byrne in 2010, human rights lawyer and former president Mary Robinson described how her attitude to the Catholic Church was heavily influenced by the missionaries whom she witnessed working with the world's poor. 'When I am in African countries and I meet these priests and nuns… and you just look into their faces and you know that they have an additional element in their lives which is transcendent: it is their faith, and it is the fact that they live it, and I have never rejected that. I aspire to the highest beliefs and morality of the Christian faith… To me the simple gospel is a wonderful standard that we can all aspire to live to.'[40]

Missionaries themselves are cautious about wading into this debate, and as a whole are slow to claim credit for conversions. As Dan Fitzgerald, veteran of the Columban mission to China, said, 'Working as a priest anywhere you have to accept it isn't you who turns the key to bring people into the Church. It is the holy God and you are just an instrument.' Asked to assess their own legacy, missionaries tend to speak of relationships built rather than of minds controlled. Quizzed on the matter, Fr Eamon Aylward, executive secretary of the Irish Missionary Union, said, 'The great legacy is that there are millions and millions of people and their families alive today because of the work of missionaries. Also, in terms of education, they brought the Christian message, and they did so in their own context.' That's about as detailed a response as you are likely to get from a missionary. There are many of them who are loath to speak of any material success out of a sense that 'the greatest work is that which cannot be measured'. It is a fine sentiment and there is some truth in it, but taken to extremes it can lead to self-delusion. There are some missionaries who plead exceptionalism to avoid scrutiny, and it is widely decreed among missionaries that because the best work is not measurable then any external evidence suggesting their work is not so great can simply be dismissed.

The difficulty in assessing the legacy of missionaries – past and present – is exacerbated by the fact that they have often worked in isolated locations. This, coupled with a propensity among missionaries to pursue their own particular 'charism' or divine inspiration, makes them somewhat elusive, or even slippery at times. Traditionally, missionaries have operated with different values, as well as markedly different objectives, to other development workers. And, frequently, they are accountable only to themselves. Measuring success in such circumstances is like judging performance art.

Take, for example, Sr Cyril Mooney. At the Loreto Sealdah Day School in downtown Calcutta (now officially known as Kolkata), she has pioneered a form of education that crosses the social classes and turns barefoot street children into successful professionals. The school today caters for 1,400 students and since the early 1990s has provided accommodation, food and clothing for the poorest among them. It is estimated that Mooney has directly assisted up to 450,000 people during her half century in India, and their uplifting has mirrored a transformation of the country. Travelling to the heart of Kolkata today, one finds that shopping malls and five-star hotels have replaced some of the city's notorious slums. Kolkata's first McDonald's opened in 2007, and flashing neon, from Siemens to Mountain Dew, is springing up on buildings like ivy. But social divides are widening in modern-day India, with a swelling middle class and an increasingly detached and expanding lower class.

Away from the construction and the plush resorts, Mooney relaxes in the office of Loreto Sealdah adjacent to a city highway. On her desk sits the Padma Shri, one of the highest honours bestowed by the Indian president. The Indian government generally gives the award to Indian citizens, and just over 2,000 people have received the honour since its inception.

Inside her office, children lie scattered around the floor, reading Indian folk tales or playing cards and ludo. Some are practising spelling by writing with chalk on the ground. Others finish up the day's chores, scrubbing pans or mopping the tiled floors. It's almost time for bed. Mooney takes down a red whistle and blows. Hundreds of kids come scuttling out from every corner, demanding bedtime hugs. Mooney embraces each child individually.

The Loretos established their first school in India in 1842. Seven sisters and five postulants from the Irish order were sent to the country the previous year, never expecting to see their homeland again. In the decades that followed, the Loreto sisters concentrated their efforts on educating the children of the colonial and merchant classes, and Mooney admits that little had changed by the time she arrived in India in 1956. 'We lived the same conventional life as we did in Ireland… we didn't really get very involved with the real poor.'

The nuns introduced an outreach dimension to their work in the mid-1960s but it wasn't until 1979 that the reform of their schools began when Mooney converted a 120-year-old private college – which had been geared for a privileged few – into the self-proclaimed 'rainbow' project Loreto Sealdah. Half its students would be taken from deprived backgrounds and half from affluent circumstances, and fees gathered from the latter would help subsidise the former. Since the early 1990s, the school has provided accommodation for children who would otherwise be on the streets, as well as assisted living programmes that can help them gain a profession and embark on a successful life. A pioneering aspect of the school is the fact that children from both privileged and non-privileged backgrounds are educated under the one roof, breaking taboos on people from different castes or social backgrounds mixing.

'The poor kids are an asset in that they challenge the others by judgements that are not based on social rank,' says Mooney. 'At first when kids come off the streets, they can't keep clean clothes, do homework or care for books. We have created a space where they can come and sit down and study in a safe environment. They can also get a meal or have a bath if they want. But we never make anyone feel ashamed by telling them they have to wash. Usually within a week of coming they'll keep clean by themselves. The transformations sometimes are amazing to watch. The kids come in looking like little rats and we see them through to starting their first day in work as bright, confident young adults.'

Funding the project hasn't been easy. Mooney gets donations from a range of private and public sources but there is little certainty from year to year. In fact, the school almost closed in the early 1980s because of a lack of finances, and it was only saved by the impulsive generosity of the Irish public. 'What had happened was that the Indian government had raised salaries so I was in a bit of a fix.' She takes up the story, 'Someone in Ireland lent me a Fiat Panda and I began to drive to most of the Loreto Convents in the country to collect funds… I would drive to a place, talk to the nuns in the evening, sleep there, and then talk to the school the next day at five or six different times. I did this for about seventeen schools, but we were still way behind our target. Then someone wrote to the Mother General in Rome and asked if they could put me on *The Late Late Show*. She agreed but as it turned out it wasn't convenient, so instead they got me on the Gay Byrne radio show. I was told he'd ask me a question and I was to keep talking until he interrupted. I was warned not to clam up on him. He had some nun on earlier that just gave yes and no answers. Remember though I had told this story for the previous seventeen days so when I went into him it flew out of me. We talked for a whole hour and we mentioned if anyone wanted to make a donation they could send money to the Loreto Convent in Bray. When I went out to Bray later, fellas were driving up in lorries saying, "Here's ten quid for the nun from India I heard on the radio." The response was incredible and helped save the school. From that point on we went from strength to strength.'

Mooney's maverick style of operation is not untypical among Irish missionaries. By necessity they are inventive and innovative but, by the same token, they are prone to short-term planning and sometimes run on a hand-to-mouth basis. Missionaries have also been guilty of duplicating the work of one another, and their insistence on absolute independence has the potential to dilute their overall impact.

'Half the work in education and health in sub-Saharan Africa is done by the Church,' former World Bank president James Wolfensohn told the World Economic Forum in Davos in 2008, 'but they don't talk to each other, and they don't talk to us.' His exasperation is shared by many who believe faith-based organisations could have a bigger and better impact if they improved their levels of cooperation and competence. Research in development argues that Church-run institutions have the capacity to mobilise communities to action because they 'inspire levels of trust and confidence unmatched by governments, donors, or secular non-government groups'. Faith-based organisations score high on criteria like 'value for money' and 'reaching the poorest of the poor'. Moreover, they have a long track record of service. A 2008 study by a Catholic development agency estimated that the Church sponsored 26.7 per cent of all Aids-related services in the developing world.[41] 'Approximately one million members of Religious Institutes (consecrated religious) and three million lay persons – work in close to 1,000 hospitals, over 5,000 dispensaries and 800 orphanages in Africa alone,' the same study remarked. However, it said, 'the breadth and role of these Catholic individuals and organisations is largely unrecognised and under-funded.'

Compared to professional aid workers, 'I would bet anything the missionary would stretch money further, and often have a more thoughtful approach – often but not always,' says Gerry O'Connor, an advisor to the Irish government on overseas development policy.

A mid-forties former Goal volunteer, built like a second-row rugby player and a fanatic supporter of Munster rugby too, O'Connor is well placed to evaluate the respective value of different types of development work. He has worked in Sudan and Darfur, in Rwanda in the aftermath of the 1994 genocide and in Brazil, has served on Goal's executive committee and since returning to Ireland has run a community project in drug-ridden Cherry Orchard in Ballyfermot, Dublin. An accountant by training, his expertise in the aid sector was acknowledged in 2003 when he was appointed chairman of the audit committee of the Department of Foreign Affairs, which has an annual budget of €1 billion. O'Connor also happens to be a Redemptorist priest.

'I would believe that the value for money from missionaries is better than from NGOs,' he reiterates. 'If you were to ask about a straight trade-off between an NGO and a missionary I would be very confident that a missionary would be better value for money – unless the NGO, because they are so good at fundraising, can turn your euro into four euros, whereas the missionary might only use that one euro.' Missionaries can also have a huge 'multiplier effect' by being advocates for change, he says. 'If you have 500 people in front of you every Sunday you have great capacity to change mindsets, for positive or negative.'

O'Connor was an unlikely recruit into the Church. He was radicalised politically during the 1983 'pro-life' referendum when he decided to vote 'No' because of what he perceived as its flawed wording. His parents were 'aghast' and the principal at his school had stern words with him. When his local parish priest announced from the altar that anyone voting 'No' couldn't consider themselves a Catholic, 'I took that seriously – perhaps unnecessarily seriously – so I didn't go to church in my college years.' After graduating, he worked as an accountant with KPMG and then went with Goal to Sudan in 1988–1989. 'You couldn't live in Sudan and not be philosophical – asking questions about life and death.' He had a number of experiences that were 'frightening, where the end was close', and during these moments he had 'some sense of someone being close to me at those times of danger'. They were 'warm, spiritual experiences'. Once he was in a plane that seemed to be crashing. 'I expected to die, and I felt it was OK. There was something happening… as a religious person now, I would love to be able to catch moments like that again, the reality of it, the richness of it was quite tangible in terms of energy and warmth. It was like something reassuring you; this is OK. That is where the curiosity came.'

Another eye-opener in Sudan was the way in which Western diplomats and aid workers began to evacuate as soon as the security situation worsened. 'Some of those on the highest wages started to go, then other NGOs, Goal stayed a bit longer. The only ones who stayed in the end were four Irish Kiltegan priests. It left a huge impact on me at the time. I said, "There must be something motivating them." I was hugely impressed by their commitment to the people.' On his return to Ireland he enquired about joining the priesthood and opted for the Redemptorists. 'Where I ended up in life is quite a bit of a surprise to my family and others,' he laughs.

He went to Brazil as a missionary rather than a Goalie and initially found the transition difficult. He had no translator and no social life with other aid workers. Instead he spent evenings and weekends with local people at their funerals and parties. There were lots of meetings – endless meetings – at which he'd talk to local people about their problems, 'trying to be an animator and trying to find solutions'. It was a simpler life, 'a life that is not totally dissimilar to the people – even though it can never be the same'.

Comparing his experiences as an aid worker and as a missionary, he says: 'Both were very satisfying positions. My experience with Goal was a wonderful one, and I can still think back to some of the achievements and some of the difference we made. But I was very fulfilled by my life as a Redemptorist. It wasn't glamorous but there was great integrity to it. As a missionary I had a better appreciation of where people were at in their lives… There was a longer-term perspective taken – often without a lot of resources.' He adds: 'I felt I was less condescending. I don't mean "condescending" as a negative word. But I had a greater understanding of how people survived… I had a greater sense of the whole of people; their aspiration for education and health and jobs but also what keeps them going in terms of their family connections, or their sense of a spirit from God being amongst them.

'Poor people generally need to see the skin of your commitment before you really get to know them. They can be strategic in their relationship with you if they know there are going to be benefits from it… That isn't just in Africa or Brazil. I found the same in Ireland, sometimes it takes four or five years before people will potentially really open up to you and not just as someone who can be strategically helpful to their families and community.'

Measuring success is difficult as a missionary, he admits. One of the most satisfying things is seeing attitudes change, or watching community leaders emerge, but 'it can take fifteen to twenty years to see it'. He cites the example of a fellow Redemptorist in Mozambique who goes from village to village, teaching a human rights course. He pitches up his tent and asks locals who do they think is better: a man or woman? The reply always comes back 'a man'. The priest isn't instantly changing people's minds but he's 'hoping to get a different answer' to the question in five or ten years' time, O'Connor says.

But is this sort of work not just futile? 'A lot of missionaries would have a very strong sense of the importance of presence,' O'Connor replies. 'We are inspired by the idea that God is our creator, and that Jesus dwelt amongst us.' While he liked to see concrete results, 'there are others who trust in the fact that they are present' and who believe 'all sorts of good things will come' from simply residing in a community.

Rather than arguing, one is better than the other, O'Connor says the missionary approach and the development approach focus on different things: the former relationships, the latter 'engineering'. 'The development approach takes the log-frame,' he says, citing one of the latest development buzzwords, 'it starts looking at what the problem is, what are the inputs and expected outcomes – and then it tries to match the inputs with the expected outcomes and impacts. The relational approach is one where you live with the people, and you might even take time with the people before you even decide what it is you want to change here, and particularly you decide, even if it takes time, that you want the community to shape the agenda.'

Development specialists complain that missionaries 'go at a different speed' but this can just as easily be seen as a strength rather than a weakness. UK-based analyst Mary Myaya says, 'A sister who has only been working somewhere for four years will say "I'm still learning", whereas the Concerns or Trócaires will say after four years "We know everything".' The missionaries' long-term perspective puts them 'at odds with development orthodoxy and practice', says Dr Gerard Clarke, a development economist at Swansea University who has written extensively on faith-based organisations. 'Development policies are short term. They are designed for three or five years, whereas some missionaries will work in the same place for 30 or 40 years.' It is this deep loyalty to a community that distinguishes Irish missionaries not just from secular agencies but from other European missionaries, he argues. 'Because they are unmarried they can make that long-term commitment' and because they are not planning to hop between postings, Clarke adds, Irish missionaries are less likely to be involved in proselytising or doing anything else that might get them alienated from the local population. While some evangelical Western churches have targeted developing countries to boost their numbers, he says, 'Irish missionaries will not be involved in stirring up trouble in multicultural, conflict-ridden societies.'

Missionaries also command a high degree of trust by virtue of their modest lifestyle. 'NGOs go around in four-wheel drives and have good salaries and live in the capital city, whereas missionaries live a very simple life, close to the people. They don't have fancy vehicles, and communities value that,' says Clarke. Myaya recalls visiting a mission-run hospital in Tanzania which received identical funding as a state-run hospital nearby but was far better maintained and managed. 'I wouldn't classify myself as religious in any way,' she says, but 'maybe there is something about starting the day confirming you are trying to help people. You don't necessarily have that same type of motivation in a government hospital.'

On the downside, because they are so focused on the needs of their communities, missionaries can lack a wider, strategic vision. 'They tend to carve out their own little space, and then don't go outside of that, while development groups are always thinking about wider change,' says Myaya. 'Development, like any sector, moves on, and if some of the missionary sisters and fathers don't keep up with that then they will have difficulty getting funding in the future.' Missionaries can also be overlooked on grounds of scale. Like NGOs, they tend to be project-focused and choose a few areas of speciality, as they haven't the capacity to transform entire health and education sectors. That's why Gerry O'Connor says he backs the Irish Aid policy of 'budget support', or government to government funding, as well as giving grant aid to Irish NGOs and missionaries. 'The work of missionaries and NGOs will fail if the government in the country in which you are working doesn't have the capacity and ability to plan, or predictability of funds.

Without these you will have an oasis of interesting projects but no real progress.'

For funding organisations, the way missionaries are set up is quite problematic. Government and civil society donors like to know exactly where their money is being spent. They also like tangible results, and in the development sector there is a penchant for changing aims and objectives every few years. For priests and nuns, systematic reporting is anathema, performance reviews unheard of. It's not just that missionaries think filling out forms to be a waste of time (because they do), they resent having to explain themselves to anyone who hasn't travelled the same hard miles they have travelled.

This has left Irish missionaries in an increasingly vulnerable situation financially. For years they could rely on grants from the Irish government, handed out informally through its embassy network or through its overseas development wing, Irish Aid. Since 2004, however, all state funding has been directed through the missionary support agency Misean Cara, which is controlled by a board of directors drawn from missionary congregations. In recent years, missionaries have been in the privileged position of receiving personal funding for their work. When Apso, the volunteer funding agency, was abolished in 2004, missionaries were able to continue to avail of a standard grant, averaging about €12,500 per person in 2009. This facility, however, was scheduled to be phased out from 2010 onwards, with Misean Cara putting greater emphasis on strategic funding in the sector.

O'Connor admits there are weaknesses in the missionary approach. He says the 'accountant' in him emphasises strategic planning but the missionary in him knows people in developing countries have different values. 'Volunteerism, trust and faith' are important in the south – but not very important to us. 'A strategic plan that is based on the culture of efficiency, targets, excellence and quality will struggle in a culture premised on church and extended family that emphasise love, concern and harmony as a way of life.' Relationships are more complex in that setting. 'If your life is about trusting [that] you will get through tomorrow . . . asking to predict what will happen in the next two to three years is very difficult.'

The tension over funding leads to conflict on occasion, and Misean Cara takes the brunt of criticism from missionaries. That said, Trócaire, the Catholic aid agency, also gets abuse for its perceived 'unfriendliness' to missionary appeals for funding. The organisation was initially set up to support priests and nuns overseas but very little of its money goes to them today, and missionaries feel the charity is now embarrassed by its Catholic roots. Among development specialists, however, it is easy to find critics in turn of the missionary model. There are members of the aid profession who regard missionaries as too insular, and even self-important, describing them witheringly as 'dinosaurs' and 'impossible to deal with'. In truth, there are unrealistic expectations on both sides. Some missionaries just want to be given a cheque with no questions asked, while some development specialists want missionaries to be shoehorned into mainstream aid practice.

O'Connor says there is a dilemma because 'some of the best missionaries can be quite maverick. Some of those who impress you most, the congregational leader mightn't have a clue how they get their money. They don't want to be sidelined into training novices, or whatever... Some have done it on their own. It is strength of character and not always linked into the goals of the organisation.'

A deeper obstacle to funding is a suspicion that, no matter how much they deny it, missionaries are primarily engaged in evangelisation. O'Connor hears the argument all the time and replies: 'I have a view that the development sector is good at evangelising too. They have their Bible, something which is a flavour of the month, and then a few years later, they have a completely different Bible.' But what of missionaries? Is evangelisation still a goal of theirs today?

Few say so outright, even though bishops as a rule still demand figures from them every year on the number of baptisms they carry out, along with other sacramental statistics. Fr Kieran Creagh says conversion is not something he actively pursues in South Africa, but 'it would be disheartening if your church numbers were declining'. He usually baptises about twenty adults a year. 'It's humbling,' he says. 'You wonder: what are they seeing that has touched them?'

This is a pretty typical missionary response. When religious personnel see people join the Church they regard it as a small compliment. But they also tend to see it as a mere by-product of their work, and one over which they have little or no control. Carmelite priest Robbie MacCabe has spent more than thirty years driving around the Turkana desert in Kenya in a clapped-out Land Rover with a small bag of medical supplies, treating problems like cholera, malaria and trachoma. The veteran 'Father Doctor' or 'Doctor Father' (he's not hung up on titles) says he baptised about twenty-six people in 2009 'at a little outstation' for desert nomads. Asked to explain why these people became Christians, he is more than a little vague: 'The Turkana are very good people. They pray to God for what they need – the rains, or good pasture. The word for God is equivalent to that for the sky – *akuj*. So when you tell them the God of love is the creator of all these things then they accept it and become Christians, which is very nice.'

There is a certain innocence in this explanation, and critics of the missionary movement might detect a little presumptuousness, but the elderly MacCabe makes no attempt to disguise his motives, which are – on face value – humanitarian. 'The Turkana people suffer a lot. If they get one meal a day they are very pleased,' he remarks. 'If you said to them, "How are you keeping?" They would just say "*Akoro*", which is their word for hunger.' MacCabe himself sometimes goes days without a proper meal, and his daily diet in the desert is usually a bowl of porridge in the morning, and an egg and a tomato for tea. He has to contest with poisonous snakes and scorpions while doing his medical rounds, but his main concern at this time is an outbreak of kala-azar, a disease spread by sand flies which is usually fatal without treatment. He has just over a dozen patients but not enough medicine for them all and, on a fundraising trip back to Ireland in his eighty-third year, he is thinking of nothing else. 'I could not rest here comfortably knowing there are thirteen patients and we only have medicine for two. Are the other eleven going to pass away? I have a sort of feeling I must get back and do the job.'

To many missionaries, such questions about evangelisation seem outdated. They argue that their congregations moved away years ago from the 'conversion' model of mission work. Asked about the evangelising aspect of her work, Sr Cyril Mooney replies with an exasperated air: 'We do occasionally get people asking about becoming Roman Catholics. But you get much more changes in attitude, or changes in heart, which I see as evangelisation. For example you get well-off parents bringing in clothes and other things for the street children. A lot of hearts get touched when you start working with the poor, and that also contributes to a change in society later on.'

Mooney has little patience for those who perceive missionaries as having ulterior motives. The British author and filmmaker Christopher Hitchens once described Mother Teresa of Calcutta as 'a demagogue, an obscurantist and a servant of earthly powers', and, in his 1995 book *The Missionary Position*, claimed 'the true address of the missionary is to the self-satisfaction of the sponsor and the donor, and not to the needs of the downtrodden'. But Mooney, who was a friend of the revered Albanian nun, says such 'nasty' claims have no basis in fact. 'At no stage did she [Mother Teresa] ever advocate conversion; it was more about converting people to a good life – because conversion is something that can only come from God; it doesn't come from us. We have to live our own lives and love our neighbour as ourselves. That is what I am trying to do. That's my message if you are a Christian: love your neighbour as yourself. That means if you have a kid out on a garbage dump you pull them out and put them into school you don't leave them there saying "poor, poor thing, sad, sad, sad"; it means going there and doing it.'

Mooney's defending of her late friend doesn't mean she has no mind of her own when it comes to assessing charitable works. 'The approach of Mother Teresa is to give help to people who are starving. If you are starving there is no point teaching them philosophy. That was her way of tackling it. We have another way of tackling it.' Was Mother Teresa's work a sustainable or long-term solution? 'No it's not long term and it's not developmental. If you keep handing out food to people they keep on coming back – so it's so much down the drain. On the other hand it is assuaging a very basic need in some people.' It is the closest Mooney will come to striking a critical note. 'People would say, yes, different approaches should be taken. I feel the education way is the best way.'

Notwithstanding Mooney's assurances on the way in which missionaries approach evangelisation, suspicions do linger about their motivation, and these have deepened in the wake of recent Church scandals. Trust in priests and nuns has been badly dented by the catalogue of clerical sexual abuse and its cover up, and missionaries have not escaped criticism. The 2009 Ryan and Murphy reports, which investigated the Church's handling of abuse allegations in residential institutions and the Dublin Archdiocese respectively, showed missionary congregations to be little different from other Catholic institutions in the way in which they mismanaged, or colluded in, abuses.

One of the worst cases cited in the Murphy Report was that of Fr Patrick Maguire, a Columban priest who served in Japan between 1961 and 1974 before working in the UK and Ireland. Born in 1936, Maguire travelled between postings with 'no supervision', the report said. This was despite the fact that there was evidence that the Columbans had concerns about him as early as 1968. After thirteen years in Asia, Maguire was sent back to Ireland in 1974 when a nun in the missions complained to a bishop about his inappropriate conduct with young males. A letter from a member of the society in Japan to the head of the society in Ireland reported that Fr Maguire had a 'problem' which 'involves young male children'. Neither this nor subsequent warnings were acted upon and Maguire was later put in charge of the society's mission promotions. Between 1976 and 1979, he travelled from parish to parish speaking at Masses and in schools about the society's work. This was 'a particularly disastrous move', the report said, as it 'gave him access to every Catholic church congregation and to every Catholic school in the country, in effect, to virtually every child in the country. He duly took advantage of that access.'

In 1997, Maguire admitted to having abused about seventy young boys in a number of countries, including thirteen in Japan, as well as abusing at least one girl and grooming others. He was convicted of indecent assault in the UK and Ireland and served prison sentences in both countries. The Murphy Report said the Columbans were 'to be commended for supervising him' in recent years 'and not expelling him from the society'. However, it concluded, 'Complaints about Fr Maguire were handled very badly by his society over a period of about twenty years. A number of complaints seem to have been largely ignored or avoided; in other cases, the response was to move him somewhere else.' The report continued, 'It appears that the culture of confidentiality, the overarching concern for the welfare of the priest and the avoidance of scandal were the major contributory factors to the quite disastrous way in which this case was handled.' In a statement after the report's publication, the Missionary Society of St Columban said it was 'shamed by the findings', adding, 'It is particularly chastening that, as a society with a history of standing with the poor and the disadvantaged in many cultures, we so continuously failed vulnerable children.'

The Ryan Report was similarly damning of a number of religious congregations, citing 'endemic' physical, emotional and sexual abuse in industrial schools and reformatories. While the inquiry's remit was to focus on institutions in Ireland, its conclusions cast a pall over religious-run schools and projects in the missions where some of the same personnel operated.

One of many disturbing cases involving Christian Brothers was that of the pseudonymous Brother Adrien who was removed from St Joseph's Industrial School, Artane, Dublin in the 1960s after allegations of sexual abuse were made against him. The report said he had been identified by the residence manager in Letterfrack as early as 1959 as 'not suitable at all to handle young boys', and 'positively dangerous' in their company. Yet, the report said: 'He later spent ten years on missionary work. There is no reference in his personal card to his ever receiving any sanction or warning in relation to his abuse.'

There were other references in the report to religious personnel who had either worked in the missions or had been sent to work there after abuse allegations surfaced. These included Sr Ronja (again, a pseudonym), who was accused of beating and hitting children and being an autocratic manager at the Sisters of Charity-run St Joseph's Industrial School, Kilkenny. The report said she resigned her position at the school in 1990 and was assigned to a missionary post overseas, where it can only be assumed she continued with the same managerial style.

In the case of the Rosminians, the most missionary-oriented society among the eighteen congregations investigated by the Ryan inquiry, the report found that abuse took place at schools in counties Cork and Tipperary where young priests were trained for work in developing countries. Three former members of the Rosminian order were convicted of sexually abusing children in its care. The society told investigators it had been under pressure to keep up admissions to the school so as to maximise income from the state's capitation payment system and this created a 'trap'. The report praised the society for its candidness on this and other matters – a small comfort in the circumstances. 'The biggest contrast between the Rosminians' position and [that of] other orders,' the report said, 'was in its acceptance of responsibility for what happened in their industrial schools. Even when factors such as inadequate resources were involved, they took responsibility for tolerating them and doing nothing about it.'

It is important to stress these inquiries dealt with a mere sample of sexual abuse cases within Ireland, and it was not within their remit to investigate allegations of abuse overseas. Neither religious congregations nor the Catholic hierarchy has shown any desire – or indeed willingness – to examine the extent of wrongdoing in missionary settings. The fact that abuse victims have not – as yet – come forward in large numbers in developing countries would appear to have much to do with the taboo attached to discussing the subject there, allied to the relative difficulty in pursuing complaints. The scale of sexual abuse in remote parts of Africa, Asia and South America, where Irish missionaries held high positions of authority in schools and parishes, can therefore only be speculated upon.

Among many causes for concern is the fact that some of those clergy convicted of abuse in Ireland had previously worked as overseas missionaries. Father Gus Griffin, for example, a Holy Ghost Father who was jailed in 1998 for seven and a half years by the Dublin Circuit Criminal Court for sexually abusing two young boys, had spent several years working in Sierra Leone. Ordained in 1955, Griffin was also a former director of vocations of the Holy Ghost Fathers and former editor of its missionary magazine, *Outlook*. Thomas Naughton, who was convicted and jailed for abusing a number of altar boys while working as a priest in the Dublin Archdiocese, had previously served under the St Patrick's Missionary Society, Kiltegan, operating in Nigeria and Grenada from 1963 until 1976.

Not only has the Church shown little appetite for investigating abuse committed by missionaries, but it has largely ignored alleged crimes committed *against* them too. In 1994, Sr Maura O'Donoghue of the MMMs prepared a report on the alleged sexual abuse of nuns in more than twenty countries, mainly in Africa. She cited cases of priests demanding sex from nuns and defending it on the grounds that were they to go outside of the Church they might have a greater risk of contracting HIV. O'Donoghue referred to a 1988 incident in Malawi where leaders of a women's congregation were dismissed by a bishop when they complained that twenty-nine nuns had been made pregnant by diocesan priests, and the Clare woman reported another case where a priest took a nun for an abortion during which the sister died. The hypocrisy was complete when he officiated at the nun's requiem Mass.

In February 1995, O'Donoghue briefed Cardinal Eduardo Martinez Somalo, prefect of the Vatican's congregation for the religious life, on the content of the report. But details were not made public for a further six years, and then only because they were leaked to the US weekly, the *National Catholic Reporter*. The Vatican then acknowledged that 'the problem is known' but it claimed it was 'restricted to a limited geographic area', namely Africa. It added the matter was being dealt with in collaboration with bishops and religious superiors. However, there has been no evidence of any follow-up in the Church.

Asked whether further abuse in the missions has yet to surface, Maura O'Donoghue replies, 'Who knows? This is something the Church will have to face up to. Is there a risk? Is there a risk today? If so, it has to be addressed.'

Nairobi-based Sister of Mercy Angela Hartigan is more emphatic, having investigated, along with her colleague Sr Mary Killeen, several allegations of abuse against Kenyan clergy. While she wouldn't speculate on whether or not certain priests were likely to be prosecuted, she said, 'I think this halo of superiority [around the priesthood] is very soon going to wear off. I see it coming in my lifetime.'

A further category of abuse, the scale of which can only be guessed, is bullying. Religious congregations have a policy of keeping human resource disputes in-house, but if even a fraction of the stories missionaries tell of authoritarian superiors and vindictive colleagues are true then the sector has a serious problem with personnel management.

Former Columban James Kennedy is still bitter at some of the things he experienced and witnessed while a member of the order. He recalled how one colleague who had put in a request for laicisation was ordered by his bishop to spend the remainder of his days in the priesthood picking up litter in Phoenix Park. Along with other ex-Columbans, Kennedy formed a support group, initially called – somewhat jokingly – 'Judas Iscariot FC'. Some members testified to becoming penniless and destitute after leaving the Columbans. Others were emotionally scarred. One member of the group later wrote in confidence to its members about how he had been forced out of the Columbans after falling out with one of his superiors – a not untypical complaint. Describing exactly how he was treated in the last years of his vocation, the ex-missionary quoted the philosopher William James when he said: 'No more fiendish punishment could be devised, were such a thing physically possible, than that one should be turned loose in society and remain absolutely unnoticed by all the members thereof. If no one turned around when we entered, answered when we spoke, or minded what we did, but if every person we met "cut us dead" and acted as if we were non-existent things, a kind of rage and impotent despair would before long well up in us, from which the cruellest bodily torture would be a relief.'

In 2002, Kennedy published his memoirs, *Fat God Thin God*, a book that got a frosty reception from the Columbans. 'What really bothered me was that all of us were airbrushed out of history and I resented that very much, and that is why I said I will put my neck on the line and I will tell my story honestly and without anger.' Today, he is still riled by his experiences, and he believes some of those running Church congregations are 'now far more devious' than superiors in his day. At the last census he identified himself as Catholic but 'I was signing documents in the clinic the other day, and it came to religion and I said "none". I hope it stops there because I am not anti-anything. My policy has always been to let everyone do their own thing.' Is he happy? The married father of two puffs absent-mindedly on a cigarette before replying: 'I am enjoying the freedom of being another person, to catch up where I left off aged eighteen.'

Whatever the scale of psychological or physical abuse in religious orders, the potential for it would seem to be even greater in the missions than in Ireland due to the low standards of supervision, and the patchy reporting mechanisms, in typically remote and isolated locations. There also appears to be have been an excessive tolerance for maverick behaviour in the missions, and rogue clergy were sometimes moved overseas to avoid scandal at home. Allegations have surfaced in recent years suggesting that a number of missionary societies were aware that certain members were engaged in sexual relations and turned a blind eye to them on the presumption that they were 'consensual'. Even if this were strictly the case, however, and even if the number of individuals involved was relatively small, it is hard to justify societies overlooking what were very dubious power relations. A missionary priest who adopted a local 'wife' might try to excuse his behaviour on the basis that he was adapting to local custom. But how did the other half of such a union feel? In 2009, a Nigerian woman went public over an alleged twenty-year relationship with one of the country's archbishops, Richard Burke, a missionary from the Kiltegan Fathers, claiming the relationship began when she was a teenager and in a vulnerable situation. Archbishop Burke was suspended by the Vatican in October 2009 over the allegations. He resigned as bishop of Benin City in Nigeria in June 2010.

The fine line between consensual sex and sexual or psychological abuse can be seen in the case of a priest identified in the Murphy Report as Fr Laurentius. He had numerous sexual relationships with women in all countries and areas in which he ministered, and two young women in Dublin claimed they had been abused by him. He denied the charges but, in October 1997, provided the head of his order with a list of women who had been in his life. This showed he had a sexual relationship with eight women while in Africa, twenty-six in Ireland, and twelve in other First World locations. They included a woman who he had been counselling at the time for child sexual abuse and marital difficulties. The Murphy Report said, 'It was very clear that he was using his status as a priest and as a counsellor to meet women with whom he then had sexual relationships. This is clearly predatory, exploitative behaviour and, at a minimum, is unprofessional conduct.' Describing him as 'promiscuous man' who had resisted all attempts at disciplining him, the report also noted, 'Church authorities seem to be remarkably tolerant of breaches of their rules where sexual activity with adults is concerned.'

As a whole, missionary societies appear to have dealt with abuse allegations no better or worse than other religious congregations. They have been afflicted by the same dysfunctional channels of communication and at times skewed priorities as Irish dioceses. Within the missionary cohort, however, there are some individuals who emerged from the scandals with some credit. One of these was Fr Michael Mernagh, an Augustinian priest who walked from Cobh to Dublin in solidarity with clerical child sex abuse victims after the publication of a 2008 Catholic agency report which strongly criticised child-protection measures in the diocese of Cloyne. The idea for the 'walk of atonement' came when the 70-year-old priest returned to Ireland for a Christmas break from South Africa, where he had been working on a township community project. Horrified by the details of the report and uncomfortable with his own awareness of rumours and stories of clerical sexual abuse over the previous twenty years, he did what came naturally to missionaries: he took action, ill-defined and instinctive, but action nonetheless.

'The day of thinking and talking was over,' he recalled, 'so I said, "I will walk the walk."'[42] He woke in the middle of the night before Christmas Eve and, telling no one, got into his car in Meath Street, Dublin and drove to Cobh. There he maintained a three-day vigil outside St Colman's Cathedral, seat of the bishop of Cloyne, Dr John Magee. He then began a 300-km walk back to the capital, finishing at Dublin's Pro-Cathedral on 6 January 2009, where he was applauded by a waiting crowd and embraced by Archbishop of Dublin, Dr Diarmuid Martin. Two months later, Dr Magee, who himself had a missionary background, having served for eight years as a Kiltegan priest in Nigeria, stood down from governance in the diocese of Cloyne. He resigned as bishop in March 2010.

Other missionaries have expressed genuine remorse at the way in which abuse allegations were handled, and have advocated a new era of transparency. In the wake of the Ryan Report, the Kiltegan priest and theologian Donal Dorr confessed that even those 'who had no immediate or direct responsibility for what happened' had a responsibility to make some reparation. In an article for *The Irish Catholic* under the headline 'I'm Sorry', Dorr said he agreed with the view that power, sex and class were the sources of the abuse. 'How could we have lived so long with such a warped approach to sexuality?' he asked, adding, 'It did not occur to me to consider, still less to enquire more deeply into, the abusive nature of a system which I see now could scarcely have existed or continued were it not for the deficiencies in our theological teaching and understanding in the past. I want now to say that I am deeply sorry about this.'[43] Those who worked closely with vulnerable children, migrants and victims of abuse overseas, have felt the betrayal of offending peers more than most. Asked whether she believes the legacy of missionaries has been damaged by the abuse scandals, O'Donoghue replies, 'I think legacy is a minor detail really for most people. The effects, the consequences, for people who have been abused are what have upset people. It is why I am now involved in anti-trafficking.'

Many missionaries describe the issue of abuse in their field as a 'timebomb', implicitly acknowledging the probability of skeletons lurking in cupboards. Their fear is palpable, as is their depression over existing scandals. With vocations in Ireland all but wiped out and the reputation of the Church at a low ebb, the more pertinent question appears to be not 'what future will missionaries have?' but 'will they have a future at all?'

Adding to the gloom is the sight of traumatised peers in Ireland. By being out of the country during the various domestic Church scandals, many missionaries feel like they dodged a bullet and as a result have something close to survivors' guilt. Fr Joseph Kearny, a Jesuit who has spent thirty-six years in Zambia, told *The Irish Catholic* during a visit to Ireland in the wake of the Ryan Report that the 'real heroes of the day' were not the missionaries but 'the ones that stayed behind'. He said 'the real heroes are the ones that battle it out here in the face of so much opposition and the low morale and even being humiliated. For me they are the ones who have the strongest faith, to be able to carry on like that.'[44] Such expressions of sympathy for Irish-based religious are common among missionaries. 'I think missionaries would feel less disappointed than the priests and religious here in Ireland,' says Fr Aylward. 'They feel a great sense of accomplishment and it's a downer for them to see how the Church is viewed in this country.'

The legacy of the countless Sr Colombière Kellys and Fr Robbie MacCabes can't, and shouldn't, be erased from the history books because of the crimes of a relatively small minority of Irish clergy. In the absence of full transparency of their operations, however, missionaries are inadvertently leaving a question mark hanging above themselves. Where wrongdoing has been identified, moreover, they have proven to be their own worst enemies. This was shown especially in the MMMs' handling of successive controversies at Our Lady of Lourdes Hospital in Drogheda. When serious failings in obstetric care were identified, affecting more than 100 women, the MMMs stubbornly denied responsibility and then refused to contribute to a state compensation scheme for victims. An inquiry into the high number of hysterectomies at the hospital showed the nuns' style of patient management left a lot to be desired. It was revealed that the MMMs, among other things, sought and took advice from the late Cardinal Tomás Ó Fiaich on medical and legal matters rather than getting independent, professional help.

'I think congregations as a whole are suspicious of the outside world and the Ryan Report has pushed them down a bit further,' says Anne Garbutt, an Oxford-based development specialist who has been involved in assessing the work of Irish missionaries for funding agencies. There is something of a vicious circle: reticence breeds suspicion, which in turn tarnishes the missionaries' reputation and legacy. Even when discussing purely developmental work, missionaries tend to open up only on their own terms. Thus, all we are left with are snapshots of missionary work that we must take on trust, or not – snapshots like that of Sr Cyril Mooney in Kolkata.

'Essentially what we have here is a good Catholic school with close to 1,400 children. We don't have any glass on our notice boards and yet nothing is ever scribbled on or spoiled,' she says proudly. 'For some of these children, they have no mothers. This is their home.' As the conversation turns to religion and spirituality, she remarks: 'God is very much part of everyday life here. If someone loses their father they have no problem going around in a bit of thread, shaving their head and letting everyone know their father has died and now they are doing all the religious rituals necessary. You'd never get that in Ireland. Hardly anyone admits they have belief there anymore.'

And with that, the lights go out on Sealdah Day School. The pressures on energy in Kolkata mean power shortages are an almost daily occurrence. Mooney searches for a torch, makes do instead with three candles and helps light her exit. In their rooms the children giggle and chatter excitedly, unable to sleep because of the blackout. Mooney picks up a copy of *The Chronicles of Narnia*.

'Who's for a bedtime story?'

CHAPTER 8: IDEOLOGY – THE MISSIONARY POSITION

'He has sent me to bring the good news to the poor, to proclaim liberty to captives and to the blind new sight, to set the downtrodden free, to proclaim the Lord's year of favour.' (Luke 4:18)

At a cursory glace, Irish Catholic missionaries seem fairly homogenous. Sure, don't they all read the same scripture? Aren't they all pursuing the one goal? In truth, the missionary field – like any other occupational sector – has its disagreements, personality clashes, bitching and splits. And these divisions run deep within the movement. Missionary priests and nuns do a lot of thinking about their work because they have committed their entire lives to it. They have made sacrifices and have foregone the comforts of family, marriage and home. So, understandably, they are capable of expressing strong views about why they do what they do. And, as you'd expect from a group of people whose job-spec includes reflection, prayer and contemplation, they have each developed their own idiosyncratic and highly personal outlook. All things considered, there are probably as many ideologies of missionary work as there are missionaries.

Take Michael Lynch. He is not what you'd expect from a Christian Brother. A rapid-talking, humorous character who likes to quote Albert Einstein and is disparaging about man-made institutions, he has made a name for himself advancing the cause of penal reform in Paraguay. 'My aim is to close prisons, and any opportunity I get I advocate it.' On a brief trip back to Ireland to visit his elderly mother, he agrees to talk, but with the usual proviso for a missionary interviewee that anything that's put down on paper will avoid puffing him up. 'If someone says after reading this, "Isn't he a great fella," I would be disappointed,' he says. 'I want them to think about closing prisons.'

Lynch went to Paraguay after spending fifteen years in Christian Brothers schools in Ireland, teaching woodwork and technical drawing. His colleagues had proposed missionary life for him but 'I ran from it' – until his fortieth birthday. 'I said, "I have twenty years or more left," and I said, "Is this what I want to do with the rest of my life?" I was very happy with what I was doing. But I don't think it's the job of the religious to be too happy. You are meant to be a bit uneasy, a little different, odd maybe.'

After speaking to his superiors about a possible vacancy overseas, he went back to his mother's home in Drimnagh, Dublin and took out an atlas. 'I didn't know where Paraguay was,' he admits, and – as a nature lover – he was disappointed to find it 'landlocked and flat'. A crash course in Spanish later and he was on a plane to Asuncion, with no clear plan as to what he would do when he arrived.

On one of his first outings in the city, he walked past a prison. He was told not to even think about going there. He was warned that prisons were a lost cause; there was too much violence, drugs and corruption. But that just spurred him on. 'Where do you go? You go where nobody wants to go. And who do you speak for? You speak not only for those who don't have a voice but for those who society doesn't want to listen to. They were my mission statements.'

In the cramped conditions – 'the smell of urine is still in my nose' – he met young men and children in bad physical shape. They had nothing to do but sit around, take drugs and trade their criminal expertise. 'I said, "OK, I have a decision: I could walk out of here, or I can try to do something." I said to myself, "I'm a teacher, I can teach."' He pulled a twig off a dead tree in the yard and used it to start teaching maths in the dust on the ground. 'I thought it was great: I could write in the sand, and rub it out. And that's how it started, a little group around me, teaching simple maths, addition and subtraction.'

The informal classroom moved indoors, and eventually it grew into a school, with computers and more teaching staff. Lynch became a state employee, first as a teacher, then as a social worker, then as a deputy governor and finally as a governor of not one but two prisons. These included Panchito López, a notoriously overcrowded lock-up where violent clashes between guards and prisoners were commonplace. Despite the many risks, he had stayed healthy. Now aged 56, he looks like a man at least ten years younger. His tightly-cut dark hair and beard are only partly turning grey, and he retains an athletic physique, a firm handshake and a bright, expressive face. He is comfortable in any company and had a policy, when he started his prison ministry, to sit with prisoners and sip *tereré*, a communal brew of cold tea which was passed around from one hardened criminal to the next and sucked through a shared metal straw. Sure, it was unhygienic but Lynch wanted to 'avoid offence' and 'the Lord has looked after me', he says. Needless to say, the phrase 'hardened criminal' is not in his vocabulary. 'There is no such thing as a bad person. There are people who do bad things.'

In a discussion of the ideology of missionaries, Lynch – and his views about human nature – is as good a place to start as any. The Dubliner, who talks about his work in a circumlocutory manner, sees people as inherently good. He is optimistic. He is practical. All these are typical missionary characteristics. But, as Lynch flits from one subject to another (and another, and another), it's hard to discern a concrete philosophy – other than firm opposition to 'fear and anger', what he calls 'the two cancers in society'. Refusing to be pigeonholed on the left or right, he criticises lazy teachers in one breath and laments modern consumerism in another. He quotes socially radical scripture, while also invoking businessman Ben Dunne as a role model for prison management – because 'he would see income and expenditure and say, "These prisons are not value for money".' (Lynch, it need be stated no more, advocates the closure of prisons.)

Are there contradictions in Lynch's outlook? He doesn't think so. His faith provides consistency. Asked what keeps him motivated, he leans forward and his dark, deep-set eyes sharpen in focus. 'I believe in it,' he says. 'I believe in it. I believe in it.' His accent wavers between South America and the south-east, where he spent many of his teaching years. 'I feel very sorry for the person who fails. I have an auld soft spot for the guy who is down.'

What is the missionary position? Lynch is an example of how difficult it is to attribute an ideology. Even to suggest that missionaries have such a thing will prompt much questioning and resistance. Priests and nuns prefer to speak of having a 'spirituality' or a 'charism'. An ideology sounds much too permanent and missionaries are chameleonic by nature. They have to be in order to survive in the very different settings where they work. Being a committed Marxist doesn't make much sense if, say, your community's greatest need is micro-finance. The fluidity of missionaries also comes from the fact that they tend to do their theology on the hoof. Rather than using a theory to try to sort out a problem, they generally prefer first to practise – get their hands dirty and directly engage with the situation – and then make sense of their actions afterwards.

'Irish missionaries are like Irish people. We are basically not hugely intellectual as a whole,' says Donal Dorr, Kiltegan priest and author of several books on the missions, including the influential *Option for the Poor: A Hundred Years of Vatican Social Teaching.*

As the closest thing we have to an intellectual Irish missionary, it might sound like he is taking a potshot at his peers. Far from it. Turning Irish anti-intellectualism into an asset, he says: 'By and large, theology would be a reflection of reality; that would be my view of the nature of theology. In that sense, although this sounds a bit arrogant, I think missionaries – because they are on the frontiers – are developing the practice and the theory is coming along behind it.'

What of the theory? The Vatican periodically issues encyclicals which are meant to guide Catholics in their life and religious personnel – missionaries included – in their work. The first such instruction with a modern, social dimension came in 1891 with *Rerum Novarum* (Of New Things), on the condition of the working classes. It warned against unbridled capitalism, supporting the right to private property but also the right to form trade unions. This message – gently critical of the economic status quo – changed little for the next seventy years. Regarding 'Catholic Social Doctrine' during this period, Dorr wrote, 'While theoretically offering "a third way" that was neither capitalist nor socialist, in practice it gave solid religious legitimation to the "free enterprise" model of society.' He said: 'The Church still challenged the ideology of liberal capitalism; but its opposition to socialism was far more explicit, systematic and effective.'[45] The Church's insistence on 'rendering unto Caesar that which is Caesar's' was paramount. Before the Second Vatican Council in 1962–5, the Church saw itself almost exclusively as a vehicle for personal salvation. Crudely speaking, it did not think its job was to address causes of injustice in society but rather to teach people to grin and bear them. It proclaimed itself to be above politics which, in practice, meant it was politically promiscuous. The Vatican would get into bed with either democratic or dictatorial governments so long as it would be free to run its churches unmolested.

The Church's relative disinterest in social justice in the pre-

Vatican II era filtered down to parish level. For the average Catholic, faith was not measured by your commitment to fighting homelessness or child poverty but rather your ability to memorise the 'Penny Catechism'. In line with such thinking, missionaries were charged with teaching personal salvation, or crudely 'saving souls'. Matthew 28 was the catch-cry: 'Go then to all people everywhere and make them my disciples: baptise them in the name of the Father, the Son and the Holy Spirit, and teach them to obey everything I have commanded you.' Those who answered the call didn't care much about the political milieu in which they worked. Performing the sacraments was all.

'There was a kind of religious imperialism,' says Spiritan Fr Brian O'Toole. 'And the missionary was seen as a hero – the Marlboro man, or the Lone Ranger.' Those missionaries who left Ireland did so without any specialist training. Their main task – articulated forcefully by their bishops – was to secure a rising number of baptisms one year after the next. But how they would go about that was left unsaid. Unprepared, and typically ignorant of local customs and even the basics of the local language, missionaries often fell back on the authoritarian and paternalistic culture with which they had grown up in Ireland. 'We had bad theory but good practice,' Dorr insists. 'If you ask some of the older missionaries what they were doing they would say we were going out to save souls, or something along those lines. But in practice they were far better than that.' He cites the case of a now deceased Kiltegan, 'a very saintly guy' but 'old-style evangelical', who worked in a predominantly Muslim community fifty-odd years ago. 'I asked him about the Muslims: "Did you think they were saved?" And he replied, "Ah well!"' Dorr puts on a deep, gravely voice. '"The mercy of God was looking after them." His heart was saying something far better than the old theory. I don't think anyone really believed the theory, that's what it boiled down to.'

Dorr's verdict is perhaps overly sympathetic to the early missionaries. In truth, there were no serious questions asked about the nature of missionary work for long stretches of the twentieth century, and this generated an uncritical approach in the field. The righteousness of the work of Irish priests and nuns was assumed. No one stopped to ask whether they should be trying to convert people of other faiths or whether they should be running colonial schools and hospitals – usually, somewhat ironically, under a British flag. *Herder Correspondence*, a religious affairs periodical edited by the writer Desmond Fennell, put it thus in an article in 1968:

> The Irish missionary movement hitherto has been a combination of Irish vitality, generosity, skill in human relations, intellectual incuriosity, and general mental uncultivatedness with Anglo-Saxon pragmatism. Its predominant spirit has been that of the man who hacks his way into a burning house to rescue people trapped there. Unreflective, rushing to answer call after call of dire need, working under the tyrannous pressure of necessities seen as urgent and unlimited, the Irish missionaries have not paused to get to know themselves and the specific culture… which they brought with them and embodied. They have not taken the time off to survey the human landscape of their endeavours, to study its contours.[46]

Things began to change with Vatican II, which sought to modernise Church teaching and reorder the relationship between parishioner and priest. One of the most radical declarations of the Second Ecumenical Council, which sat under two popes and finished its work in 1965, was in relation to faiths such as Buddhism, Confucianism and Islam. 'The Catholic Church rejects nothing which is true and holy in these religions,' the Council concluded.

'She looks with sincere respect upon those ways of conduct and of life, those rules and teachings which often reflect a ray of that Truth which enlightens all men.' This was alien thinking to many missionaries in the field and a world removed from the philosophy of Blowick and Galvin.

Instead of indoctrination, the buzz word post-Vatican II was 'inculturation'. Missionaries were urged to be more sympathetic to other cultures; to work *with* them rather than against them. In tandem with this was a more fundamental shift that Dorr associates with the Irish word *lách*, or solidarity. 'The first shift was simply about having a more human relationship with people; having an ease with them,' he says. 'There was a kind of humanising that came in after Vatican II, a kind of softness. Words we would put on it afterwards were "being in solidarity with people, being open with people, having an open house".'

This was not a seamless transition. Older missionaries found the new theology hard to take. Dorr recalls the liberal theologian Enda McDonagh giving a talk at Dalgan Park in the late 1960s 'and some of the older missionaries were absolutely shocked. They felt their traditional understanding of mission – which they felt was the only one – was being completely undermined'. On the other hand, younger religious were pushing for more radical change, and new recruits were asking some very awkward questions. 'Vocation directors suddenly found themselves required to provide well-reasoned arguments for missionary work,' wrote Edmund Hogan in his history of the missions, 'and were unable to turn to a serious mission literature for answers.'

Liberation theology and development theory were now in vogue. In his 1967 encyclical *Populorum Progressio*, Pope Paul VI famously said 'development is the new name for peace'. *The Wall Street Journal* called the encyclical 'warmed-over communism'. A meeting of Latin American bishops in Medellin, Columbia in 1968 further radicalised the Church. Citing growing demands for 'full emancipation' and 'liberation from every form of servitude', the bishops proclaimed: 'We perceive the first indications of the painful birth of a new civilisation.' As well as committing the Church in Latin America to combating social injustice, the Medellin conference gave rise to a wave of new, liberal voices. These included the Spanish missionary Fr Pedro Arrupe, who first used the phrase 'the preferential option for the poor' in reference to the duty of Christians. The 'option' spoken of here was not a choice but rather a positive discrimination for the poor that Arrupe and others felt should be institutionalised in the Church. Much of this new thinking was brought about by the major global upheavals of the late 1960s. Old-style colonialism was dying out, but in its place came the Cold War and proxy battles between East and West.

Fr Jim Crowe, who arrived in Brazil a year after the Medellin conference, was one of those swept up in the liberation theology movement. Would he have been political before arriving in Brazil? 'I would have been, I suppose. I was always, even as a student in the seminary, very much preoccupied with the whole thing of religion and life, faith and life – which is political.' Inasmuch as it would have impinged on life in his homeland of rural Clare, Crowe feels he had a one-sided view of the Cold War until he came to Brazil in the late 1960s. 'We were brought up in a situation where America was good and communism was bad… When Kennedy became president, that highlighted that for the Irish especially. If you wanted to save the world, it was America that was going to save it. And you had to be saved from the bad boys – the communists.'

Not every Irish missionary working in South America in the early 1970s would have been caught up in radicalism of Medellin ('half and half' is how Crowe remembers it), but few would have taken a stand against it. He remembers a Redemptorist priest called Joe Hanrahan, who was made a bishop in a very poor area.

'Liberation theology would not have been a strong point for him, but at the same time he wouldn't have gone against. A very short time after he went in there [as bishop], there was a parade for land reform. They stopped in front of his house and asked him to join them, and he said, "If it's for land, no Irishman will go against it." And he joined them. Shortly after that, two French priests – they were of his diocese – were jailed for supporting the land-reform movement. This was by the military regime. He took on their defence, and every court case, he was at it. He died very quickly of a bleeding ulcer, but there was a strong rumour at the time that it was poisoned he was.'

Pope Paul VI gave the liberation theologians further succour when in 1975 he published *Evangelii Nuntiandi*, an apostolic exhortation on freedom from oppression. Many people ignored such documents, and perhaps Irish religious were more prone to do so than others, but 'they give me a context to work; they give me a clout,' says O'Toole who joined the Spiritans in 1980 and spent thirteen years in Ethiopia. 'I got the go ahead and imperative to do mission from those two encyclicals – *Populorum Progressio* and *Evangelii Nuntiandi* – they were the breakthrough.' These papal statements also influenced formation at missionary colleges. At Dalgan Park, young priests were instructed in how to set up co-ops and credit unions, and a number of them were sent to university to study tropical agriculture. 'We moved,' says Fr John Guiney, a Jesuit who cut his teeth politically on civil rights and anti-apartheid marches, 'and with that, we moved almost to the other side from having a religious or spiritual ideology to promoting a social ideology. It was almost like swinging with the signs of the times and the challenge was always trying to find a balance.'

The pope himself had difficulty striking such a balance. In January 1979, John Paul II gave a significant address at a Catholic conference in Puebla, Mexico. With liberation theology in vogue, the pope reaffirmed *Evangelii Nuntiandi* and said the Church should not back down from Medellin. But he spoke out strongly against those who 'purport to depict Jesus as a political activist, as a fighter against Roman domination and the authorities, and even as someone involved in the class struggle'.

Other papal statements followed, notably in 1987 when John Paul II published encyclicals on social concerns, *Sollicitudo Rei Socialis*, which addressed the question of underdevelopment. This was followed by *Redemptoris Missio* in 1990, which spelled out the Church's missionary mandate with a view to revitalising missionary work. Over time, the Vatican grew uncomfortable with liberation theology, and the assassination in March 1980 of Óscar Romero, the outspoken Archbishop of San Salvador, reminded the Church that engaging in politics carried serious risks. Reinforcing the point cruelly was the murder of six leading Catholic intellectuals in El Salvador in 1989. These included Fr Amando López, who studied theology at Dublin's Milltown Institute and was ordained there in 1965. López preached that the root cause of the conflict in El Salvador was 'wealth distribution' but along with his colleagues he was shunned by the Salvadorian bishops, one of whom was chaplain to the armed forces. The murder of the six Jesuits, killed alongside two women to leave no witnesses, silenced what was one of the last major fronts of liberation theology in the Church. The left-wing author Noam Chomsky has described the killings as nothing less than the 'end of Christianity'.[47]

In the last twenty years, there has been a further shift in missionary priorities. While Irish missionaries are firmly embedded in development work, they are now more involved in areas like community building and peace and reconciliation. 'You are not a handyman anymore,' says O'Toole, 'that concept is a thing of the past.' Instead missionaries emphasise their role as facilitators, catalysts for change or 'capacity-builders' – to use the development sector jargon.

Events like the 1994 Rwandan genocide gave missionaries cause for deeper reflection. How could such bloodshed occur in a largely Catholic country, people asked? The general conclusion was that the Church had passed on its teaching in a very superficial way, in Rwanda and in other countries. In the wake of such deliberations, many missionaries felt they could be best deployed in conflict resolution. Others turned to inter-faith dialogue, a principal concern of Pope Benedict XVI. 'Mission life has moved from "doing" more into "witnessing",' says O'Toole. 'There is no such thing as an individual missionary anymore because every missionary is working in the local church. You are coming not as a crusader but as a guest.'

This evolution in missionary thought occurred in all Catholic missions, not just the Irish ones. Is there, then, a specific Irish missionary philosophy? Many missionaries themselves would believe so, and they typically cite Ireland's history of famine and colonialism as having created a shared empathy for the world's poor. These two historical experiences have contributed to a 'closeness' between Irish missionaries and the people with whom they work, according to the Jesuit Fr Michael Kelly. 'The memory of the Great Famine is something that is written into our psyche. Irish missionaries are not able to go to bed easy each night with the knowledge that across the world thousands of people are dying of hunger, most of them children.' As for the colonial experience, it helped Irish missionaries to relate better to people in the newly independent countries of the 1960s and 1970s, he says. Dorr agrees with this analysis, saying: 'I am from the west of Ireland, and one thought that came to my mind one time was the nearer I can be to the mentality of Mayo, where I grew up, the closer I am to Africa.'

An Irish culture of flexibility and casualness – and a disdain for strict rule-keeping – has also rubbed off on missionaries. Irish religious congregations have traditionally decentralised decision-making, which suits the mentality of rural populations, especially in Africa. Asked if he thought there was a specific Irish missionary identity, Dorr replies, 'I do. I really do… We are not too ideological. The French have this *analyse logique*, and this theory about what should be done, and it's extraordinarily valuable and thank God for it; that's their strength. And the Dutch, the Dutch are fabulous, amazing. There is a kind of doggedness in the Dutch personality,' he stops for a moment and giggles. 'Somehow, the Irish are a bit more fluid. I hope that is not boasting. I am talking about something in the Irish character.'

It would be a mistake to generalise, though, as different congregations have different styles. Marists, for example, are deliberately low key and go about their work 'quietly, because', as they say in their literature, 'that is how Mary carried out her role in the early church'. The Marist philosophy is to be present with people, to sit with them and to be still. They don't want attention. They will live with people on the margins – prisoners, for example – without becoming an advocate on penal reform. In contrast, the members of a society like the Redemptorists attract more publicity. They are more involved in community development and not afraid to agitate on behalf of others. In a domestic setting, a classic of the Redemptorist model is Fr Alex Reid, whose work with deprived Catholic communities in west Belfast brought him close to many leading Republicans. (He went on to play a role in brokering the IRA's ceasefires in the 1990s.) In short, Marists would be less political than Redemptorists, but does that mean one is better than the other? 'I think both are valid,' the Redemptorist priest Fr Gerry O'Connor replies. 'You will get people who have a wonderfully articulate voice on human rights but will never have spent much time with someone in pain, or who is anguished.'

Trying to identify a single missionary model is also undermined by generational differences. Sr Majella McCarron, Shell Oil's irritant, says people who joined the missions in the 1960s and 1970s are more likely to have shifted from a 'theology of redemption' to a 'theology of liberation'. The former, in its crudest form, decreed that those who were baptised were 'saved' and those unbaptised damned. And it followed from this thinking that your energy, as a missionary, should be devoted to performing the sacraments. 'If you have been working in one theological paradigm, and you attach your whole internal meaning to that paradigm, then it's very hard to move to another one – as the move to liberation theology would require. It's like asking you to be a Marxist if you are a Catholic,' she says. 'I don't think you should even demand it. Nobody over forty could negotiate the transition easily without being totally disrupted mentally. It's as strong as that.'

The generational influence can be seen in someone like Fr John Guiney who was born in 1953 and cut his teeth on protests when he was in his early twenties. He studied politics at UCD and French and philosophy in NUI, Maynooth. 'The 1970s was a time of change in the air, and there was a tremendous sense as Jesuits and students at UCD that we were part of this change and we were going to change the world. There was a great idealism – and naivety… At that time, I spent most of my time on the streets. We were protesting about the Irish going to South Africa to play rugby. We were protesting against Outspan oranges coming into Ireland. We were protesting against the bombings of the IRA. We were a very politicised generation – both within and without the Jesuits. It was a time of excitement.' What were his key influences? He lists three: Mahatma Gandhi; Paulo Freire, the educationalist; and Julius Nyerere, the Tanzanian president whose promotion of *ujamaa* – becoming a person through the community – 'fascinated me'. The Jesuits moved its offices from Milltown to Gardiner Place, and many of its members – Fr Peter McVerry included – started new works with the poor. 'The thinking at the time was, "Be inserted with them. Don't do your studies and theology just from a desk at Milltown Park or UCD, or in Trinity, but do it in the community and among the people." There was a strong feeling in the Jesuits that they wanted to take option for the poor seriously.' After joining the Jesuits, Guiney was sent to teach in Belvedere College – 'to cool down' – and later assigned to Tanzania. 'Probably any other congregation would have kicked me out. The Jesuits had a tremendous breadth of formation. They said you have to test out your beliefs in the real world, and you are given enough rope to hang yourself, and you are allowed to make choices.' Thus began a career which took Guiney to Ethiopia, Kenya, Sudan and Uganda, working for long periods with refugees and displaced people.

Looking back on his first trip to Africa thirty years ago, he admits both he and his peers were somewhat innocent about socialism and how it would cure all the continent's ills. It turned out *ujamaa* wasn't quite so perfect as Tanzania went into a tailspin of corruption and incompetence. Guiney says he realised there was a difference between promoting the 'equality of people' and the 'equalisation of people' by suppressing individual initiative. 'We are all equal but we are not all equal in the same skills, in terms of initiative, and to impose equality is to impose a standard of life that is actually dehumanising, and that is what happened to many people in Tanzania. We did not allow people with initiative to generate wealth, and that was the key issue in practice.' The disappointment he felt in Tanzania was replicated by left-leaning missionaries in other parts of the world. 'I think a lot of thinking within the Church at the time was probably a bit naive. My contemporaries might bark at me for saying it but I think so.'

He says those missionaries who campaigned for the poor in developing countries were 'on the right side – in terms of standing in solidarity with the reality of what people were experiencing. But, you have to say, what we are not experts on is creating sound models of economic development.' You must show solidarity if you want to achieve justice but, he says, there is a question over how to secure justice 'in the long term, given the realities of our economies, and how economic rules work in our world.' He continues: 'There has to be a pragmatism. I think that has been the great wake-up call to the social activists of the 1970s, to the social activists of the 1980s and 1990s. Put it like this, some of us in our social justice campaigns in the 1970s and 1980s put ideology before the gospels.'

Listening to Guiney speak about the need for 'people with initiative to generate wealth' in society, it might be tempting to think missionaries are really misunderstood capitalists. Even the placard-wielding rebel Majella McCarron doesn't want to be labelled a socialist. 'I wouldn't be trapped by a system, or party, or ideology. Every system is beset by the human condition. Every system, just like every organisation, has to be monitored and regulated,' she says. 'The human condition has to be confronted. I call it "sinfulness". Other people call it "evil".'

In Brazil, Fr Jim Crowe says many of the missionaries he knows have, with age, grown wary of ideological extremities, but he proudly describes himself as a socialist and wonders how anyone could fail to be drawn to the principles of wealth redistribution 'if they're living in the situation we're living in'. He is still fond of the phrase made famous by Hélder Câmara, the late Archbishop of Olinda and Recife: 'When I give food to the poor, they call me a saint. When I ask why the poor have no food, they call me a communist.'

On reflection, the difficulty in nailing missionaries to a particular ideology should be expected. For the likes of Guiney, McCarron and Crowe the division between capitalism and socialism is nothing compared to the chasm between material existence and the word of God. 'I would say the Bible guides me,' says Crowe. 'There are different ways of reading the Bible or reading the Gospel in any situation… I would say after all my years in the seminary, studying the

Bible every day, I only understood the Bible and the gospel in the Brazilian situation. You can take hundreds of examples. The gospel statement that "all may have life and have it in abundance". What does that mean for those who are in the shantytowns? "Peace be with you." What does that mean in a violent situation? "Do not be afraid." What does that mean when you're circled by guns? It takes on a very practical, down-to-earth meaning.'

If Jim Crowe is any way representative of missionaries it explains why their thinking can be contradictory. How could it be any different when the Bible itself is open to so many rival interpretations? Missionaries, then, are perhaps best described as members of a club, a very broad-based club, with old, young, conservative and liberal. Some members barely relate to one another. Some are close-knit, like family. As such, they are capable of disagreeing with one another – and disagreeing strongly – while also having deep affection for one another. Sr McCarron notes that when she goes to her motherhouse, of the seventy nuns there, sixty-five are still in traditional veils. 'That is very symbolic for me. It's not symbolic of either left, right, back or front but of a specific paradigm.' While she has close bonds with these elderly nuns, she tends not to discuss her work with them, 'because it's too disturbing and it's too demanding. I've great sympathy for that, and I treat that with great gentleness because people who have been thirty, forty years in mission have a very particular understanding of their religious call.'

Within this missionary club, there are inevitably those who look to the future and those who are nostalgic for the past. There are those who call for change and those who want more of the same. 'We've got to get away from this idea that missionaries only go overseas,' says Lynch, the Christian Brother who falls into the reformist category. 'We got caught up some time ago in a kind of preferential option for the poor, and that got tied down to whether people had money or did not have money, and it lost its focus. In fact, every person in society is called to be a missionary – to care for the weak and the vulnerable.'

Some missionaries believe that the collapse of vocations in Ireland should be used as an opportunity to refocus the direction of the missionary movement. As well as trying to bring missionaries 'home', congregations should create more opportunity for lay involvement, it is argued. Not everyone agrees, though, and some pose the uncomfortable question: if a lay person can be a missionary, then what's so special about those priests and nuns who make a lifelong commitment to the job?

A significant number of missionaries believe the decline in vocations is linked to the very process of modernisation. They point to the fact that the congregations which have done best at attracting new recruits – the Dominicans, for example – are at the conservative end of the Catholic spectrum. To tap into the idealism of young people, the argument goes, you need to offer certainty and a unique life-goal, rather than a wishy-washy notion of religious commitment. The difference of opinion on this matter is mirrored in a broader dispute over the purpose of missionaries. Liberal theologians like Donal Dorr and the Columban Seán McDonagh are very vocal but far from representative. The rather more silent majority is cautious of reform, believing that undermining the foundations of the missionary movement could further demoralise its members and accelerate its decline. Elderly missionaries are particularly conscious of how the 'opening up' of the Church in the 1970s and 1980s coincided with thousands of defections. As celibacy was increasingly questioned, scores of priests and nuns became laicised and a large proportion of them went on to get married.

The debate in this area can get hot and heavy at times, as illustrated when Fr Seán McDonagh and Dr Vincent Twomey, prominent theologian, staunch defender of Pope Benedict and member of the Divine Word Missionaries, traded public insults over the question of whether evangelisation should still be part of missionary work. In an exchange on the letters page of *The Irish Catholic*, McDonagh suggested Twomey was downplaying the importance of peace and justice issues, while Twomey accused the environmentalist of being 'blinded by his ideological blinkers'.[48] At the heart of the argument was a key question of emphasis. While 'justice, peace and the integrity of creation' quite evidently had their place in the mission of the Church, Twomey wrote, 'What I see as the undermining of the missionary zeal of the Church is the reduction of that mission almost exclusively to such concerns.' Arguing that missionaries needed to address people's 'spiritual and moral poverty' as well as their 'material poverty', Twomey claimed 'the way the Church leads people out of the desert is primarily through evangelisation. This is a term that has almost disappeared from discourse on the missions.'[49]

Whatever about the merits of Twomey's thesis, he has a point about evangelism being laid on thin these days. If you spoke to someone like the former accountant turned priest Gerry O'Connor, for example, you might be lured into thinking he is simply a highly committed and extremely professional aid worker. Until, that is, discussion drifts to his faith. 'I always come back to this sense that missionaries trust that God has created the world, and so we are called to love the creation, which includes the people and the earth,' he says. 'Our inspiration is Jesus Christ who was of God and dwelt amongst the people. So, as missionaries, our job is to dwell among the people and feel their pain as Jesus felt our pain.' It's a highly demanding mission statement, and it articulates a sort of theological backstop for many missionaries. This holds, roughly, that everyone on Earth is part of the Body of Christ and therefore we have a responsibility to all; we are all brothers and sisters. Call this philosophy creationist if you like but, really, it's more to do with egalitarianism. Missionaries have a deep commitment to, or profound appreciation of, the equality of humankind.

But, using these broad brush-strokes, are we any closer to articulating a specific Irish missionary identity? At best perhaps we have some 'family resemblances', and these include: a strong practical emphasis; physical strength or energy; courage in the line of fire; single-mindedness and occasional contrariness; a good work ethic; excessive humility; a fluid ideology; a belief system not fixed in dogma but rooted in the circumstances of the day; and a willingness – or even impulse – to go against the grain. As a general point, you might say Irish missionaries are not ideologues, they are personality types, and what defines them best is not their beliefs – or indeed the words they speak – but their actions.

Brother Michael Lynch proves this point. When faced with the challenge of reforming a broken prison, he didn't have a firm idea as to what he would do – or how he would do it – but almost instinctively he acted. He had no notion to where his actions would lead and was necessarily uncertain about the future, as he admits. 'If you'd asked me at 40 would I go down this road, knowing what I do now, knowing that I'd see all that I saw, I would say "No". It's maybe better not to know what is on the road ahead of you.'

Is it fair to say missionaries act before they think? Perhaps so, when looking at the great sweep of missionary history. But in individual cases the relationship between the mind and the body is more complex. Lynch, for example, is informed by both scripture and experience when he approaches the issue of crime and punishment. He is guided on the one hand by a strong sense of the equality of humankind and on the other by practical lessons learnt as governor of a tough prison. He is inspired by the theoretical example of Jesus Christ but also the very tangible example of the prisoners' mothers. They inspire him, he says, by sticking by their children even when they fail and fail again. 'I think mothers are saints,' he says, 'and it's that fire in the belly that we all need, that example of motherhood that says we are not going to abandon anyone – be it our family, or the larger family in society.'

Explaining his attitude to crime and punishment, he continues, 'When healing is done that's justice. It is nothing to do with revenge, and equalling the scales.' But how do we go about healing? It starts, counterintuitively, with helping the perpetrator, Lynch believes. You provide him with clothes and documentation – basic stuff that might help him get a job. You get him an appointment with a doctor to try to get him off drugs. You get him into a home when he leaves prison. You support his family so he doesn't have to steal to put food on the table. You encourage him to face up to his crimes and to make amends. Sometimes it works, sometimes it doesn't. Lynch describes how one of his clients redeemed himself by paying compensation to his victim and how another was shown charity by a neighbouring family and repaid them by robbing them of all their furniture. It is tough work, fuzzy and uncertain, and it shouldn't be confused with 'restorative justice', Lynch insists. This he deems to be too restrictive a framework – because it requires the perpetrator to admit his crime at the outset and some people are 'not mature enough' to acknowledge their guilt. 'In dealing with the human person,' he grabs a menu from the restaurant table in front of him and jabs a finger at its list of options. 'I cannot say that works for you but it doesn't work for him… but I would prefer to err on the side of helping the person rather than crucifying them.'

Coming from a Christian Brother, it is hard not to think of the leniency that his religious congregation showed to abusive peers down the years – leniency many would say was not within their gift. Beyond that, Lynch's view appears overly idealistic. How, for example, can we be expected to be mothers to everyone in society? Lynch admits there are issues of practicality to overcome but, then, he turns the question on its head. Is not the current attitude to law and order hopelessly flawed? Arguing that the medical or scientific approach is to tackle the cause rather than the symptom, he points out: 'Einstein once said, when he was speaking about inventors, "You will never solve a problem looking at it with the same point of view as you had when you encountered the problem," which I thought was excellent. If you are looking at the prison system and you want to reduce crime rates, we are always looking backwards not forwards. We are building more prisons and we are having stiffer sentences. We are using an old system to try to solve a present problem. With any of the inventors, they had energy, and they had a new way of looking at things and a willingness to try something. It's that energy that is needed to bring society forward. That is very important, whether here or abroad: to come to something with a bit of fresh air, and to have the guts to try it out. There is courage needed to say, "OK, I don't understand what you are doing but try it out".'

To Lynch, this is the core of the missionary ideal: to offer 'a new way of looking at things'. He says, 'Missionaries are supposed to offer a bit of fresh air, a different point of view.' In his case, 'We deal with the person where they are at, while also challenging the system. It is not just "doing good". It's looking at it from a very professional point of view… We need to be practical. Otherwise we are just do-gooders. And missionaries were never meant to be do-gooders.'

The missionary ideal envisaged by Lynch is something of a tightrope act. Be 'a bit of fresh air' but not a do-gooder. Be both realistic and visionary. Be professional but don't get sucked into the system. The image Lynch keeps coming back to is Simon of Cyrene, the man who – in the New Testament story – helped Jesus carry the cross on the road to Calvary. 'Simon of Cyrene did not change the sentencing of Jesus, he did not change the attitudes of the people, he did not change the law but he saw a person in need of help and he did an act of kindness. And I think everyone in society is called to do that – not to change the world but to give someone a helping hand – without judging, without looking at our history, to do something in this moment of time… It's not saying "I have the answer". It's rather, like Simon of Cyrene, saying "I will help you along the way", or "Will we try this one?", or "How about this?" And it is done on a very friendly, human level. Because if it's not it's almost… *prepotente*, is the word in Spanish. Presumptuous, yeah.'

As an example of missionary thinker, Lynch captures all of the infuriating blend of practicality and other-wordliness; radical and irrational thinking. He doesn't so much have an ideology as a way of approaching ideology. He strives to be logical within the framework of a deep and profound faith.

Of course, Lynch says, some people dismiss him as a dreamer. And, of course, he says, 'There is a conflict. You are dealing with reality and practice that has gone on for years… but I go back to the inventors. They had no proof of what would work and what wouldn't work but they had the energy, the enthusiasm and a novel way of thinking – "let's try this". Not only that but when it doesn't work they would say "let's try another way". You see, inventors never go back. They always look forward. And in Church, in society, we have got to reach forward.' Broadening his thoughts to Ireland's current societal woes, he adds: 'The banks, the politicians, the Church, the professionals have all let us down. We should be saying, "This was the old system, it has let us down so let's try something new. But there is one place we won't go and that's back."'

CONCLUSION: THE FUTURE

'I want you to be happy, always happy in the Lord; I repeat, what I want is your happiness. Let your tolerance be evident to everyone: the Lord is very near. There is no need to worry.'

(Paul's Letter to the Philippians 4:4–7)

The drenched earth is drying despite the humidity. It's the start of the rainy season but as yet the downpours are intermittent. When one deluge comes, a cluster of schoolgirls at Loreto Rumbek scatter amid peels of laughter. Their 37-year-old school principal, Sr Orla Treacy, watches bemused. A soaking in the rain is the least of her worries. Tensions here can surface at any time, either among her students or in the wider southern Sudanese society. In this fraught and battle-scarred community, the slightest provocation can ignite any number of potential flashpoints, often abetted by the rampant poverty, high rate of male unemployment and prevalence of guns.

'When the cows are moving, there's a lot more tension,' says Treacy, from Bray, County Wicklow. One of the first things she learnt about the local Dinka culture was the importance of cattle for the people. When cows wander from the land of one clan into another's in search of water it can be perceived as an attempt to steal a herd and so 'old fights' are reignited. Entire villages have been wiped out in cattle raids, creating fresh atrocities in a region already traumatised by war. 'Violence is here constantly,' adds Treacy, who was robbed at gunpoint in November 2008 when thieves broke into her convent. 'There are times when you feel it more than other times, but you can't live in fear.'

Loreto Rumbek is located on 100 acres of scrubland which is being cultivated to produce food for the boarding school. A major school building programme is also underway. It is an indication of the esteem the local community has for the nuns that it permitted them to settle on a site which is considered 'sacred'. Right beside the school lies a burial plot where up to 500 people were massacred at a wedding feast during Sudan's long-running civil war between the mainly Muslim north Sudan and the mainly Christian, or Animist, south.

The decision by the Loreto sisters to set up a school here in 2006 – in the aftermath of a conflict that claimed 2 million lives and despite the instability and violence in Darfur, a few hundred kilometres north of Rumbek – in a certain sense defies logic. The congregation held a general meeting the previous year to discuss its future against a backdrop of dwindling vocations and an ageing workforce. The heads of each national Loreto branch met in Rome and decided that instead of adopting a policy of retrenchment they would try to recapture the spirit of the congregation's founder, the English nun Mary Ward, and of its Irish figurehead, Frances Mary Teresa Ball. That meant starting new missions despite a relatively small number of sisters. The Kenyan Loretos decided to go to Ghana to open a rural school, the Australians to East Timor to start a teacher-training project. The South Africans went to Zambia and the Spanish to Equador. As for the Irish, 'We had a strong feeling we should go to Sudan, and set up a girls' school, because that was seen as the area of greatest need,' Treacy explains.

Loreto Rumbek is the first secondary school for girls in Lake

State, a province of 40,000 square kilometres with a population of 350,000. 'Traditionally, in the Dinka tribe, a woman is valued by her cow value. She is rated by how many cows they can marry her for.' Women are very much second-class citizens, and it galls Treacy when students are pulled out of school indiscriminately by parents who don't value their daughters' education. 'One of the big things for us would be if the kids become pregnant. I would say to the family, "Please do not beat your daughter, please do not marry off your daughter, please allow your daughter to complete her education." That's all you can do, and only hope they can listen to you.' Sometimes she has to bite her tongue because, 'If the parents think we are trying to take from their culture, or tell them what to do, we will find ourselves in trouble and what could happen is they will put us on a plane and there will be no school.'

Her sensitivity to local culture is quite different to the approach of early missionaries like Teresa 'Mother Kevin' Kearney, who chopped down the sacred tree of Nkokonjeru in Uganda, a country next door, to try to displace local beliefs with Catholicism. Treacy says the Loreto sisters are in Sudan primarily for the girls' education and 'if evangelisation comes out of that it's an extra'. Tall and slim with copper-coloured hair, Treacy mixes easily with her young charges, passing on more words of encouragement than discipline on a typical day. Unlike at the nearby bush school, where children who misbehave are beaten with a stick, there is no corporal punishment here, and when it comes to religion, there is an 'open' dialogue, Treacy stresses. 'I'd have an abhorrence about pushing religion on people but where I am people are searching and wanting instruction because they see Christianity as something that could be positive for their lives.' While discussing the topic, she notes approvingly that one of her students has a T-shirt with the slogan 'Africa by Africans'. 'They want Africa to be led by Africans. So if we become redundant here it is because others are qualified to do the work. That achievement would be the greatest gift for all of us.'

Asked whether people like Mother Kevin or MMM founder Marie Martin were an inspiration for her, she replies with a laugh: 'Never heard of them. I was never one of those pious ones who read the lives of the saints. I always say that I missed that day of lectures in the novitiate.' Her mother was 'deeply religious', her father a 'more religious, questioning type'. One of her uncles, Frank Laverty, was a Spiritan missionary, 'so I would have grown up with the stories of Biafra', and missionary magazines would have piled up on the coffee table at home. Despite this, she met 'a lot of opposition' to her decision to join religious life.

'It wasn't so much cruel opposition, it was just confusion: why would any young person want to serve the Church?' She confesses: 'It was certainly something I did not want to do. I did not want to be a nun.' The decision to follow this path was influenced by a number of factors. 'When I was a fifth-year student in Loreto Bray, there were a number of Loreto Sisters in the school and one in particular who was very youthful, vivacious, intelligent and alive. I think she changed my stereotypical image of what a nun was. I began to realise that you could in fact be young, youthful, vibrant, maybe a bit half-crazy as well, and be a sister. That probably planted the seed.' Today, she is seen as something of a curiosity by her peers and former schoolmates. Revelations about sexual abuse in the Church, and its cover-up by the religious authorities, has 'hugely affected' her, although she says 'my friends and my family don't associate me with that'.

To the Loretos, the youthful Treacy is a welcome shot in the arm. But she is a different type of missionary to her predecessors, and she doesn't see herself staying in Sudan forever. Moreover, Treacy's joining the missions won't buck a historical trend. The figures indicate the Irish missionary movement is coming to an end rather than enjoying the 'Second Spring' which congregations have been predicting periodically over the past forty years. In 1965, there were over 7,000 Irish priests, nuns and brothers working in developing countries. By 2009, the number had fallen to 1,981. With their average age now well over 70, Irish missionaries are largely heading for extinction in the next decade.

More significant perhaps than the dwindling numbers is the way in which missionaries are drifting out of the public consciousness. A chasm has formed between those still active in the field and the society they've left behind, and it's widening. Many missionaries don't want to return home and wish to be buried in the countries where they now live. The Ireland they left thirty, forty or fifty years ago has changed beyond recognition. The pace of life is faster, and hostility towards priests and nuns is on the rise. Those who drift back to their convents and seminaries, now converted in large part into retirement homes, tend to spend their last years in quiet anonymity. They might help out in their local parish, or find the odd job to do in their congregation, but their glory days are over.

At the Drogheda convent of the MMMs, all but three of the eighty elderly residents are now retired. This place was once teeming with young nurses being trained for export, but today those filing through the canteen are to a woman of pension age. They gather for their daily meal together under an unusual picture of *The Last Supper* in which their founder Marie Martin is depicted sitting at the head of the table; she is being introduced by the Virgin Mary to an inquisitive Jesus Christ. The painting – which hangs across almost the entire length of one side of the room – was specially commissioned in 1967 when the MMMs were at their height and when Ireland was unselfconsciously, uniformly Catholic.

It was in that same year too, Helen Ahern first went to Africa. The Corkwoman joined the MMMs after seeing *Visitation* in her local cinema. 'There was footage of a nun crossing a river on a rope bridge, with a bicycle. This nearly blew my mind. I thought, "There is plenty of room for excitement there, and challenge."' Ahern spent a total of thirty years in Tanzania and another ten in Uganda. In between, she had a stint in the US, running a counselling service for drug addicts and alcoholics. While in Tanzania, Sr Ahern picked up cerebral malaria – which will kill her, doctors say, if she gets it again. But she doesn't want to return to Ireland – not yet. She feels she still has work to do.

Her latest mission is tending to prisoners in Masaka, in southern Uganda. She started going to the city's main prison in 2001 and was struck by the lack of rehabilitation – 'there is no library, no books'. Inmates have just one meal a day. There are 800 of them in cells built for just 250. She had initially planned to do 'some social work, a bit of prayer and crafts' but after a couple of visits the governor asked her to have a look at the clinic room. 'It was just a room, with no running water – that's how it still is – and no drugs… I decided to give it a shot and started looking for funding.' Today, she uses the room for HIV-testing and for dispensing medication.

Recently, she began visiting women prisoners on death row in a high-security institution in the capital, Kampala. 'We pray a bit, we talk a bit. Sometimes they'd cry, sometimes they'd laugh. When we are finished I always say, "One day you'll be free and you'll be coming out with me."' The women, mostly jailed for murder, have begun to depend on her. While she is back in Drogheda, she sends them text messages to keep their spirits up. She also tries where possible to support their children and helped to arrange funding to put one condemned woman's daughter through secondary school; the girl has since gone on to college. Everyone who she speaks to in Ireland wants to know the prisoners' stories – 'What did she do, and what did he do?' – but it doesn't interest Ahern. 'At this stage, I see them all as people, unfortunate people.'

Her worry now is passing on the work. Like many a veteran missionary – she turned 70 in 2009 – she is struggling to find someone to replace her. It is a sorrowful thought: that her project will collapse when she is gone; that there will be no legacy. 'My prison work is non-sustainable… No one wants to do it, and also it's voluntary. I couldn't do it only for the support of the Irish government' (she gets funding through Misean Cara). She has tried – and failed – to find a replacement within the ranks of the MMMs. Now she is looking for a Ugandan to do the job.

'I have to be realistic. I can't do this forever.' Visiting the motherhouse offers a stark reminder of this fact. A few years ago, the MMMs opened a public nursing home at the Drogheda convent – with the hope of creating a new income source for the order. Now all thirty places at the home are occupied by retired nuns from the MMMs.

'This is where I'm going too,' she sighs. 'You see yourself going into it.'

Down a side street from the convent is another reminder of time's inexorable passage. A grey, pebbled plot marks the site where Marie Martin is buried, along with scores of her disciples. Amid the row upon row of charcoal headstones is a single bowl of flowers. It rests on the concreted grave of the foundress. Standing before the plot, Sr Ahern explains that each grave used to take two sets of remains but 'they now go down triple'. In one month alone in early 2009, the MMMs buried four of their members.

Next to the gravestones is a row of smaller monuments. They are carved with the names of those who died overseas and the places where they fell. Exotic places like Ibadan and Abakaliki that evoke clear blue African skies. The general rule in religious orders, the MMMs included, is that if you die overseas you are buried there. It's cheaper.

It is also what most missionaries want for themselves. After decades away from 'home', priests and nuns can feel more Brazilian, or Zambian, or Korean, than Irish. A few go so far as renouncing their Irish citizenship. Lots more try to avoid returning to what is now an alien land.

Missionaries should, of course, assimilate in other cultures but, says Ahern, 'It's a very sad thing if you don't see Ireland, if you don't see your motherland, as your home. I think that's a very sad thing. Sad, yeah.' Thinking of those with whom she works in Africa, she adds, 'We could never live at their level, the level of poverty and just existence. You could never be satisfied with that, once you are Irish, English or American.'

Back in Dublin, Kiltegan priest and theologian Donal Dorr also reflects on life, and death, after the missions. The modest nature of his home – a poky upstairs bedsit – provides a near physical reminder of the status of the missionary movement today. Not that Dorr is too downbeat. 'Instead of trying to change it, or saying it is good or bad, we have to accept it,' he says, having just bounded up several flights of stairs without pausing for breath. 'It would seem that a particular phase of missionary work is coming to an end. But it has taken other forms – more pluralistic forms.' He cites the work of volunteers and the peacekeeping missions of the Irish Defence Forces. 'A compassionate outreach has become more diffuse. It is only to be expected that the narrower mission, which takes in that compassionate outreach but also other things, like the commitment to celibacy, has become kind of unusual. The question is not "Why is that mission less?" but "Why was it ever more?"'

Other missionaries – but not all – are similarly philosophical about the movement's decline. The child protection campaigner Shay Cullen says it would be 'no harm' if certain religious orders were disbanded, and he is largely indifferent about the fall in vocations, noting that his Filipino charity Preda has thrived on the support not of clergy but of dedicated volunteer lawyers and social workers. Cullen says he has spoken to his superiors – 'though they don't listen to me' – about the possibility of recruiting 'apprentices' who may or may not go on to be ordained. 'If someone has a faith and enthusiasm and idealism and they want to burn it out in service then throw them into the fray right away so they learn their spirituality day by day,' he argues. 'They should be listening to the cries of the poor, not the sweet strains of Gregorian, medieval chants. If that is translated into action for justice then you are going to have a very strong missionary movement.' But, he says, if missionary societies ignore such reform 'they miss the boat. If they want to survive they have to reinvent themselves, and the only way to do it is practically engage in the face to face, *mano a mano*, combat of the battle for good and evil, and challenge the inspiration of young people.'

Like many missionaries who are active in peace and justice, Cullen has mixed feelings about entering religious life. Forty years ago, options for young men like him were limited and it seemed like he couldn't help the developing world unless he signed up for the full priestly package, celibacy included. 'There was a great thirst to get outside the insular cage that Ireland was in those days. In the 1960s you were hearing about revolutions and the Vietnam War and you were thinking, "Gosh, what is happening in the world?"' But why did he join the Columbans specifically? 'Because it was convenient.' He shrugs. 'It had a good recruitment system.'

In an interview with *The Irish Times* in 2009, Cullen admitted that he thought about leaving the priesthood when he was in his forties after falling in love with a woman. She was a Jamaican who worked for the UN in New York, a 'Michelle Obama type'. But he let her go, after counting the cost to Preda of the inevitable scandal that would have ensued.[50] Asked whether he'd join the missions if he was a young man today, he replies: 'One can never know. The opportunities I've had presented themselves because I became a

Columban and happened to go to the Philippines. That was a good vehicle.'

Cullen is not alone among priests and nuns in feeling that the traditional missionary model has outlived its usefulness. Idealistic young people today have different – and maybe better – ways to make a difference. This sort of *à la carte* missionary can be seen in the ranks of volunteers and aid workers who do anything from a week's house-building in South Africa to several years teaching schoolchildren in Nepal. Having a religious faith is not necessary to do this kind of work, but Christian belief can be a motivation. It was striking, for example, that when the kidnapped Darfur aid worker Sharon Commins was released from captivity in October 2009 she chose to thank the people of Ireland for their support through a letter to the Archbishop of Dublin Diarmuid Martin. In what was an arresting statement of faith in these relatively secular times, the Goal employee wrote that she and her fellow hostage Hilda Kawuki 'sought sanctuary in prayer during our 107 days in captivity'. They prayed to St Jude, patron saint of hopeless causes, St Thérèse, the Little Flower, and St Anthony, patron of lost items 'that we would soon be found'. Expressing 'no doubt' that their combined prayers 'made a difference', Commins wrote, 'We both survived because we had the strength and willpower and love of our families stored in those deep caverns of our souls. And we had the love of God.'

Some missionaries take comfort in people like Commins who have made a contribution to former mission countries. But 'there would be some,' admits Gerry O'Connor, the Goal veteran turned Redemptorist priest, 'who would be saying, "Where is the faith-dimension to this?" If they didn't see people back involved in the parish after volunteering overseas some might say, "What the hell is that all about?"' O'Connor's own charity, Serve, which recruits people aged 20–40 years for projects in six different developing countries, is necessarily pragmatic when it comes to faith. Adopting the slogan 'Solidarity in Action', Serve has its own moderately trendy logo: a cartoon image of a pair of sandals, and its mission statement has no mention of religion. Instead, it says it's committed to 'tackling poverty' by 'working in solidarity, service and partnership with marginalised and oppressed communities'. The main requirement for volunteers, says O'Connor, is that they have 'fire in their belly' rather than being on good terms with Rome. Of about 400 volunteers who joined Serve between 2003 and 2010, four went on to join the Redemptorists. Not bad, you might argue, from a recruitment viewpoint, but elderly missionaries find it hard to see the positives. 'Most of the older generation would be disappointed if they thought volunteering was their legacy,' says Eamon Aylward, chief executive of the IMU and a former missionary in Mozambique.

Whatever the reason for the decline in vocations, missionary societies are gradually coming around to accepting it. The Columbans made a landmark decision on 1 May 2008 to move their superior general from Dalgan Park to Hong Kong, effectively relocating the society to a new headquarters outside of Ireland. At the time, the number of ordained priests in the Columbans stood at 500, with about 400 of them aged over 60. There hadn't been a new entrant from Ireland in a decade but there had been modest growth in Asia. 'Years ago we talked about a five-year plan,' says Fr Tommy Murphy, the Columbans' superior in 2010. 'Now, no one even talks about a three-year plan. Really, we review things year after year.' A key decision in the Columbans was made in 1982 to accept young men from countries outside of Ireland into the mission. The Philippines produced the largest number of recruits, and some of them are now working in parishes in Ireland, engaging in the sort of social work and pastoral duties that made Irish Columbans famous worldwide.

Whether the Columbans opened up in sufficient time to secure their future is uncertain. The latest IMU survey shows just under

6 per cent of their members are from mission areas, compared to 40 per cent of Missionary Sisters of the Holy Rosary and 33 per cent of MMMs. Other congregations are believed to have moved far too late, with the Kiltegans listing just six members from mission countries out of 305 priests in December 2008. It is clear some missionaries feared losing control over their organisations, and cynics say they only changed their minds when it became evident that they'd need younger members to look after them in their old age. There are other problems in the field of recruitment: resources are wasted on students who avail of a church-run education and then vamoose, while those who enter the Church are not necessarily 'formed' in the way Irish congregations would like. African seminaries are frequently accused of turning out highly conservative and status-obsessed young priests, a bit like Irish clergy of old perhaps. The irony is that liberal-minded young missionaries leaving Ireland today can find themselves in conflict with their African peers on a whole range of issues, from the role of the laity in the church to the Vatican's stance on homosexuality.

Sr Angela Hartigan, who works in the slums of Mukuru, near Nairobi, says the Church in Africa got 'too caught up in the numbers game. We have a huge number of people in formation but you have to ask whether there is a trade-off between quantity and quality.' The Sister of Mercy recalls a friend in the priesthood telling her twenty-five years ago 'the Church triumphant has to learn to become the Church suffering' and this still resonates with her today. 'My reading of the situation in Kenya is they have set out on the same road of arrogance and superiority that we set out on in Ireland fifty years ago, and it pains me to see it. There is a false belief [among priests] that they are better than their lay colleagues and that frightens me.' She sighs. 'But, then, my hair is white, and the Church in Ireland has nothing in the way of credibility to explain that to people.'

Dorr remains upbeat, even about the recruitment challenges. If a priest leaves the Kiltegans after training, 'I see that as a good thing,' he says, 'because they see they have options and they grab them.' Describing those men who complete their training in African seminaries as 'very impressive', he adds: 'A colleague of mine and I used to joke that our main aim should be to make sure no other chancers like us get in.' Most missionaries don't share this sort of optimism, however. They are perturbed at the fall in vocations, and they see their way of life steadily disappearing. Some are ordered home as financial and staffing constraints force the closure of foreign projects. Missionaries also have a heightened sense of being judged these days. There is a changed, less friendly environment that is almost reflected in the altered landscape back home.

For Cyril Mooney, each time she returns from Kolkata to Loreto's hilltop convent in Bray, County Wicklow for a break, it seems like another one of the fields on which she played as a child has been sold off to developers. Private housing estates creep ever closer with the passing years. Rooftops arrow towards a mossy Bray head in the distance.

Opening the convent's stately front door one crisp, spring morning, Mooney wrestles with a clunky bolt-lock and a large brass key which dangles above the handle from a piece of string. 'We had a few people here with Alzheimer's so we put this in to stop them wandering off,' she explains. Now in her mid-seventies, Mooney walks with a slight stoop; the wide-rimmed glasses hanging around her neck seem to propel her forward through a high-ceilinged entrance hall. Inside the ground-floor reception room are a number of display books, typifying some of Loreto's areas of interests. There is a glossy hardback on Mother Teresa, a former member of the order. There are picture books on Irish emigrants, local history and astronomy. Few visitors call to the convent these days, and Mooney – like the other nuns – can walk down the hill to the shops without being approached or spoken to. A small mercy in Ireland, you'd think. But a stark contrast with India where

Mooney can't cross the street without a glance, a wave or a snatched conversation with some friend or former student. 'The bonds, my God.' She lets out a hollow laugh. 'You meet them all over the place – all over India wherever I go. "I'm a Loreto girl," they say.' In Kolkata, she is a well-known sight zipping around in a minivan between her various street projects (she used to ride a Lambretta 175 motorbike but, to her regret, had to trade it in because she couldn't find the spare parts to keep it on the road). She feels more liberated there, knowing that, at her age, she wouldn't be allowed run a school in Ireland. 'The teachers' unions would be up in arms,' she grins.

The contrast between her persona in India and Ireland is stark. In Kolkata, she is valued, still seen to be making a contribution and even fêted. In Ireland, what do the eyes that follow her down the street see? A helpless old woman? An old nun? Just some relic from a discredited Church?

It is no wonder many missionaries never want to come home. Any time they return to Ireland to visit friends and family, they are dreading what the mood will be like and wondering what revelation in the Church will surface next. They have a sense that their reputation is in constant flux and a fear that they may not be judged so well in the future. What's worse, this predicament is part of their own making. Reluctant to investigate abuses within, and loath to discuss past mistakes, missionary congregations are actively contributing to their self-alienation. 'They agree to engagement, but only on their own terms,' says one experienced aid worker. By lacking transparency, missionaries run the risk of having their reputation reduced to a mixture of suspicion and innuendo. It is not the end these old men and women would have imagined for themselves when they first left Ireland decades ago, hailed as heroes for Christ.

Among those who believe there is some good in missionary work, there is some regret attached to this decline. Once missionaries commanded awe, they now tend to attract pity. It is hard not to feel sympathy and even a sense of unfairness. Here is a unique movement, Ireland's very own compassionate foreign legion, a peace corps that would be celebrated in probably any other Western country, and it is being extinguished without proper recognition of its qualities – or its genuine faults – so that the best of it can be preserved for the future. A generation of Christian entrepreneurs, who have gained an extraordinary, grass-roots perspective on the world, and on its trials and injustices, are dying off without passing on their wisdom. The irony is that missionaries were largely ignored during the Celtic Tiger years, when some of their outlook might have been useful. In recent times, they are perceived to offer little practical value to Ireland Inc. Yet Ireland's missionaries have served the country in some very practical ways. Over decades, in different parts of the world, they gave Ireland a reputation – perhaps undeservedly – for compassion and humanitarianism. President Mary McAleese has described them as 'our primary ambassadors'.[51] The goodwill they have created has opened doors for politicians and businesspeople. Peter Sutherland, chairman of Goldman Sachs International, and former director general of the World Trade Organisation, has spoken of the 'fantastic reputation' Ireland gained in the developing world thanks to 'our priests and nuns', as well as Irish NGOs. 'Everywhere, Africa and South America, I went people said, "I was educated by an Irish priest or Christian Brothers. I knew the Irish." It was amazing for a small country. It is a huge advantage that the Irish have.'[52]

Businessman Denis O'Brien describes missionaries as 'advance point people' for Irish companies trying to break into emerging markets, and he can attest to their assistance himself. 'I am involved in very controversial licences, OK. But I can tell you this much, we got most of our licences in the Caribbean because we were Irish.' While Ireland's artistic or cultural heritage might open doors in the United States, he continues: 'If you take these [poorer] countries they have never heard of Seamus Heaney. So it's really because of the work of missionaries. It's the same in Africa and the same in parts of Asia and India. Missionaries have effectively created unbelievable goodwill towards Ireland.'

By way of example, O'Brien cites a meeting he once had with the Samoan prime minister over the contentious issue of import duties. The Irish business tycoon was trying to negotiate a better deal for a mobile phone company which he had just bought in Samoa. It was O'Brien's first venture in the Southern Pacific telecommunications market, and he recalls: 'The meeting was going badly. I could feel it. I was trying to talk about rugby.' He groans, reminiscing about the stilted conversation. 'Eventually I said, "Have you ever been to Ireland?" and he said, "No, I haven't but I know everything about Ireland – your culture, your music, your writers." He said, "I was educated by the Christian Brothers; it was an Irish school and three of the priests were Irish." After that…' O'Brien clicks his fingers. 'He talked to me about Ireland for twenty minutes. Going out the door he said, "We will give you duty-free status." I came away and said, I am going to have to thank the Christian Brothers who educated this man – because we were getting nowhere, and that's why small Irish companies who go off to these emerging markets to do business will do extraordinarily better than German, French, British companies.'

How many other practical benefits have flowed – and will flow – to the Irish people from their association with compatriot missionaries? And how can their debt be repaid? How many Irish soldiers, aid workers and journalists have escaped tight corners in conflict zones by name-dropping a locally admired activist priest? How many citizens have been given the privilege of connecting directly with the world's poor through an introduction by some Irish 'Mother Teresa'? We commemorate the war dead, the martyrs of 1916 and those who have given their lives in the service of the state. Is there not a case too for celebrating those who made great sacrifices – and sometimes the ultimate sacrifice – out of a sense of solidarity with the world's poor and who in the process brought a good deal of honour to Ireland? By their nature, missionaries themselves are not clamouring for public recognition, but that should not necessarily deter the state from acknowledging their contribution honestly and fairly. A modest proposal might be to put missionaries at the heart of an annual commemoration in Ireland of World Humanitarian Day, designated by the UN as 19 August and first staged internationally in 2009.

For the state to celebrate missionaries today would be somewhat countercultural but it would also be a mature and perhaps necessary gesture. That the Catholic Church in Ireland has committed great crimes is beyond contention but that shouldn't erase from history the contribution of many caring, compassionate priests and nuns who worked not just in the missions but also at home. It's not just a question of putting the record straight. Where good was done it should be acknowledged for the mental health – or, if you like, the self-esteem – of the nation, and especially of an Irish nation that is mired in anger and anxiety. In the aftermath of the 2008 banking collapse, the novelist Colm Tóibín made a plea for celebrity economists to be banished from the airwaves and to be replaced by people who are 'not nuns, but like nuns … people with a certain sort of wisdom, people who have some sort of set of spiritual or material values that are serious; who are asking fundamental questions.'[53] Well, why not nuns? It would be a sign of collective childishness if we thought women like Dr Maura Lynch, Cyril Mooney or Orla Treacy had nothing to teach us because they happened to believe in God. At the very least, we might be able to learn something about handling setbacks – because there's one thing missionaries hate and that's self-pity.

If Irish missionaries do feel undervalued they can comfort

themselves in the knowledge that they are part of a long tradition of personal disappointment. The joint patron saints of the missions, Francis Xavier and Thérèse of Liseux, had nothing like comfortable retirements. The former died of a fever thousands of miles from home, the latter of TB aged just 24. Mary Ward, founder of the Loretos, was condemned as a heretic by Rome and died in isolation in 1645. Bishop Joseph Shanahan, one of the founding fathers of the Irish missionary movement, ended life as a pauper, isolated by his own congregation. A young Holy Ghost priest recalled meeting the bishop in his last years. The veteran of African adventures had been ostracised by the Holy Rosary Sisters at that stage; a cloud of suspicion hung over his head. The priest James Finucane, a cousin of Concern's Jack and Gus Finucane, recalled, 'He walked over to me and said, "Father I feel ashamed to have to ask you for money but could you give me the fare in and out to the city? I brought a pound note with me, but a poor man came up to me saying he had not eaten anything since morning, so I gave it to him."' James Finucane said he gave Shanahan two half-crowns with tears in his eyes. 'That example of humility and charity,' Finucane wrote, 'did more for my spiritual life than all the conferences I got in the scholasticate.'[54]

Pat Whitney had a similar end: removal from office under a cloud of suspicion attached to his illness. Then there was Blowick, who suffered from depression as he saw the Columban mission to China collapse. Galvin perhaps saw it clearer than most – how failure was inevitable in their business. Dan Fitzgerald recalls Galvin's attitude when they were expelled from Hankow, how he looked at a crucifix on the wall and said 'what else would you expect?' And Fitzgerald said when Galvin told him to put the great Irish saints in front and behind him as he ploughed on, 'he was saying to me: think of St Patrick, what had he? He had druids hunting him, and he hadn't much time to be thinking about how he spread the gospel. St Columban was thrown out of his monastery in France and was hunted and finished up in northern Italy. So if you think things will turn out the way you expect, you'd be wrong.' Fitzgerald continued: 'He [Galvin] saw very clearly that almighty God planned his kingdom would come through, not succeeding, but failing. Because if you analyse the story of incarnation and the redemption, what have you there? You have the story of a man who allowed his whole world be destroyed, because there he was on the cross, but 'twas there that the battle was won.'

By any earthly measure, missionaries are failures. Each one of their declared enemies – fear, hunger, exploitation and poverty, not to mention paganism – will outlive them. But there is honour in failure, and there is integrity in swimming and swimming and swimming against the tide. Ironically, moreover, in continuing to fail, and fail again, opting out of conventional life, missionaries may offer us a model for survival. At their best, they live humbly, at the interface between different cultures, with tolerance and integrity. Their kind of life might even be called sustainable. It is certainly simple and more in tune with the real world than the self-centred, compartmentalised existence that most of us enjoy. Missionaries may have their egos but if they really craved attention they'd have changed jobs long ago. After his kidnap ordeal in 2009, Fr Michael Sinnott returned to his work with disabled children in the Philippines, proclaiming, 'I'm hoping I can now fade into obscurity again; for me notoriety is worse than captivity.' A favourite poem among missionaries is 'The Prayer of Óscar Romero', which was composed by the Salvadoran bishop and given added poignancy after he was murdered while saying Mass on 24 March 1980 by a right-wing death squad. It ends with the lines:

> We may never see the end results
> but that is the difference

between the master builder and the worker
We are the workers, not master builders
Ministers, not messiahs
We are prophets of a future not our own.

Missionaries in this tradition are happy to live and die with anonymity. With no sense of unfinished business, they'll honour their fallen colleagues quietly and without fanfare, until the last one of them is gone. But is this how it should end? Those of us who are outside the missionary movement looking in might rightly feel an opportunity being lost. Are we humble enough to try to learn from these men and women, while they are still around to teach us? Our time is running out.

BIBLIOGRAPHY

Akenson, Donald Harman, *The Irish Diaspora: A Primer* (PD Meany Co, Ontario, 1993)

Barrett, William E., *The Red Lacquered Gate: The Early Days of the Columban Fathers and the Courage and Faith of its Founder, Father Edward Galvin* (Author's Choice Press, Lincoln, 2002)

Boner, Kathleen, *Dominican Women: a Time to Speak* (Cluster Publications, South Africa, 2000)

Buchanan, Andrew, *Visitation: The Film Story of the Medical Missionaries of Mary* (MMMs, 1948)

Byrne, Tony, with a foreword by Frederick Forsyth, *Airlift to Biafra: Breaching the Blockade* (The Columba Press, Dublin, 1997)

Claffey, Patrick, and Egan, Joe (eds), *Movement or Moment? Assessing Liberation Theology Forty Years after Medellin* (Peter Lang, Bern, 2009)

Coogan, Tim Pat, *Wherever Green is Worn: The Story of the Irish Diaspora* (Random House, London, 2000)

Crowley, Michael, *To Cape Town and Back: Story of Sacred Heart Missionaries in Apartheid South Africa* (Mission Support Centre, Cork, 2008)

Cullen, Shay, *Passion and Power* (Killynon House Books, Mullingar, 2006)

The Diary of a Medical Missionary of Mary (Richview Press, Dublin, 1957)

Dorr, Donal, *Mission in Today's World* (Columba Press, Dublin, 2000)

Dorr, Donal, *Option for the Poor: A Hundred Years of Vatican Social Teaching* (Gill & Macmillan, Dublin, 1983)

Dunn, Joseph, *No Tigers in Africa! Recollections and Reflections on 25 Years of Radharc* (Columba Press, Dublin, 1986)

Farmar, Tony, *Believing in Action: The First Thirty Years of Concern 1968–1998* (A&A Farmar, Dublin, 2002)

Fennell, Desmond, ed., *The Changing Face of Catholic Ireland* (Herder Correspondence, London, 1968)

Fischer, Edward, *Maybe a Second Spring: The Story of the Missionary Sisters of St Columban in China* (Crossroad Publishing Company, New York, 1983)

Forristal, Desmond, *Edel Quinn 1907–1944* (Dominican Publications, 1994)

Forristal, Desmond, *The Second Burial of Bishop Shanahan* (Veritas, Dublin, 1990)

Hitchens, Christopher, *The Missionary Position: Mother Teresa in Theory and Practice* (Verso, London, 1995)

Hogan, Edmund M., *The Irish Missionary Movement: A Historical Survey, 1830–1980* (Gill & Macmillan, Dublin, 1990)

Hurley, Paul, *The Word* (The Divine Word Missionaries, Maynooth, December 2008)

Keaney, Marian, *They Brought the Good News: Modern Irish Missionaries* (Veritas, Dublin, 1980)

Kearney, Paddy, *Guardian of the Light: Denis Hurley – Renewing the Church, Opposing Apartheid* (Continuum, New York, 2009)

Kee, Robert, *The Green Flag: A History of Irish Nationalism* (Penguin, Harmandsworth, 1972)

Kennedy, James, *Fat God Thin God* (Mercier Press, Cork, 2002)

Kiggins, Thomas, *Maynooth Mission to Africa: The Story of St Patrick's, Kiltegan* (Gill & Macmillan, Dublin, 1991)

Louis, Sister M., *Love is the Answer: The Story of Mother Kevin OSF* (Fallons, Dublin, 1964)

Lynch, Irene Christina, *Beyond Faith and Adventures: Irish Missionaries in Nigeria Tell Their Extraordinary Story* (Ross Print Services, Wicklow, 2006)

Maathai, Wangari, *My Hero's Hero* (The My Hero Project, 2005)

Maathai, Wangari, *Unbowed: One Woman's Story* (Random House, London, 2007)

Maye, Brian, *The Search for Justice: Trócaire, A History* (Veritas, Dublin, 2010)

McGrath, Aedan, and Moreau, Theresa Marie (ed.), *Perseverance Through Faith: A Priest's Prison Story* (Xlibris Corporation, Bloomington, 2008)

O'Brien, Niall, *Revolution from the Heart* (Oxford University Press, New York, 1987)

O'Brien, Niall, *Seeds of Injustice* (O'Brien Press, Dublin, 1985)

Ó Maille, Padraig, *Living Dangerously: A Memoir of Political Change in Malawi* (Dudu Nsomba Publications, Glasgow, 1999)

Pilger, John, *Freedom Next Time*, (Random House, London, 2006)

Purcell, Mary, *To Africa with Love: The Life of Mother Mary Martin, Foundress of the Medical Missionaries of Mary* (Gill & Macmillan/MMMs, Dublin, 1987)

Quinn, Richard F., with Carroll, Robert, *The Missionary Factor in Irish Aid Overseas* (Dominican Publications, Dublin, 1980)

Smyth, Bernard T., *The Chinese Batch: The Maynooth Mission to China 1911–1920* (Four Courts Press, Dublin, 1994)

Films

Mary Ward: Dangerous Visionary, Sarah MacDonald & Ciaran O'Connor (New Decade DVD, 2009)

On God's Mission, Ruán Magan (Tyrone Productions/RTÉ, 2010)

NOTES

Chapter 1: The Other Rising

[1] Smyth, Bernard T., *The Chinese Batch: The Maynooth Mission to China 1911–1920* (Four Courts Press, Dublin, 1994), p.57
[2] Ibid., p.62
[3] Hogan, Edmund M., *The Irish Missionary Movement: A Historical Survey, 1830–1980*' (Gill & Macmillan, Dublin, 1990), p.146
[4] Kee, Robert, *The Green Flag: A History of Irish Nationalism* (Penguin, Harmondsworth, 1972), p.568

Chapter 2: New Leaders

[5] 'Pioneer missionary nun was wife of Trinidad governor', *The Irish Times*, 17 August 1959
[6] Louis, Sister M., *Love is the Answer: The Story of Mother Kevin OSF* (Fallons, Dublin, 1964), p.94
[7] Forristal, Desmond, *Edel Quinn 1907–1944* (Dominican Publications, Dublin, 1994), p.42
[8] Barrett, William E., *The Red Lacquered Gate: The Early Days of the Columban Fathers and the Courage and Faith of its Founder, Father Edward Galvin* (Author's Choice Press, Lincoln, 2002), p.230
[9] Kiggins, Thomas, *Maynooth Mission to Africa: The Story of St Patrick's, Kiltegan* (Gill & Macmillan, Dublin, 1991), p.145

Chapter 3: The Recruitment Drive

[10] Quinn, Richard F., with Carroll, Robert, *The Missionary Factor in Irish Aid Overseas* (Dominican Publications, Dublin, 1980), p.41–42
[11] Hurley, Paul, *The Word* (The Divine Word Missionaries, Maynooth, December 2008), p.47
[12] The history of the use of clofazimine is explored in greater depth in Manton, John, 'The Roman Catholic Mission and Leprosy Control in Colonial Ogoja Province, Nigeria 1936–1960', Nuffield College, University of Oxford, thesis submitted to Modern History Faculty for PhD in 2004
[13] Forristal, Desmond, *The Second Burial of Bishop Shanahan* (Veritas, Dublin, 1990), p.310

Chapter 4: From Sacramental to Social Work

[14] Byrne, Tony, with a foreword by Frederick Forsyth, *Airlift to Biafra: Breaching the Blockade* (The Columba Press, Dublin, 1997), p.21
[15] Ibid., p.22
[16] Farmar, Tony, *Believing in Action: The First Thirty Years of Concern 1968–1998* (A&A Farmar, Dublin, 2002), p.23
[17] Myers, Kevin, 'You have to fight like hell to do any good', *The Irish Times*, 9 March 1991
[18] *The Irish Times*, 14 February 1968
[19] Speaking at launch of Misean Cara, Croke Park, Dublin, 24 June 2008
[20] Coogan, Tim Pat, *Wherever Green is Worn: The Story of the Irish Diaspora* (Random House, London, 2000), p.508
[21] Speaking on *The Late Late Show* tribute programme for Fr Jack Finucane and Concern, RTÉ, 16 May 2008

[22] Speaking on *What If: There Were no Radharc Documentaries?*, RTÉ Radio 1, 9 March 2008
[23] Ibid.
[24] Dunn, Joseph, *No Tigers in Africa! Recollections and Reflections on 25 Years of Radharc* (Columba Press, Dublin, 1986), p.133

Chapter 5: Rebels and Revolutionaries

[25] Pilger, John, *Freedom Next Time*, (Random House, London, 2006) p.214
[26] Ó Maille, Padraig, *Living Dangerously: A Memoir of Political Change in Malawi* (Dudu Nsomba Publications, Glasgow, 1999), p.152
[27] 'Madcap militarism no solution for Colombia', *The Irish Times*, 19 August 2000
[28] Walsh, Declan, 'A turbulent Irish cleric with a mission', *The Irish Times*, 10 March 2001
[29] *Daily Nation*, 11 October 2009

Chapter 6: Missionaries Today – Where Do They Belong?

[30] 'A Misean Cara discussion paper on responses by missionary organisations to the challenges of health care and HIV and Ireland', Misean Cara, Dublin, 2007

Chapter 7: Evaluating the Work, Assessing the Legacy

[31] Maathai, Wangari, *Unbowed: One Woman's Story* (Random House, London, 2007), p.70
[32] Coogan, p.543

[33] Maathai, Wangari, *My Hero's Hero* (The My Hero Project, 2005)
[34] Crawford, Caroline, 'India's queen mum mourns "kind and generous" Irish nun', *Evening Herald*, 26 October 2009
[35] Cullen, Paul, 'Irish emigrants ruined native cultures, professor says', *The Irish Times*, 26 September 1997
[36] Speaking on *The South Bank Show*, UTV, 10 May 2009
[37] Maathai, *Unbowed*, p.8
[38] Hogan, p.8
[39] Quinn, p.31, notes there were 6,532 gardaí in 1970 and 8,663 soldiers in the defence forces in 1971
[40] *The Meaning of Life*, RTÉ 1, 14 Feburary 2010
[41] 'In Loving Service: A Global Analysis of the Commitment of Religious Institutes against HIV and Aids', 2008, USG–UISG
[42] Gartland, Fiona, 'Journey of atonement nearly over for priest who vowed to walk the walk', *The Irish Times*, 1 January 2009
[43] Dorr, Donal, 'I'm Sorry', *The Irish Catholic*, 4 June 2009
[44] Tanner, Siobhán, 'The Hero of the Day', *The Irish Catholic*, 27 August 2009

Chapter 8: Ideology – The Missionary Position

[45] Dorr, Donal, *Option for the Poor: A Hundred Years of Vatican Social Teaching* (Gill & Macmillan, Dublin, 1983), p.211
[46] Desmond Fennell, ed., 'The Changing Face of Catholic Ireland', *Herder Correspondence*, (London, 1968), pp.148–49
[47] Cullen, Paul, 'Israel's worst enemies are those who support its policies, claims Chomsky', *The Irish Times*, 4 November 2009
[48] McDonagh, Seán, 'In defence of missionaries', *The Irish Catholic*, 22 October 2009
[49] Twomey, Vincent, 'Mission of the Church', *The Irish Catholic*, 15 October 2009

Conclusion – The Future

[50] McNeill, David, 'Every day without compromise', *The Irish Times*, 9 June 2009

[51] Speaking on *On God's Mission* (Tyrone Productions/RTÉ, 2010)

[52] Interview with Simon Carswell (some comments contained in 'The Ultimate Social Networker'), *The Irish Times*, 30 January 2010

[53] McKeon, Belinda, 'An Irishman in America', *The Irish Times*, 25 April 2009

[54] Forristal, *The Second Burial of Bishop Shanahan*, p.246

Index